WHY THE WORLD NEEDS ANTHROPOLOGISTS

Why does the world need anthropology and anthropologists? This collection of essays written by prominent academic anthropologists, practising anthropologists and applied anthropologists aims to answer this provocative question.

In an accessible and appealing style, each author in this volume enquires about the social value and practical application of the discipline of anthropology. Contributors note that the problems the world faces at a global scale are both new and old, unique and universal, and that solving them requires the use of long-proven tools as well as innovative approaches. They highlight that using anthropology in relevant ways outside academia contributes to the development of a new paradigm in anthropology, one where the ability to collaborate across disciplinary and professional boundaries becomes both central and legitimate. Contributors provide specific suggestions to anthropologists and the public at large on practical ways to use anthropology to change the world for the better.

This one-of-a-kind volume will be of interest to fledgling and established anthropologists, social scientists and the general public.

Dan Podjed is Research Fellow at the Research Centre of the Slovenian Academy of Sciences and Arts and Assistant Professor at the University of Ljubljana, Slovenia.

Meta Gorup is PhD Candidate at Ghent University, Belgium.

Pavel Borecký is PhD Candidate at the University of Bern, Switzerland, and Convenor of the EASA Applied Anthropology Network.

Carla Guerrón Montero is Professor of Anthropology at the University of Delaware, USA.

WHY THE WORLD NEEDS ANTHROPOLOGISTS

*Edited by Dan Podjed, Meta Gorup,
Pavel Borecký and Carla Guerrón Montero*

Routledge
Taylor & Francis Group

LONDON AND NEW YORK

First published 2021
by Routledge
2 Park Square, Milton Park, Abingdon, Oxon OX14 4RN

and by Routledge
52 Vanderbilt Avenue, New York, NY 10017

Routledge is an imprint of the Taylor & Francis Group, an informa business

British Library Cataloguing-in-Publication Data
A catalogue record for this book is available from the British Library

Library of Congress Cataloging-in-Publication Data
Names: Podjed, Dan, editor. | Gorup, Meta, editor. | Borecký, Pavel, editor. |
Guerrón-Montero, Carla María, 1970– editor. | Routledge (Firm)
Title: Why the world needs anthropologists / edited by Dan Podjed,
Meta Gorup, Pavel Borecký and Carla Guerrón Montero.
Description: First Edition. | New York: Routledge, 2021. |
Includes bibliographical references and index.
Identifiers: LCCN 2020023837 (print) | LCCN 2020023838 (ebook) |
ISBN 9781350147140 (Hardback) | ISBN 9781350147133 (Paperback) |
ISBN 9781003087397 (eBook)
Subjects: LCSH: Anthropology. | Anthropologists.
Classification: LCC GN25 .W49 2021 (print) | LCC GN25 (ebook) |
DDC 301—dc23
LC record available at https://lccn.loc.gov/2020023837
LC ebook record available at https://lccn.loc.gov/2020023838

ISBN: 978-1-350-14714-0 (hbk)
ISBN: 978-1-350-14713-3 (pbk)
ISBN: 978-1-003-08739-7 (ebk)

Typeset in Bembo
by codeMantra

CONTENTS

FIGURES

CONTRIBUTORS

Lenora Bohren, Senior Research Scientist and Director, National Center for Vehicle Emissions Control and Safety, Colorado State University, the United States.

Pavel Borecký, PhD Candidate, University of Bern, Switzerland.

Sophie Bouly de Lesdain, Anthropologist and Expert Researcher, Electricité de France.

Joana Breidenbach, Co-founder, betterplace.org, betterplace lab and Das Dach, Germany.

Thomas Hylland Eriksen, Professor, University of Oslo, Norway.

Meta Gorup, PhD Candidate, Ghent University, Belgium.

Carla Guerrón Montero, Professor, University of Delaware, the United States.

Steffen Jöhncke, Senior Lecturer, University of Gothenburg, Sweden.

Anna Kirah, Founder and Director, Kirah Co, Norway.

Jitske Kramer, Founder, HumanDimensions, the Netherlands.

Riall W. Nolan, Professor, Purdue University, the United States.

Sarah Pink, Professor and Director, Emerging Technologies Lab, Monash University, Melbourne, Australia.

Dan Podjed, Research Fellow, Research Centre of the Slovenian Academy of Sciences and Arts, Slovenia.

Rikke Ulk, Founder and Director, Antropologerne, Denmark.

Tanja Winther, Professor, Centre for Development and the Environment, University of Oslo, Norway.

ACKNOWLEDGEMENTS

Dan Podjed kindly thanks organizations which have continuously supported his work on this book and assisted him to organize *Why the World Needs Anthropologists* symposium: Research Centre of the Slovenian Academy of Sciences and Arts, Institute of Slovenian Ethnology; Institute for Innovation and Development of University of Ljubljana; and the University of Ljubljana, Faculty of Arts, Department of Ethnology and Cultural Anthropology. He also acknowledges the financial support of the Slovenian Research Agency in the research projects DriveGreen: Development of an Ecodriving Application for a Transition to a Low-carbon Society (L7–6858) and Invisible Life of Waste: Development of an Ethnography-based Solution for Waste Management in Households (L6–9364) and in the research programme Cultural Spaces and Practices: Ethnology and Folklore Studies (P6–0088).

Meta Gorup would like to thank Ghent University, Faculty of Political and Social Sciences, Belgium, for travel funding which supported her organization of and participation at the *Why the World Needs Anthropologists* symposiums between 2014 and 2016.

Pavel Borecký expresses his gratitude for moral support and travel funding provided by University of Bern, Walter Benjamin Kolleg, that allowed him to co-organize *Why the World Needs Anthropologists* symposium from 2017 to 2019.

Carla Guerrón Montero wishes to thank the Department of Anthropology at the University of Delaware for its unwavering support of her long-term engagement with the *Why the World Needs Anthropologists* symposiums from 2015 on, and for its encouragement to continue to develop connections with the European Association of Social Anthropologists and its Applied Anthropology Network.

Editors of the book also thank the European Association of Social Anthropologists and its Applied Anthropology Network. Without the association and the network, this book most probably would not exist.

INTRODUCTION

Why does the world need anthropologists?

Dan Podjed and Meta Gorup

Anthropology is the study of humans, their cultures, behaviours, habits, practices, values and motivations, seeking in-depth understanding of cultural variations in the world. As a discipline, anthropology provides 'methods and theoretical perspectives enabling the practitioners to explore, compare and understand the varied expressions of the human condition' (Eriksen 2004: 7). Its trademark method is ethnography, which typically involves participant observation and extended researcher presence in the selected field site. The goal of such an approach is for the anthropologist to gain detailed, first-hand knowledge of the studied local culture as well as a deep understanding of its broader context.

But how is such detailed knowledge of cultural peculiarities and complexities relevant to the contemporary world and the problems facing humanity and the planet at present? And how about those problems we are about to face in the future? How can anthropology help to address major global issues such as climate and environmental disasters, migration and refugee crises, the rise of identity politics and concerns related to the fast-paced technological advancement? Why *does* the world need anthropologists? These are the questions explored in the present book by renowned anthropologists who have been using their anthropological knowledge and skills – many of them for several decades – in areas as varied as globalization, solutions to air pollution, social entrepreneurship, emerging technologies, sustainable energy, organizational change, design and international development.

Looking at the successful careers of and the important work done by these anthropologists, the book at a broader level aims to contribute to reshaping the discipline of anthropology as it has largely been known since its beginnings in the nineteenth century. Anthropology – with its focus on small, often far-off localities, and its unconventional research design – has commonly been perceived by the public as irrelevant to resolving 'real' problems, and many anthropologists have themselves been wary of practicing anthropology beyond their academic studies. Thus, before introducing in more detail the background of the present book and the remainder of the chapters, this text first examines anthropology's stereotypical image, the discipline's contested history – particularly in relation to its applied aspects – and finally, calls for breaking the mould of anthropology as an interesting but not a very useful endeavour. Instead, we call for an anthropology that moves beyond the description of academically interesting phenomena and towards informing change for the better.

'Sandals-with-socks obsessives' doing research in 'the Upper Volta valley'

If anthropology is to be perceived as a valuable and useful discipline and profession, the first step is to understand its currently prevalent stereotypical image and the origins thereof. Anthropology seems to remain closely associated with the late-nineteenth- and early-twentieth-century representations of the discipline's forefathers such as Bronisław Malinowski, Alfred Reginald Radcliffe-Brown and Franz Boas. For example, Malinowski's photo taken during his fieldwork in the Trobriand Islands, portraying the acclaimed anthropologist sitting on a log, dressed in white, flanked by four locals in their traditional clothing, has become exceptionally famous. Somehow, these kinds of images have stuck in people's imagination for over a century.

Most people still imagine anthropologists as 'pith-helmet-wearing colonial adventurers living with "hidden tribes" in the jungle'. Another image that comes to mind is 'bearded, sandals–with–socks obsessives going bonkers somewhere in the outback' (Strang 2009: 1). In the BBC show *Thinking Aloud*, in which a broadcaster asked people for their perceptions of anthropologists, the three answers were 'quite picky, argumentative, very critical of others' behaviour', 'bearded, long-haired men [sic.]', and 'serious people but sometimes a bit dotty' (cited in MacClancy 2005: 549). Such stereotypes – often hinting at anthropologists' unconventional methodologies, irrelevant topics of interest and their eccentricity – are commonly reproduced in cartoons and 'memes' shared on social media. One such cartoon portrays a man sitting in an armchair, anxiously looking at a woman observing him through the window. The man is making a phone call, saying, 'Hello, police? I'd like to report a peeping anthropologist'. Meanwhile, a woman – who could be Jane Goodall – observes the man through the window and comments, 'The big male senses danger and adapts a ritualized threatening posture'. Another cartoon circulating in various media since the 1980s shows 'natives' in a hut, one of them looking through the window and shouting, 'Anthropologists! Anthropologists!' as two anthropologists approach the village. Meanwhile, two other 'natives' hurry to hide away a lamp, phone, television and video recording set. Some of the more recent jokes and memes about anthropologists point to their supposed uselessness and inability to find 'real' jobs. For example, 'How many anthropologists does it take to change a light bulb?' The possible answers include, 'One, but it takes nine years', 'None. The point isn't to change the light bulb but to attempt to understand how the light bulb experiences its own reality', 'It depends on the context', and so on.

This commonplace mocking of anthropological work is, in most cases, harmless, and there is a grain of truth in these jokes, memes and stereotypes. Many anthropologists continue to carry out their fieldwork in remote parts of the planet among 'hidden tribes' and, to be honest, we have seen some of them wearing sandals with socks. However, such public image of anthropology sometimes translates into ideas and actions that can have a negative impact on the public's perception of anthropologists' usefulness in addressing societal issues facing us at present. Given the prevalence of the above stereotypes, it does not come as a surprise that anthropological methods and research designs are frequently perceived as 'unconventional', too 'time-consuming' and resulting in 'idiosyncratic stories with no implications for broader contexts' (Podjed, Gorup and Bezjak Mlakar 2016: 54; see also Sillitoe 2007; Stewart 2014). Similarly, the notion of anthropological training as a waste of public money has also been persistent. As reported by Jonathan Benthall in 1985, a British cabinet minister defended cuts in education funding by explicitly referring to the anthropological study of 'the pre-nuptial habits of natives of the Upper Volta valley' to point out that one cannot expect that research not resulting in 'the creation of wealth' would be heavily funded (Benthall 1985: 18). While the reference to the year 1985 may seem outdated, there have been much more recent vocal characterizations of funding anthropology programmes as a waste of public money. In 2011, the then Florida governor suggested public money should not be invested into anthropology students who may later struggle to find a job (see e.g. Morais and Briody 2018).

The discipline's contested history

Not only have anthropologists commonly been perceived by the broader public as studying 'exotic' peoples, interesting but irrelevant cultural phenomena and often historical rather than contemporary aspects of human societies (Podjed, Gorup and Bezjak Mlakar 2016), but persistent criticism from inside the discipline of those anthropologists who have sought to apply their knowledge and skills outside the academic circles has also further hindered the perception of anthropologists as professionals who can importantly contribute to a number of pressing societal concerns. The reasons for such critiques lie in the discipline's controversial history, a very concise version of which we present below (for detailed accounts of the history of anthropology with an emphasis on its applied components, see e.g. Hill and Baba 2006; Sillitoe 2006; van Willigen 2002).

The precursor of anthropology as we know it today first began to flourish during the era of Western colonialism and expansionist politics of the nineteenth and early twentieth centuries. In Europe, for example, the British colonial administration began to view anthropology as a tool that could assist them in their domination over the colonized peoples across the globe through the deep understanding of their societies. This resulted in colonial administrators receiving training in anthropology as well as anthropologists' employment by the empire (Rylko-Bauer, Singer and van Willigen 2006; Sillitoe 2006). On the other side of the Atlantic, anthropologists were similarly serving the government, although assisting the United States in internal affairs, via the Bureau of American Ethnology. The latter was created with the idea for anthropologists to inform the policies and assist the administration of Native Americans (Rylko-Bauer, Singer and van Willigen 2006; van Willigen 2002).

These connections between anthropology and colonial and expansionist regimes resulted in critical views of anthropology's applications in the service of dominating powers, especially in the United Kingdom. Although there are doubts about whether anthropologists and their insights were ever taken seriously by administrators – and anthropologists' efforts were often seen as having largely academic orientation or focussed on the preservation of cultural artefacts (Baba and Hill 2006; Nolan 2017; Pink 2006; Sillitoe 2006; van Willigen 2002) – anthropology's image has, nevertheless, remained tainted due to its involvement with the governments' colonial and expansionist efforts. In the United States, where it remained common for anthropologists to work for the federal government, anthropology's image became particularly tarnished by anthropologists' engagement in what became viewed as unethical governmental endeavours during and following Second World War, such as Japanese internment camps, Project Camelot in Latin America and Thailand Project, the latter two characterized as 'counterinsurgency research' (van Willigen 2002: 51; see also Nolan 2017).

The so-called 'colonial hangover' and anthropologists' more recent engagements in ethically problematic projects resulted in a broader critique of applications of anthropological knowledge and skills. These views among anthropologists have to an extent persisted to this day; anthropologists who earn their living by working 'within the system' are sometimes accused of supporting and sustaining oppressive political and economic systems (Rylko-Bauer, Singer and van Willigen 2006: 182; see also Baba 2009; Nolan 2017). This reinforces the long-held idea of anthropology as split into two: 'pure', 'theoretical', 'academic' anthropology versus 'applied', 'practical' anthropology. From sustained perceptions of applied anthropology as less rigorous, as likely to threaten the discipline's 'scientific integrity' (Foster 1952: 5) and as being even referred to as a 'scientific prostitute' (Embree 1945: 635) to continuous arguments that applied anthropological endeavours are very likely to be ethically charged and thus problematic from the perspective of anthropologists engaged in 'purer' versions of anthropological research (Baba and Hill 2006; Briody and Meerwarth Pester 2014; van Willigen 2009), applied anthropology has frequently been perceived as the lesser of two anthropologies (Baba and Hill 2006; Briody and Meerwarth Pester 2014; Rylko-Bauer, Singer and van Willigen 2006; Sillitoe 2006, 2007; van Willigen 2002).

What often remains implicit, however, is the close intertwinement of anthropological practice and theory since the discipline's very beginnings (Baba 2009; Nolan 2017; van Willigen 2002, 2009). First anthropology departments at British universities were established largely due to the empire's need to train colonial administrators in anthropology (Rylko-Bauer, Singer and van Willigen 2006; Sillitoe 2006; van Willigen 2002). A number of classical ethnographies of the colonized peoples began as reports for the administration and were funded by the latter (Rylko-Bauer, Singer and van Willigen 2006; van Willigen 2002). It has been argued that 'applied' anthropology paved the way for academic institutionalization of the discipline, provided the social context for the development of anthropological theories and has continued to enrich the discipline through anthropologists' engagement in new environments and with novel topics, sometimes yielding innovative research methodologies and designs (Nolan 2017; Rylko-Bauer, Singer and van Willigen 2006; van Willigen 2002; van Willigen and Kedia 2005). Ethical challenges pertaining to anthropological research were first formally addressed in the ethical code of the Society for Applied Anthropology in 1949, with the American Anthropological Association issuing their ethical guidelines only about twenty years later (Rylko-Bauer, Singer and van Willigen 2006; van Willigen 2002). At the same time, 'academic' anthropology with its theories and methodological approaches has clearly informed applied anthropological endeavours, pointing to a continuous interlinking of 'applied' and 'academic' anthropology (Rylko-Bauer, Singer and van Willigen 2006; Strang 2009).

The persistent divide between anthropological theory and practice, between 'academic' and 'applied' anthropology (cf. Guerrón-Montero 2008), has thus been viewed by some as 'unhelpful' (Sillitoe 2006: 15), and the calls for bridging this gap have become louder (Baba and Hill 2006; Briody and Meerwarth Pester 2014; Nolan 2017; Peacock 1997; Pink 2006; Sillitoe 2006, 2007).

Breaking the stereotypes

Clearly, it is high time to change the public perception of anthropology as an interesting but obsolete endeavour as well as to dismantle the notion of 'applied' anthropology as the 'evil twin' (Ferguson 1997, cited in Baba 2009: 383) of 'academic' anthropology. As the academic job market for anthropologists shrinks (Baba 2009), universities should be preparing graduating anthropologists to enter the workforce outside academia. Fortunately, a number of anthropology programmes are already placing a stronger emphasis on the applied aspects of anthropological work (Nolan 2017; Podjed, Gorup and Bezjak Mlakar 2016). What is more, it is not just about anthropology graduates *having* to work outside the more traditional forms of anthropological employment because they have no other choice but about many of them *wanting* to do so (Nolan 2017). And many have already embraced opportunities beyond academia, building successful careers in a variety of fields. Anthropologists have held prominent positions in international technology companies, such as Intel, Microsoft and Nissan, where they have contributed to developing autonomous vehicles, smart buildings and user interfaces of emerging technologies. They sit in important positions in various governmental and international agencies and are establishing non-governmental organizations supporting social and environmental causes. They are teachers, researchers, developers, designers, managers and consultants, working in all sorts of domains: governance, social policy, development, migration, intercultural relations, social work, health, organizational change, management, marketing, design, communications, law, technology, environment, sustainability, tourism, cultural heritage, art – and we could go on and on.

Despite the growing numbers of anthropologists employed outside academia or collaborating with non-academic partners, much remains to be done if we are to break the stereotype of the eccentric anthropologist working in far-off places, studying issues most people do not care about or understand. Anthropology should be presented to the public as a discipline adjusted to the present, using approaches that enable to record contemporary social phenomena and can assist in solving local and global issues. An important step in this direction is the dissemination of new anthropological knowledge – that nowadays very often has to do with important contemporary issues in societies similar to our own – to the broader public. Only in this way can we encourage public engagement and convince people of the important contributions of our discipline (Eriksen 2006). But beyond this, making anthropology more accessible and applicable to the world outside the academic walls will often require changes to how we *do* anthropology. Not least, we might have to adjust our methods. Extended ethnographic fieldwork, arguably one of the trademarks of anthropology, might not always be well-suited to the demands of a faster paced world outside academia. It has been argued that ethnography can be accelerated by a better planned research process and the use of digital technologies (see e.g. Ladner 2014). Participatory approaches, wherein the researched actively collaborate in shaping the research agenda and the formulation of findings, may also speed up the research process. At the same time, and very importantly, they enable for 'indigenous knowledge' to transpire in solutions applied to the identified issues (Sillitoe 2007). Furthermore, as we engage head-on with societal, organizational, environmental and other problems in need of solutions, interdisciplinarity becomes unavoidable. Anthropologists increasingly work across disciplinary boundaries, and many of them have become 'intellectual hybrids coexisting simultaneously in anthropology and other professional realms' (Baba and Hill 2006: 197; see also Kedia 2008; Strang 2009).

These developments do not always have an easy relationship with anthropology as conceived in more traditional ways. Changing the way we present our knowledge, adjusting the research method that to many represents the very core of what anthropology is and crossing disciplinary boundaries raise an important question: is this still anthropology? Add to this the inevitable ethical concerns associated with applied anthropological practice and one might not hesitate long to opt out of this reformed configuration of anthropology. But at the same time these transformations and shifts towards creating more applicable forms of anthropology may allow for 'constructing a more engaged' discipline as a whole (Rylko-Bauer, Singer and van Willigen 2006: 178). And as James L. Peacock, the then president of the American Anthropological Association, put it over twenty years ago, 'if we do not use it, we may lose it' (1997: 14). Yes, one can argue that in one way or another 'all anthropology is applied' (Darnell 2015: 4; see also Ingold 2018). But in our view anthropologists should more openly and actively engage in developing 'positive proposals' and inform social change rather than only observe and comment on the society as 'social critics' (Peacock 1997: 14): anthropology should be 'interventionist' and future-oriented (Future Anthropologies Network 2014; Pink and Salazar 2017). Anthropologists need to 'get their hands dirty' and intervene, but they should do so responsibly and always with an eye towards the politics and ethics of their engagement (Future Anthropologies Network 2014). Rather than feeling restricted by ethical challenges, 'examples of limited success or unintended consequences' should serve as 'lessons in the challenges of engagement' (Rylko-Bauer, Singer and van Willigen 2006: 186). The ethics of anthropology should move beyond the principle of 'Do No Harm' and instead seek to 'Do Some Good' (Briody and Meerwarth Pester 2014: 30). Careful reflection will always remain necessary, but intervention is urgently needed to change the world for the better.

Rebranding anthropology

One such attempt to break the stereotypes typically associated with anthropology is the annual international symposium *Why the World Needs Anthropologists*. After the Applied Anthropology Network of the European Association of Social Anthropologists had gotten off to a flying start in 2010, we, as convenors of the network, began to reflect on how we wanted to move forward. We were determined to prove to the non-anthropological – and a large part of the anthropological – world that anthropology was there to be applied and to contribute to resolving a host of contemporary societal issues. Thus, in the fall of 2013, the first symposium *Why the World Needs Anthropologists* took place, setting the direction for the symposiums to follow: we wanted to create an annual event which would bring together anthropologists – of different ages and backgrounds – and non-anthropologists representing various disciplines and organizations.

Since its beginnings in 2013, *Why the World Needs Anthropologists* has developed from a fringe symposium to one of the main annual anthropological events in the world. The concept has travelled seven cities in different countries – from Amsterdam to Padua, Ljubljana, Tartu, Durham, Lisbon and Oslo. Along the way it transformed from an afternoon meeting to a three-day event where participants can interact with plenary speakers, get to know academic and non-academic organizations working to apply anthropological knowledge and skills,

FIGURE 0.1   Dan Podjed and Meta Gorup on the stage at *Why the World Needs Anthropologists* international symposium in Tartu, Estonia, 2016. The purpose of the fourth edition of the symposium was to encourage cooperation between engineers and anthropologists, and to present new possibilities for developing human-friendly technologies. Courtesy Aivo Pölluäär.

attend hands-on workshops and present their own work. Symposium plenary speakers – with backgrounds in anthropology and various other disciplines – have addressed topics as varied as organizational change, climate change, sustainable energy solutions, smart cities, refugee crises, artificial intelligence and human-technology interaction, self-driving cars, social media, people-centred design and user experience. Over the years, thousands of participants from all over the world have joined us in person and via live streaming, and thousands more are connected to and engaged with us through our social media channels.

The obvious next step? The wealth of knowledge, experiences, insights and skills that have been shared over the years at the symposiums needed to be put on paper and distributed even more widely. To develop an edited volume representative of the kind of ideas our participants encounter at the annual events, editors of this book approached renowned anthropologists, most of whom have previously participated at *Why the World Needs Anthropologists* symposiums, and whose work arrangements and backgrounds cover a wide spectrum: from those firmly rooted in academic institutions to those working outside universities and others who regularly cross the boundaries between the two, anthropologists working with professionals across a variety of fields and in interdisciplinary teams and those studying the societies' past and present to inform our future, at home and in other parts of the world. The following eleven chapters offer our authors' viewpoints on why the world needs anthropologists, their experiences, stories and career trajectories, together forming a comprehensive insight into the current state of applied anthropology while providing an informed idea of the direction in which we are heading; this final point is discussed by the editors in the last chapter of the volume.

If anything, these accounts of anthropologists with very different backgrounds and career paths make one thing clear: anthropology has most certainly moved beyond its prevalent stereotypical public image, thus, in the process, continuously striving to make the world a better place.

Addressing the burning issues of our planet

While anthropology might not be *the* solution to the problems of our overheated – literally and metaphorically – planet, authors in this volume suggest that the many crises humanity is facing will not be resolved without anthropologists' engagement either. As Thomas Hylland Eriksen, professor of social anthropology at the University of Oslo, Norway, put it at the *Why the World Needs Anthropologists* symposium in Ljubljana, 'The bad news is that anthropology is never going to solve the global crisis, but the good news is that without us, *nobody* is going to because our knowledge is a crucial piece of the jigsaw puzzle' (Eriksen 2015; emphasis in the original).

Following this introduction, we continue with more insights from Eriksen. In his engaging style, he explains that the world does not consist of straightforward facts and quantifiable models alone – and this is precisely why it needs anthropologists who can make sense out of complex and often contradicting data. In Eriksen's opinion, anthropology provides a toolbox which enables anthropologists to tackle the numerous problems currently facing humanity. Introducing some of the main features of the anthropological approach – cultural relativism, ethnography, comparison and contextual understanding – Eriksen shows how they are crucial in grasping our increasingly globalized, transnational and connected world characterized by extensive 'ambiguity, complexity and ambivalence' (Eriksen, this volume).

Lenora Bohren further expands on the 'big issues' anthropologists – in fact, humans in general – need to deal with: refugee crises, cultural diversity and depletion of the environment. Bohren is director of the National Center for Vehicle Emissions Control and Safety (NCVECS) at Colorado State University, the United States, where she has been investigating the interface between culture, technology and environment. Drawing on her extensive knowledge of our 'love affair with the car', Bohren (this volume) convincingly argues for the need to recognize the relevance of cross-cultural solutions to air quality issues resulting from car emissions rather than hoping there is a universal solution to the problem. Her chapter provides an excellent example of how anthropology can be used to address problems which may appear to be very technical but are, in fact, social and should be addressed locally. Once again, the emphasis is placed on the importance of understanding cultural differences, diversity and complexity if we are to address our planet's burning issues.

Bringing anthropological theory into practice

In the words of a book title by Pink, Fors and O'Dell (2017), the next three chapters combine 'theoretical scholarship and applied practice', describing how anthropological knowledge and skills can be transferred and successfully used in governmental agencies, non-governmental organizations and industry.

Joana Breidenbach, a 'serial entrepreneur' with – for now – three successful careers, describes how in her life and work she has always drawn on some of the basic anthropological premises: embracing multiperspectivity, suspending judgement, acknowledging the fluidity of life and the importance of various inner and outer dimensions, answering big questions by studying the very concrete phenomena – and how she has been doing so by listening to people's stories. This has taken her from popularizing anthropology and anthropological approaches in Germany to co-founding betterplace.org – Germany's largest crowdfunding platform for non-governmental organizations – and betterplace lab – a 'Think-and-Do Tank' researching digital-social innovation, and most recently to co-founding Das Dach, a project devoted to developing a 'new operating system for society and the economy' (Breidenbach, this volume) in order to enable building a world that serves humanity's highest potential by supporting and implementing entrepreneurial and non-profit businesses.

Professor Sarah Pink, director of the Emerging Technologies Research Lab at Monash University, Australia, takes us on a journey through the past, present and future. Drawing on her expertise in emerging technologies, Pink envisions a new form of anthropology, breaking with how we have traditionally seen the discipline. In her view, anthropological endeavours should be interdisciplinary, team-based, methodologically creative and, very importantly, interventional and future-oriented. Constantly on the move between institutions, switching between Europe and Australia, simultaneously inside and outside academia and industry, Pink with her 'deterritorialized' – in Appadurai's words (1990) – endeavours makes a great example of the relevance that anthropology has in almost any context we can think of, due to its consideration of the very specific local and cultural details that inform 'how people really live in the world' (Pink, this volume).

Transcending the 'unproductive split between academic and non-academic anthropology', Steffen Jöhncke (this volume) illustrates how anthropological practice, teaching and research co-evolve through the collaboration with partners based outside universities. Building on his rich experience as an activist, a researcher, a practitioner – and an anthropologist – working in the fields of social work and health, combined with insights gained through his leadership role within AnthroAnalysis, a centre for applied anthropology based at the University of Copenhagen, Jöhncke introduces two key components of applied anthropological work. In his view, anthropologists' job is to translate our collaborators' problems into anthropological questions, which are to be addressed by drawing on anthropological theory and method. However, 'collaboration is key' (Jöhncke, this volume), and this goal can only be achieved through close collaboration between anthropologists and those calling on them for help. Yes, the world needs anthropologists, but only if we are to address the real problems faced by humanity.

Powering the planet

The next couple of chapters are dedicated to the anthropology of energy, which has become an important research topic in the last decades. This is not surprising, given the extent to which energy shapes nearly every aspect of our everyday lives. The following chapters persuasively argue that issues traditionally considered to fall exclusively in the domain of engineering should be researched and shaped by social scientists, including anthropologists.

Among those working at the intersection of anthropology and power engineering is Tanja Winther, professor at the Centre for Development and the Environment of the University of Oslo, Norway. With a master's degree in power engineering and a doctorate in social anthropology, Winther has been intertwining what one might see as two radically different disciplines. However, this is not the way she has experienced it; she believes engineering and anthropology provide complementary insights, and she has found it inspiring to combine them in her work on the social dimensions of energy. Her contribution in this book emphasizes the anthropological approach as one that enables us to discover the variety and complexity in a non-normative way. Nevertheless, she also calls for anthropologists to inform policy-making and use their knowledge and skills to push for a more sustainable and just system.

Sophie Bouly de Lesdain, the next contributor to the 'energy section' of this book, is associate researcher at the IIAC-LAU Lab (CNRS-EHESS) and expert researcher at Electricité de France (EDF). EDF is one of the largest electricity producers in the world, and it has lately supported and promoted a transition towards the use of renewable energy sources. As Bouly de Lesdain explains, a significant challenge for the energy industry and policy makers is to find the levers of action that make acceptance of green energy technologies possible. In her opinion, anthropology's conceptual methods and tools are perfectly suited to addressing such issues and informing the solutions to them: anthropologists can provide a deep understanding of the context as well as the motivations, adjustments made and problems faced by those adopting sustainable energy technologies.

Understanding complexity from within

The following three chapters turn to the stories of practitioners and consultants who have found their way as anthropologists in the business world. This may not always be an easy path, but it can be very rewarding and dynamic, extending the boundaries of anthropology beyond the more traditional conceptions of the discipline.

Readers are invited to learn about the career of Rikke Ulk, who in 2003 founded and has ever since led the anthropological consultancy company Antropologerne (The Anthropologists). At the time of its establishment, Antropologerne was the first – and woman-led – anthropological consultancy in Denmark and Europe. What motivated Ulk to become one of Europe's pioneers in anthropological consulting was her striving to move beyond the anthropology she experienced during her studies, which was limited by academic boundaries. She wanted to reach out and bring anthropological values to more people and organizations than anthropologists solely based in academic work could. Over the years, Antropologerne has collaborated with numerous governmental and private institutions, making sense of the organizations' issues and bringing clients and users on board in the process of co-creating the solutions to them.

We then turn to Jitske Kramer, a corporate anthropologist, speaker, facilitator and entrepreneur from the Netherlands. Kramer, the founder of the consultancy firm HumanDimensions, emphasizes the importance of understanding the increasingly diverse organizations and companies. Only by grasping their ever-evolving corporate cultures can organizations engage in sustainable cultural change. According to Kramer, anthropology's tools are more than suitable to inform such endeavours: acknowledging the multiple different insider – that is, *emic* – perceptions of reality and combining them with outsider, analytical – *etic* – perspectives can assist in strengthening or changing organizational cultures. Drawing on the anthropological appreciation of 'our cultural variety', Kramer (this volume) has been especially committed to promoting more inclusive corporate cultures.

The next contributor to this section is Anna Kirah, a design anthropologist and psychologist from Norway, well known for her work with companies like Boeing and Microsoft. Spending much of her childhood abroad and often moving, she explains that understanding other people's points of view has always come natural to her. It was precisely this skill that led her to anthropology and to pioneering a people-centric approach to change, innovation and design. Kirah emphasizes the need for anthropologists to not only describe cultures but to engage in facilitating change. In this process, the most important premise is that products and services should not be designed *for* people; instead, they should be designed *with* them. Moreover, anthropologists as practitioners have a 'moral and ethical responsibility' (Kirah, this volume) to address the problems humanity faces, especially in times of accelerated change and the resulting challenges linked to globalization, sustainability, healthcare and technology.

Embracing anthropological thinking

This brings us to the reflections of the final contributor, Riall W. Nolan, professor of anthropology at Purdue University, the United States. Nolan has not only importantly contributed to the fields of international development and higher education as a practitioner, a researcher and an educator but has also been committed to widely spreading the message closely aligned with the mission of *Why the World Needs Anthropologists*: that anthropological thinking is crucial to understanding the complexities of the world we live in and that anthropology is there to be practiced (see e.g. Nolan 2017). In his chapter, Nolan is critical of the current interpretations of reality which are predominantly guided by numbers. To understand the human diversity and complexity, he argues, we need to acknowledge the importance of context. What enables us to do that is anthropological thinking. However, it is not only anthropologists who need to engage in anthropological thinking – but everybody should be doing it. Thus while the world perhaps does not need more anthropologists, we definitely 'need more anthropological thinking' (Nolan, this volume).

Hard impact of a soft science

As this introduction and the remaining chapters in this book suggest, the purpose of this compilation is rather straightforward. We want to convince the reader that anthropology has significantly changed and has outgrown its stereotypical image rooted in the public's perceptions from over a century ago. It has become relevant and crucial for addressing some of the most pressing global issues, from climate change, poverty and inequality, to migration and large-scale conflicts.

This is not to deny the vital role of the more commonly used 'hard' sciences in various fields of STEM (Science, Technology, Engineering and Mathematics) in addressing these problems. However, as Christian Madsbjerg, a management consultant at ReD Associates with a background in philosophy and political science, explains in his book *Sensemaking* (2017), if we are to solve the global problems we need a new way of thinking – one that is based in humanities and social sciences. Our opinion, mirroring the standpoints of the majority of contributors to this book, is similar: it is impossible to address and resolve the pressing global issues merely by looking at numbers, statistics, figures and diagrams. Anthropology thus becomes crucial, as a discipline and a profession enabling the collection and interpretation of 'thick data' – in addition to 'big data' – and sheds a different light on a certain problem, helping us to understand the world we live in more comprehensively (Wang 2013). Why was someone elected a president? Why is a brand new and expensive 'smart' building a disaster? What will happen in the future with passenger cars? Whom should we appoint as a CEO in a company? Our suggestion is clear: in answering such questions, we should stop relying only on questionnaires and quantitative data analytics; instead, the most important decisions should also be informed by ethnography and other qualitative methods which provide a more complete and nuanced picture of what people like, need, want and do.

Contributors of this book show from different perspectives and through examples from their careers that anthropology can provide an excellent platform for understanding human diversity and complexity on different levels and across various parts of our planet – and that it can contribute to developing new, innovative solutions to the world problems. Each chapter is divided into four parts: an essay exploring why the world needs anthropology, a story on what or who motivated each contributor to become an anthropologist and examples from authors' own careers connected to application of anthropological knowledge. Finally, the author of each chapter has added five tips about what anthropologists should or should not do in their practice and what kind of skills and knowledge they should obtain to help change the world for the better. In this way, we intended to provide an updated, contemporary image of who today's anthropologists are, how they found their way into anthropology and where and how they use it in their everyday work.

Even though the chapters are diverse and each offers a distinct point of view, we can find several commonalities among them, especially in their standpoint towards problem solving. Anthropology, the authors of the book believe, can offer in-depth and innovative ways of understanding 'equations' with many 'unknowns', which can be used to describe the global problems humanity is facing. Since there have been no algorithms developed yet to provide complete solutions to such challenges, the world needs anthropologists and anthropology. Perhaps now more than ever.

About the authors

Dan Podjed, PhD, is an applied anthropologist from Slovenia, devoted to developing people-friendly and environmentally responsible services, products and solutions. He is a research fellow at the Research Centre of the Slovenian Academy of Sciences and Arts, a researcher at the Institute for Innovation and Development of the University of Ljubljana and an assistant professor for Cultural and Social Anthropology at the University of Ljubljana. He has led several applied, interdisciplinary and industry-oriented projects, including *DriveGreen* and *Invisible Life of Waste*, and has been involved in the development of various ethnography-based solutions in EU projects (*MOBISTYLE*, *TripleA-reno*, *PEOPLE*, *U-CERT*, etc.). His main fields of research include human-technology interaction, sustainable lifestyle, altruism and volunteering. Dan Podjed served as convenor of the EASA Applied Anthropology Network from its inception in 2010 to 2018 and continues his involvement as one of the network's executive advisors. In 2013, he co-founded the *Why the World Needs Anthropologists* international symposium and co-organized it from 2013 to 2018.

Meta Gorup is an organizational researcher and a doctoral candidate in sociology at Ghent University, Belgium. Combining cultural anthropology and organizational studies approaches, her main research interests lie in understanding the complexities of university life, cultures and identities, specifically among university managers, academics and doctoral students. Dedicated to popularizing applied anthropology and related social sciences, Meta Gorup co-founded the symposium *Why the World Needs Anthropologists* and was a member of the event's core organizing team between 2013 and 2017. She co-convened EASA's Applied Anthropology Network from 2012 to 2018 and remains involved as an executive advisor. Since 2019, Meta Gorup has been a member of the Advisory Board of the Anthropology of Higher Education Topical Interest Group within the Society for Applied Anthropology.

References

Appadurai, A. (1990), 'Disjuncture and Difference in the Global Cultural Economy', *Public Culture*, 2 (2): 1–23.

Baba, M. L. (2009), 'Disciplinary-professional Relations in an Era of Anthropological Engagement', *Human Organization*, 68 (4): 380–91.

Baba, M. L. and C. E. Hill (2006), 'What's in the Name "Applied Anthropology"? An Encounter with Global Practice', *NAPA Bulletin*, 25 (1): 176–207.

Benthall, J. (1985), 'The Utility of Anthropology: An Exchange with Norman Tebbit', *Anthropology Today*, 1 (2): 18–20.

Briody, E. K. and T. Meerwarth Pester (2014), 'The Coming of Age of Anthropological Practice and Ethics', *Journal of Business Anthropology*, Special Issue, 1: 11–37.

Darnell, R. (2015), 'Applied Anthropology: Disciplinary Oxymoron?' *Anthropologica*, 57 (1): 1–11.

Embree, J. F. (1945), 'Applied Anthropology and Its Relationship to Anthropology', *American Anthropologist*, 47 (4): 635–7.

Eriksen, T. H. (2004), *What Is Anthropology?* London: Pluto Press.

Eriksen, T. H. (2006), *Engaging Anthropology: The Case for a Public Presence*, Oxford and New York: Berg.

Eriksen, T. H. (2015), Presentation given at the symposium 'Why the World Needs Anthropologists', Ljubljana, 27 November 2015.

Foster, G. M. (1952), 'Relationships between Theoretical and Applied Anthropology: A Public Health Program Analysis', *Human Organization*, 11 (3): 5–16.

Future Anthropologies Network (2014), *Our Manifesto*. Available online: https://future-anthropologies.net/2014/10/17/our-manifesto/ (accessed 9 August 2018).

Guerrón-Montero, C. (2008), 'Introduction: Preparing Anthropologists for the 21st Century', *NAPA Bulletin*, 29 (1): 1–13.

Hill, C. E. and M. L. Baba, eds (2006), 'Special Issue: The Globalization of Anthropology', *NAPA Bulletin*, 25 (1).

Ingold, T. (2018), *Anthropology: Why It Matters*, Medford (OR): Polity Press.

Kedia, S. (2008), 'Recent Changes and Trends in the Practice of Applied Anthropology', *NAPA Bulletin* 29 (1): 14–28.

Ladner, S. (2014), *Practical Ethnography: A Guide to Doing Ethnography in the Private Sector*, Walnut Creek: Left Coast Press.

MacClancy, J. (2005), 'The Literary Image of Anthropologists', *Journal of the Royal Anthropological Institute*, 11 (3): 549–75.

Madsbjerg, C. (2017), *Sensemaking: The Power of the Humanities in the Age of the Algorithm*, New York: Hachette Books.

Morais, R. J. and E. K. Briody (2018), 'Business Is Booming for Business Anthropology', *AAA Blog*. Available online: https://blog.americananthro.org/2018/02/09/business-is-booming-for-business-anthropology/ (accessed 9 October 2019).

Nolan, R. W. (2017), *Using Anthropology in the World: A Guide to Becoming an Anthropologist Practitioner*, New York and Abingdon: Routledge.

Peacock, J. L. (1997), 'The Future of Anthropology', *American Anthropologist*, 99 (1): 9–17.

Pink, S. (2006), 'The Practice of Anthropology in Great Britain', *NAPA Bulletin*, 25 (1): 123–33.

Pink, S., V. Fors and T. O'Dell (2017), *Theoretical Scholarship and Applied Practice*, New York and Oxford: Berghahn Books.

Pink, S. and J. F. Salazar (2017), 'Anthropologies and Futures: Setting the Agenda', in J. F. Salazar, S. Pink, A. Irving and J. Sjoberg (eds), *Future Anthropologies*, 3–22, Oxford: Bloomsbury.

Podjed, D., M. Gorup and A. Bezjak Mlakar (2016), 'Applied Anthropology in Europe: Historical Obstacles, Current Situation, Future Challenges', *Anthropology in Action*, 23 (2): 53–63.

Rylko-Bauer, B., M. Singer and J. van Willigen (2006), 'Reclaiming Applied Anthropology: Its Past, Present, and Future', *American Anthropologist*, 108 (1): 178–90.

Sillitoe, P. (2006), 'The Search for Relevance: A Brief History of Applied Anthropology', *History and Anthropology*, 17 (1): 1–19.

Sillitoe, P. (2007), 'Anthropologists Only Need Apply: Challenges of Applied Anthropology', *Journal of the Royal Anthropological Institute*, 13 (1): 147–65.

Stewart, A. (2014), 'Too Rare to Be a Token: An Anthropologist in a Management Department', *Journal of Business Anthropology*, 3 (2): 140–58.

Strang, V. (2009), *What Anthropologists Do*, Oxford and New York: Berg.

van Willigen, J. (2002), *Applied Anthropology: An Introduction*, 3rd edn, Westport (CT): Bergin & Garvey.

van Willigen, J. (2009), 'Disciplinary History and the Struggle for Legitimacy and Effectiveness: Reflections on the Situation of Contemporary Anthropologists', *Human Organization*, 68 (4): 392–4.

van Willigen, J. and S. Kedia (2005), 'Emerging Trends in Applied Anthropology', in S. Kedia and J. van Willigen (eds), *Applied Anthropology: Domains of Application*, 341–52, Westport (CT): Greenwood.

Wang, T. (2013), 'Why Big Data Needs Thick Data', *Ethnography Matters*, 13. Available online: http://ethnographymatters.net/blog/2013/05/13/big-data-needs-thick-data/ (accessed 9 October 2019).

1

ETHNOGRAPHY IN ALL THE RIGHT PLACES*

Thomas Hylland Eriksen

Anthropology is frequently described as the art of 'making the familiar exotic and the exotic familiar' (see e.g. Spindler and Spindler 1982). It has also been described as 'the most humanistic of the sciences and the most scientific of the humanities' (Wolf 1974). The standard textbook definition describes it as the comparative study of humans, their societies and their cultural worlds, simultaneously exploring human diversity and what it is that all human beings have in common.

Why should we care about this, in an interconnected, globalized world where virtually anyone can access other people's worlds through media old and new, and why should it matter? For one thing, we may be both less and more similar than we tend to think, notwithstanding globalization. For another, the kind of knowledge anthropologists have is more important than ever, precisely because globalization brings us closer together.

For many years, social and cultural anthropology was associated with the study of 'remote places' and small-scale societies, many of them unfamiliar with literacy and not incorporated into the institutions of the state. Although the study of human diversity concerns all societies, from the smallest to the largest and from the simplest to the most complex, most anthropologists today recognize that all societies in the contemporary world are involved in processes of enormous complexity, such as migration, climate change, global economic crises and the transnational circulation of ideas. Just as European and American anthropologists of the early twentieth century struggled to understand and describe 'the native's point of view' when they travelled to such then-remote parts of the world

* This essay has evolved from the EASA position paper 'Why Anthropology Matters' (2016), which, as president of EASA, I wrote 'with a little help from my friends' in the Executive Committee.

FIGURE 1.1 Thomas Hylland Eriksen at *Why the World Needs Anthropologists* symposium in Ljubljana, Slovenia, 2015. Courtesy Vishvas Pandey.

as Melanesia or Africa, contemporary anthropologists try to grasp their areas of inquiry as fully as possible wherever they conduct research, be it in their own backyard or in faraway locations. They then report on how the people they are studying perceive the world and act on it, still striving to understand 'the native's point of view', although the focus of their inquiry may now be consumption in a European city or ethnic politics in the Pacific.

Some of the questions that the first generations of anthropologists asked continue to concern today's generation, albeit in new ways. On a general level, anthropologists ask what it is to be a human being, how a society is put together and what the word 'we' means. Just as they did in the past, anthropologists explore the importance of kinship in contemporary societies and raise questions about power and politics, religion and world-views, gender and social class. Today, they also study the impact of capitalism on small-scale societies and the quest for cultural survival among indigenous groups, just to mention a few areas of inquiry.

Although there are different theoretical schools, as well as many special interests both regionally and thematically, the craft of social and cultural anthropology consists in a toolbox, which is shared by all who are trained in the discipline. Anthropology does not in itself profess to solve the problems facing humanity, but it gives its practitioners skills and knowledge that enable them to tackle complex questions in very competent and relevant ways. It therefore helps formulating alternatives by way of understanding the world and indeed oneself better than before. The key terms are *cultural relativism*, *ethno graphy*, *comparison* and *context*.

Cultural relativism

Anthropology does not entail judgement of other people's values, nor do its practitioners rank societies on a scale from 'underdeveloped' to 'developed'. This does not mean that anthropologists suspend all judgements about what people do; for example, few would condone violence or inequality, although it may well be perpetrated in the name of 'culture'. Rather, a professional perspective founded in anthropology emphasizes the need to understand what humans do and how they interpret their own actions and world-views.

This approach, cultural relativism, is an essential methodological tool for studying local life-worlds on their own terms. This is the view that societies are qualitatively different from one another and have their own unique inner logic, and that it is therefore misleading to rank them on a scale. For example, one society may find itself at the bottom of a ladder with respect to literacy and annual income, but this ladder may turn out to be completely irrelevant if members of this society have no interest in books and money. Within a cultural relativist framework, one cannot argue that a society with many cars is 'better' than one with fewer, or that the ratio of smartphones to the population is a useful indicator of quality of life.

Cultural relativism is indispensable in anthropological attempts to understand societies in neutral terms. It is not an ethical principle, but a methodological tool. It is perfectly possible to understand other people on their own terms without sharing their outlook and condoning what they do. As the late anthropologist Clifford Geertz (1983: 57) stated, 'you don't have to be one to know one'.

The power of ethnography

The second important tool in anthropological research is ethnographic fieldwork as the main venue of data generation. Traditionally designed as a solo endeavour, ethnographic fieldwork is neither capital-intensive nor labour-intensive, but instead, it can be very *time-consuming*. Even though ever-expanding communication networks render 'here' and 'there' of the 'field' increasingly contested, academic anthropologists typically dedicate approximately one year to the fieldwork. This is necessary because the aim of the ethnographic method is to develop sound knowledge and a proper understanding of a sociocultural world, and for this to be possible, they must learn the local language and take part in as many local activities as they can. Increasingly, however, anthropologists work collaboratively, often in interdisciplinary settings inside or outside the academy. Given the complexity of the world in which we live and the intricacies of the issues often tackled by anthropologists – climate change, global capitalism, mobile communication technologies, etc. – research questions are often dealt with most competently by teams of researchers, ideally with complementary skills (see also Pink's chapter in this book).

The teaching of methodology has often been a challenge in anthropology, and for years, learning by doing was considered a feasible, if not necessarily superior, alternative. Fortunately, methodology teaching has gradually been professional-ized, and one of the most comprehensive and widely used volumes in the area is *Handbook of Methods in Cultural Anthropology* (Barnard and Gravlee 2015), which covers the nitty-gritty of data collecting as well as subjects such as interpretation, the use of new technologies and anthropology and the media. Indeed, the devel-opment of new media and communication technologies in the last few decades has affected and, in many cases, transformed fieldwork. Research on, with or about digital platforms, usually accessed through smartphones, has become a supplement and sometimes a replacement for traditional field methods (Horst and Miller 2012).

Unlike qualitative sociology, which is usually based on intensive interviews, anthropologists do not see interviewing as a main method, although it forms part of their toolbox. Rather, they generate data through *participant observation*, during which the anthropologist simply spends time with people, sometimes asks questions and learns the local ways of doing things as thoroughly as possible. The method demands that the researcher gets to know others on a personal level, meets them repeatedly and, if possible, lives with them during fieldwork. For this reason, ethnographic data are of very high quality, although they often need to be supplemented by other kinds of data, such as quantitative or historical, as the number of collaborators whose lives anthropologists study through participant observation is necessarily limited.

The ethnographic methodology thus enables anthropologists to learn about as-pects of local worlds that are inaccessible to researchers who use other methods. For example, anthropologists have studied the world-views of European neo-Nazis, the functioning of the informal economy in African markets and the reasons why people in Norway throw away more food than they are willing to admit to them-selves and others. By combining direct observation, participation and conversa-tions in their in-depth toolkit, anthropologists provide more detailed and nuanced descriptions of such (and other) phenomena than other researchers. This is one of the reasons why ethnographic research is so time-consuming: anthropologists need to build trust with the people they try to understand, who will then, consciously or not, reveal aspects of their lives that they would not speak about to a journalist or a social scientist with a questionnaire, for example.

The challenge of comparison

New insights into the human condition and new theoretical developments in an-thropology often grow out of comparison, that is the systematic search for differ-ences and similarities between social and cultural worlds. Although comparison is demanding, difficult and sometimes theoretically problematic, anthropologists always compare, whether explicitly or implicitly. By using general terms such as kinship, gender, inequality, household, ethnicity and religion, anthropolo-gists tacitly assume that these categories have comparable meanings in different societies, yet they rarely mean exactly the same thing. Looking for similarities and differences between social and cultural worlds, anthropologists can develop insights into the nature of society and human existence. However, the objective of comparison is not to rank societies on a ladder of development, human rights or environmental sustainability but to understand and explain local life-worlds. Even if this knowledge does not have an explicit policy dimension, it is essential for anyone wishing to contribute to positive change.

Comparison has the additional quality of stimulating the intellectual and moral imagination. Anthropologists often come up with unexpected insights such as, for example, the fact that the internet can strengthen family ties (rather than isolate people; Miller and Slater 2000), that religious activity can help immigrants to integrate into European societies (rather than alienating them from these societies; Bowen 2011), and that peasants can be more economically rational than plantation owners (rather than being hopelessly backward and conservative; Popkin 1979). In this sense, a detailed, compelling study of a society where there is gender equality, ecological sustainability and little or no violence is interesting in its own right, but it can also serve as an inspiration for policy and reform elsewhere. The cool-headed method of anthropological comparison produces knowledge and offers models for coexistence that can be used as a reliable foundation on which to build social change. As such, both primary and applied research can prove to provide useful knowledge for approaching the problems that the world faces, without necessarily offering unequivocal policy advice.

That which cannot be measured

Anthropologists carry out fieldwork, make comparisons and do so in a spirit of cultural relativism, but all along they are concerned with context, relationships and connections. The smallest unit that anthropologists study is not the isolated individual but the relationship between two people and their environment. Whereas the society is a web of relationships, culture, as activated between sentient bodies, not inside them, is what makes communication possible. To a great extent, we are constituted by our relationships with others, which produces us and gives us sustenance, and which confirms or challenges our values and opinions. This is why we have to engage with human beings in their full social context. In order to understand people, anthropologists follow them around in a variety of situations and, as they often point out, it is not sufficient to listen to what people say. We also have to observe what they do, and to analyse the wider implications of their actions.

Because of the fine-grained methodology anthropologists employ, we are also capable of making the invisible visible – be it voices which are otherwise not heard, from marginal or precarious groups, or informal networks between high-status people. In fact, one writer who predicted the financial crisis before it began to unravel was Gillian Tett (2009), a *Financial Times* journalist and editor who, thanks to her training in anthropology, understood what the financial elite was actually doing, not just what they told the public. It should also be kept in mind that not only the methods of anthropology but also its subject-matter evolves rapidly. The World Wide Web appeared in 1992, the smartphone in 2007, and these platforms for communication and dissemination have created new challenges and opportunities for anthropologists. Indeed, a handful of smartphone apps now exist dedicated to ethnographic data collecting. At the same time, web-based publishing and academic discussion have contributed to shifting the conditions for communication within the discipline.

As anthropologists tend to agree, some of the most important things in life, culture and society are those that are hard to measure. Yet, as societies are becoming increasingly entangled in the information age, there is often a strong temptation to simplify complex issues. Whereas a few would doubt the existential value of love, the social importance of trust or the power of Dostoyevsky's novels, in knowledge production and dissemination, clarity and lucidity are virtues. As Einstein is believed to have said, 'Make it as simple as possible. But not simpler'. Accordingly, anthropologists resist simplistic accounts of human nature and accept that complex realities tend to have complex causes. In other words, to understand human worlds, qualitative research and interpretation are necessary.

The need for anthropology

The kind of knowledge anthropology teaches is invaluable, not least in our turbulent, globalized age, in which people of different backgrounds come into contact with each other in unprecedented ways and in a multitude of settings, from tourism and trade, to migration and organizational work.

Unlike training in engineering or psychology, an education in anthropology is not strictly vocational. In consequence, there are few readymade niches for anthropologists in the labour market other than in teaching and research in universities and research centres. Most anthropologists in Europe thus work as journalists, development workers, civil servants, consultants, information officers; they are employed in museums, advertising agencies, corporations and non-governmental organizations (Nolan 2017). Basically, one can find anthropology graduates in a multitude of professions in the public and private sectors, where they implement specific skills and knowledge much sought after by employers: the ability to understand complexity, an awareness of diversity, intellectual flexibility and so on.

There are several reasons why anthropological knowledge can help to make sense of the contemporary world. First, contact between culturally different groups has increased enormously in our time. In the nineteenth century, only a small proportion of the Western population travelled to other countries (when they did, it was usually on a one-way ticket), and as late as the 1950s, even fairly affluent Westerners rarely went on overseas holidays. These patterns have changed in recent decades. Business people, development workers and tourists travel from rich to poor countries: the flows of people who move temporarily between countries have expanded dramatically and have led to intensified contact (see Hannerz 2019). For the global middle classes, long-distance travelling has become more common, safer and cheaper than it has ever been.

As people from affluent countries visit other parts of the world in growing numbers and under new circumstances, the opposite movement is also taking place, though usually not for the same reasons. Largely because of the substantial differences in standards of living and life opportunities, millions of people from non-Western countries have settled in Europe, North America and other industrialized parts of the world. These movements have introduced new ways of acting, being and thinking. In the mid-twentieth century, it might have been necessary for an inhabitant in a Western city to travel to the Indian subcontinent in order to savour the fragrances and sounds of South Asian cuisine and music. Pieces and fragments of the world's cultural variation can now be found in virtually any sizeable city on any continent. As a result, curiosity about others has been stimulated; however, it has also become necessary to understand what cultural variation entails for political reasons. Many parts of the world have seen political upheavals and new conflicts and alignments since the turn of the millennium. In some societies, politics of identity have superseded a politics of class as the main political discourse; tensions between national and ethnic identities and cosmopolitan values founded in universal human rights are articulated, always in locally specific ways, in many countries now, from India to Hungary, from South Africa to Russia. Refugee crises, from that emerging out of the Syrian war to the exodus (and some would say genocide) of Rohingya in Thailand, the Brexit vote in the UK and the proposed wall along the US–Mexican border serve as a contemporary reminder, at times dramatic, of the increased connectedness of people and places as well as of the tension between boundedness and openness, which has been a mainstay of anthropological theorizing for generations. These and many other topical issues testify to the growing importance of anthropological knowledge and an urgent need to deal sensibly with cultural differences.

Second, the world is shrinking in other ways as well. For better or worse, satellite television, mobile phone networks and the internet have created conditions for instantaneous and friction-free communication. Spatial distance is no longer a decisive hindrance for close contact and new, deterritorialized social networks (Deleuze and Guattari 1972) or even 'virtual communities' (Boelstorff 2015; Postill 2018; Rheingold 2000) have developed. At the same time, individuals have a larger palette of information to choose from than they previously did. The economy is also increasingly globally integrated. In the last decades, transnational companies have grown exponentially in numbers, size and economic importance. The capitalist mode of production and monetary economies in general have become nearly universal in the twenty-first century. In politics as well, global issues increasingly dominate the agenda. Issues of war and peace, the environment and poverty are all of such a scope, and involve so many transnational linkages that they cannot be handled satisfactorily by single states alone. Pandemics and international terrorism are also transnational problems which can only be understood and addressed through international coordination, not to mention the arguably greatest challenge of all, that is climate change and environmental degradation (Latour 2017; Stensrud and Eriksen 2019). This ever tighter interweaving of formerly relatively separate sociocultural environments can lead to a growing recognition of the fact that we are all in the same boat: that humanity, divided as it is by class, culture, geography and opportunities, is fundamentally one.

Third, culture changes at a more rapid pace than ever before, and this can be noticed nearly everywhere (Eriksen 2016). In the West, the typical ways of life are certainly being transformed. The stable nuclear family is no longer the only morally acceptable model for procreation. Youth culture and trends in fashion and music change so fast that older people have difficulties following their twists and turns; food habits are changing before our eyes, leading to greater diversity within many countries; secularism is rapidly changing the role of religion in society and vice versa; and media consumption is thoroughly transnational. These and other changes make it necessary to ask questions such as: Who are we, really? What is our culture – and is it at all meaningful to speak of a 'we' that 'have' a 'culture'? What do we have in common with the people who used to live here 50 years ago, and what do we have in common with people who live in an entirely different place today? Is it still defensible to speak as if we primarily belong to nations, or are other forms of belonging equally valid or more important?

Finally, recent decades have seen the rise of an unprecedented interest in cultural identity, which is increasingly seen as an asset. Many feel that the local uniqueness that they used to count on is being threatened by globalization, indirect colonialism and other forces from the outside (Eriksen and Schober 2016). They often react by attempting to strengthen or at least preserve what they see as their unique culture. In many cases, minority organizations demand cultural rights on behalf of their constituency; in other cases, the state tries to slow down or prevent processes of change through legislation. In yet other cases, as witnessed in many places today, dominant majorities try to assimilate or exclude non-dominant minorities. The marketing of cultural identity as a tourist commodity is also widespread, and is naturally being studied by anthropologists as well (Comaroff and Comaroff 2009).

European cultural and intellectual identity is indebted to a long and deep history of philosophy. Giving flesh and blood to its fundamental questions, anthropology thus takes part in the long conversation about what it is to be human. Goethe (2006) once said that 'he who speaks no foreign language knows nothing about his own'. And, although anthropology is often about 'the other', it is ultimately about 'the self'. For it can tell us that almost unimaginably different lives from our own are meaningful and valuable. That everything could have been otherwise, that an alternative world is possible, and that even people who seem to be very strange to you and me are, ultimately, like ourselves. It is thus a genuinely cosmopolitan discipline in that it does not privilege certain ways of life above others but charts and compares the full range of solutions to the perennial human challenges. Nowadays, as diverse in its scope and local traditions as humans can be, anthropology teaches important lessons about the whirl of cultural mixing, contact and contestation. In this respect, anthropology is uniquely a knowledge for the twenty-first century, crucial in our attempts to come to terms with a globalized world, essential for building understanding and respect across real or imagined cultural divides.

YET ANOTHER ACCIDENTAL ANTHROPOLOGIST

It was never my intention to become an academic. In my teens, I oscillated between ambitions to write fiction (who doesn't?) and devoting myself full-time to green activism. Yet, since I needed to do something respectable while sorting out the alternatives, I went to university a year after finishing school. I was keenly aware of anthropology, not least thanks to Fredrik Barth's series of television programmes, broadcast in 1979 when I was seventeen, where he sat behind his desk at the Ethnographic Museum in Oslo, telling stories and sharing photos from his fieldwork. However, I was also attracted to existentialist philosophy (again, who wasn't?) and admired the sophistication of the kind of social theory taught in sociology departments. Therefore, I took three subjects – philosophy, sociology and social anthropology – devoting a year to each. In the end, I began to draft a proposal for a postgraduate degree in philosophy, the ambition being to discuss the relationship between Sartre's early existentialism and the Norwegian philosopher Arne Næss, the founder of deep ecology, known for his conversion from logical positivism to a Spinoza-inspired ecological philosophy. However, the gravitational pull of the anthropology department became too strong to resist, and I soon found myself at the feet of a couple of great, and complementary, teachers, namely, the exuberant and charismatic Argentinian Eduardo Archetti and the profound, occasionally sphinx-like Zen master from Western Norway, Harald Eidheim.

FIGURE 1.2 Last year of high school for Thomas Hylland Eriksen: ready to leave home and discover the world, Nøtterøy, Norway, 1979. Personal archive of Thomas Hylland Eriksen.

(Continued)

There were three main features of social anthropology that attracted me. Unlike sociology, anthropology was truly global in that it did not have the North Atlantic world as its main focus; it taught that all lives are equally worthy of serious examination. And, unlike in philosophy, the fundamental questions of existence were raised through real people's lives and not merely as conversations among academics. These two unique qualities of anthropology were enormously attractive to a young man who spent much of his spare time in the smoke-filled editorial offices of a monthly anarchist newspaper. Third, it was an indisputable fact that the anthropologists of that time, be they professors or postgraduates, had stories to tell about human worlds unknown to the listeners. At any time of the day, there would be someone in the common room who had recently returned from the field, and who enlarged our world through their anecdotes and analytical narratives about life elsewhere.

Yet it cannot be denied that there was an underlying normative, or moral, motivation dragging me into the anthropological world as well. Being politically engaged on the libertarian, green left, I saw in the societies typically studied by anthropologists not only alternative solutions to life's challenges but also potentially some solutions to the problems of my own society, then on the brink of becoming absurdly rich thanks to a lottery win, that is the discovery of huge oil and gas deposits in the North Sea. Obviously, emulating small-scale, often illiterate societies was neither feasible nor desirable. Instead, it seemed both decent and productive to think that it was not only 'them' who should learn from 'us' but that the learning process ought to go both ways.

If these aspects of anthropology created an irresistible gravitational field as I started out, it must be added that I would later come to appreciate anthropology for other reasons as well. There is an anthropological gaze, or approach, to the social world, which slowly grows on you as you study and practice the subject. We are trained to look for the interstitial spaces, that which few others notice. We were told that unless we get 'up close and personal', there is a real chance that we are missing the point about what people are up to. Sometimes, the proximity or intimacy established between anthropologists and informants creates ethical dilemmas precisely because of the proximity. Being taken into other people's confidence, partly because we are foreign and have no stakes in local matters, we establish relationships of trust. And who are we to break this moral contract? Like most anthropologists, I have made friends and close acquaintances in the field. Since our method is mainly informal, much of the time is spent with people going about their everyday affairs. They may see us as friends more than as researchers poking into their lives. As a result, they may make confessions or reveal secrets which are not meant to be broadcast far and wide. Some take drugs. Some are unfaithful to their spouses. Some reveal racist, misogynist or homophobic views. If this information is considered essential for the analysis, it has to be anonymized very carefully, lest we unwittingly create difficulties for people who trust us. One of my teachers discovered that a main source of income in the community he was researching was *moonshining* (distilling liquor illegally). He never mentioned this in any of his published work. By adhering to strict ethical guidelines, what we do is different from the work of a journalist.

Ethnographic fieldwork brings us miles beyond the mere interview. Throughout, the comparative imagination is activated; does this public demonstration resemble the rituals of rebellion in southern Africa described by Gluckman (1982 [1956])? Does this approach to technology bear similarity to Melanesian cargo cults (Worsley 1968)? And what can we learn from the way the Lele of Kasai in Congo classify the strange pangolin, if we are interested in how people create boundaries and codify dirt (Douglas 1966)? The methodology of participant observation and the cultural relativism of comparison make anthropology, with its unfashionably qualitative, interpretive and often ambiguous descriptions, more naturalistic and trustworthy than many other ways of knowing.

As you can tell, I was sold, and I soon became a believer. A believer in ambiguity, complexity and ambivalence. A believer in the importance of deep qualitative knowledge about other people's lives in order to contribute, in a modest way, to making the world a better place.

THE FORTUNATE OF THE FINAL DAYS: ANTHROPOLOGY OUTSIDE OF ACADEMIA

Having worked as an academic anthropologist since my late twenties, I have mainly used anthropological skills and knowledge I possess inside academia, but I have also thrived in the interstices between academia and the less ordered outside world. I have spoken and written about various topics with a bearing on anthropology in a rather vast number of settings. To give a flavour of my extracurricular work, I may mention that I have for more than a year written a weekly book column for an Oslo newspaper, have spoken at two green festivals about climate and capitalism in the last week or so, spoke about smartphones and work for a municipal council the week before. Soon I will finish a popular book about the smartphone in Norwegian, and so on. I have a blog and a podcast, and over the years I have intervened so often in matters of minority rights and immigration that the terrorist Breivik quoted me more than a dozen times in his manifesto, as a symbol of everything that

(Continued)

had gone wrong in Norway. I have also been involved, in a modest way, in politics, and continue to pay my membership fees to the Green Party.

As far as I can see, these forays into the wider public sphere are best understood as an extension of my regular work, not as the application of a certain way of working in an alien setting. Also, I have never done applied work *per se*. The best case of my anthropology outside of academia I can come up with is the following.

Anthropology is not for the feeble-minded. One of the features of the discipline of which we are proud, consists in our tendency to question the validity and relevance of what we are doing. The late 1990s were no exception. At the time, there was – as usual, one might say – considerable ambivalence surrounding the anthropological project. Following the deconstructive glee of postmodernism, which in turn had arrived just after the more coordinated critiques from feminism and Marxism, a certain fatigue could be perceived, from common rooms to monographs. Like many others, I began to speculate about ways of using anthropological epistemologies, methods and approaches in unconventional domains in an effort to have it both ways: anthropology without the pain of epistemological hypochondria, indigestion and academic conventions. So, I began to write a novel, which was eventually published in 1999. It was entitled *Siste dagers heldige* – there is an untranslatable pun in the title, which could be rendered, punless, as 'The Fortunate of the Final Days' (Eriksen 1999). It is a rather sprawling book which posits, as its opening gambit, that Norway has suddenly disappeared, like a present-day Atlantis. In the first chapter, an SAS flight from Copenhagen has to turn back since there is just open sea where the airport and the rest of the country used to be.

The characters of the book are a variegated cast. Some loosely based on real people (but properly anonymized), some purely invented. What they have in common is that they are shipwrecked Norwegians, stranded in foreign countries. Most of them find themselves in Delhi, where they spend much of their time in bars and restaurants reminiscing and trying to reconstruct the country that went missing. One of the characters, an academic called K, modelled on an older and grumpier version of myself, is a disappointed and angry man in his fifties who rails against everything from incipient New Public Management and routine racist exclusion to the alienation from nature experienced by modern people. He has little to say about Norway but more about late-twentieth-century modernity.

The book was explicitly comparative in that the action takes place in India but features Norwegians who talk and think about their country of origin, and it compares, explicitly and implicitly, features of the two kinds of society. As the narrator of the book points out, one might be hard pressed to find two countries so dissimilar from each other than Norway and India. One is cold, rich, almost empty of people and well organized on bureaucratic, formal lines. The other is hot, poor, teeming with all kinds of people and appears to be somewhat chaotic and disorganized. Yet my narrator and his protagonists also find similarities. One of them ponders the common roots of Germanic languages and Hindi, while another is struck by the fact that both Norwegians and some Indians seek the solitude of cold mountains but for opposite reasons: the Norwegians go into the mountains in order to become culturally integrated into the country that has made glorification of the icy winter a national virtue; Indians go there as elderly men in order to dissociate themselves from society as *sanyasins*, following the completion of their duties as workers, fathers and husbands.

There are several reasons why it would have been impossible for me to write this novel unless I had been trained as an anthropologist. First, the comparative gaze, which comes almost as a reflex, was fundamental to the book. Whenever I encounter a phenomenon – architecture, a custom, natural scenery, kinship organization, work ethic – I almost instinctively ask myself about its equivalents, or opposites, or complementary phenomena elsewhere. Looking at Norway from a vantage point in India, and vice versa, as my protagonists do, it provides unusual context.

In these and many other ways, the novel served as a vehicle for reflecting critically on Norwegian culture and society sans footnotes, exposing its oddities, double standards and its misplaced smugness. However, it is also demonstrating, through the reminiscences of the stranded Norwegians in India, that what Norwegians do share in terms of cultural representations is not necessarily what they think, but more mundane things. Besides, as any anthropologist of the day (and most days) would say: there is complexity, nuance and ambiguity. There is no single outlook shared by all members of a society.

The book was not particularly well received in the press. Some reviewers liked it, some were indifferent, while others positively detested it. In hindsight, I concur with the criticism that the book was overloaded and difficult to follow, but not with the outrage expressed by some in defence of their notion of Norwegian culture, of which I was widely believed to be a dangerous, deconstructive enemy. It would take more than a decade before I wrote another novel, *The Road to Barranquilla* (Eriksen 2012), a slimmer, tighter, more conventional story from Colombia with echoes from Gabriel García Marquez and Miguel de Cervantes. It was a more satisfactory book, but left me as an author less satisfied than my first effort. Yet, it was no less infused by anthropological thinking and seeing than 'The Fortunate of the Final Days'. Writing *Barranquilla* I was perfectly aware of the fact that with my fragmented and sketchy knowledge of Colombia, I would never have got away with an academic article from the country, while writing a novel went fine within the limitations I set myself.

FIVE TIPS FROM THOMAS HYLLAND ERIKSEN

1. **When you've seen something, look for the opposite.**
2. **Listen to the outcasts.**
3. **Stay curious and respectful of the knowledge of others,** be they biology professors or unemployed fishermen.
4. **Follow the loops and connect the dots,** even if you don't like what you find.
5. **Remember to take your quinine,** and stay off native women (and men). (Advice given to E. E. Evans-Pritchard before his departure to Sudan.)

About the author

Thomas Hylland Eriksen is a professor of social anthropology at the University of Oslo. He has written books in many genres, including two novels, two co-written books with a biologist, biographies, critical and literary essays, books about the unintended consequences of modernity and a book for adolescents about the need to be engaged, as well as anthropology textbooks, monographs and edited volumes. His research has mainly concerned globalization, identity politics and the social dynamics of ethnically complex societies. His most recent books in English are *Overheating: An Anthropology of Accelerated Change* (2016), *Boomtown: Runaway Globalisation on the Queensland Coast* (2018) and *An Overheated World* (editor, 2018), as well as the co-edited *Identities Destabilised* and *Knowledge and Power in an Overheated World* (both with Elisabeth Schober, 2016 and 2017), *The Mauritian Paradox* (with Ramola Ramtohul, 2018) and *Ethnic Groups and Boundaries Today* (with Marek Jakoubek, 2019).

References

Barnard, H. R. and C. Gravlee, eds (2015), *Handbook of Methods in Cultural Anthropology*, London: Rowland and Littlefield.

Boelstorff, T. (2015), *Coming of Age in Second Life: An Anthropologist Explores the Virtually Human*, 2nd edn, Princeton (NJ): Princeton University Press.

Bowen, J. R. (2011), *Can Islam Be French? Pluralism and Pragmatism in a Secularist State*, Princeton (NJ): Princeton University Press.

Comaroff, J. L. and J. Comaroff (2009), *Ethnicity, Inc.*, Chicago (IL): University of Chicago Press.

Deleuze, G. and F. Guattari (1972), *Anti-Oedipus*, London and New York: Continuum.

Douglas, M. (1966), *Purity and Danger*, London: Routledge & Kegan Paul.

Eriksen, T. H. (1999), *Siste dagers heldige*, Oslo: Aschehoug.

Eriksen, T. H. (2012), *Veien til Barranquilla*, Oslo: Aschehoug.

Eriksen, T. H. (2016), *Overheating: An Anthropology of Accelerated Change*, London: Pluto.

Eriksen, T. H. and E. Schober, eds (2016), *Identities Destabilised: Living in an Overheated World*, London: Pluto.

Geertz, C. (1983), *Local Knowledge: Further Essays in Interpretive Anthropology*, New York: Basic Books.

Gluckman, M. (1982 [1956]), *Custom and Conflict in Africa*, Oxford: Blackwell.

Goethe, J. W. von (2006), *Maximen und Reflexionen*, Helmut Koopmann (ed.), Munich: Deutscher Taschenbuch Verlag.

Hannerz, U. (2019), *World Watching: Streetcorners and Newsbeats on a Journey through Anthropology*, London: Routledge.

Horst, H. A. and D. Miller, eds (2012), *Digital Anthropology*, Oxford: Berg.

Latour, B. (2017), *Down to Earth: Politics in the New Climate Regime*, Cambridge: Polity.

Miller, D. and D. Slater (2000), *The Internet: An Ethnographic Approach*, Oxford: Berg.

Nolan, R. W. (2017), *Using Anthropology in the World: A Guide to Becoming an Anthropologist Practitioner*, London: Routledge.

Popkin, S. L. (1979), *The Rational Peasant: The Political Economy of Rural Society in Vietnam*, Oakland: University of California Press.

Postill, J. (2018), *The Rise of Nerd Politics: Digital Activism and Political Change*, London: Pluto.

Rheingold, H. (2000), *The Virtual Community: Homesteading on the Electronic Frontier*, 2nd edn, Cambridge (MA): The MIT Press.

Spindler, G. and L. Spindler (1982), 'Roger Harker and Schoenhausen: From Familiar to Strange and Back Again', in G. Spindler (ed), *Doing the Ethnography of Schooling: Educational Anthropology in Action*, 20–46, New York: Holt, Rinehart, and Winston.

Stensrud, A. S. and T. H. Eriksen, eds (2019), *Climate, Capitalism and Communities: An Anthropology of Environmental Overheating*, London: Pluto.

Tett, G. (2009), *Fool's Gold: How Unrestrained Greed Corrupted a Dream, Shattered Global Markets and Unleashed a Catastrophe*, New York: Simon & Schuster.

Wolf, E. (1974), *Anthropology*, New York: W. W. Norton & Company.

Worsley, P. (1968), *The Trumpet Shall Sound*, 2nd edn, New York: Shocken.

2

LIVING IN AND RESEARCHING A DIVERSE WORLD

Lenora Bohren

We live in a world that has always been very diverse in terms of adaptations to both our physical and social environments. These diversities have existed over many years of human evolution with limited conflict. Initially, when conflict occurred, it happened mostly in areas where there was competition for natural resources needed for the survival and functioning of particular societies. An example of this was the competition among the Plains Indians for territory and for buffalo. The buffalo roamed over the Plains, thus causing conflict between tribes for territory and for the buffalo which was their main food source. Although these conflicts were often severe, they were highly localized. In today's world, with mass media, the world has become less localized but is still very diverse. As a result, many cultures with diverse values, as with the Plains Indians, have come into contact and have increased the potential for misunderstanding and conflict. Anthropologists with their expertise in culture can play a very important role in addressing these problems. In this chapter, I will discuss some of these problems and the role I have played, as an applied environmental anthropologist, in tackling some of them.

Refugee crises and migrations, for example, create a world that is more in need of anthropologists than ever before. Authoritarian regimes are causing their citizens to leave in ever increasing numbers. Migrants are becoming refugees in countries around the world causing political, economic and cultural tensions of adjustment both by the citizens of the host countries as well as by the refugees themselves. Many of the host countries are unable to accommodate the numbers and needs of people seeking asylum. In such environments, where the lack of understanding of the diverse populations is at an all-time high, anthropologists can play a very important role in helping with the adaptation of refugees to their new countries. For instance, I collaborated with anthropologist Peter Van Arsdale, who is an expert in resettlement issues, on a project assisting the Hmong refugees to adjust to the Boulder, Colorado community. Many of the adjustment problems centred on the fact that locals lacked understanding of the cultural values, language and the needs of the Hmong culture. Our role was to act as mediators between the Hmong and the Boulder community (Van Arsdale and Psarowicz 1980).

Many host countries are traditionally very homogenous and do not have the skills and expertise, or even desire, to deal with this level of diversity. Thus, anthropologists with their training to navigate cultures and languages are essential to provide solutions for the emerging resettlement challenges. In other words, host countries need their assistance to help them accommodate the newcomers by making appropriate policies that take into consideration the needs and expectations of the diverse populations.

Diversity issues

As countries around the world have become more diverse due to economic and social mobility, there is a need for human resource personnel in workplaces who understand and work with the cultural differences of their employees in order to ensure a well-functioning team and to reduce the potential for conflict within their organizations. Anthropologists, especially those trained in business anthropology, are ideal candidates for this job.

In the United States, for example, workplaces have attracted employees from around the world, especially from India and China, to fill specialized technological positions. Other sites of diversity (Vertovec 2007) are universities which are attracting more student populations from countries such as India, China and Pakistan. Despite the obligation to pay higher tuitions at Colorado State University (CSU), the number of international students is increasing every year. At the same time federal and state funding for universities in the United States is decreasing due to tax reductions. Consequently, a need for anthropologists to work with international student organizations and universities to help students adjust to their new environment has evolved. As an illustration, international students' need for medical assistance is no different from American students, yet the perspectives on what care entails differ. Women from Asia, for example, often are in need of medical care since many are of child-bearing age. There has been an increase in the prevalence of caesarean deliveries in the United States and this is often not appropriate for students who have to return to a country where caesarean deliveries are uncommon. This is particularly inappropriate since, generally, if you have had one caesarean delivery you are likely to have to have another one for the next child.

I taught an anthropology course for a group of registered nurses (who were required to return to college to earn a Bachelor of Science degree) where I was able to address topics covered in medical anthropology, including the importance of cultural relativity as it related to medical practices with international patients. One case we discussed, for instance, was the use of hospital gowns. Since gowns are very short and open in the back, many Asian women have refused medical care because such designs are against their cultural beliefs. With examples like this, my students understood fairly quickly that anthropologists can be of help in translating the US medical customs to the patients as well as to assist US medical personnel understand the needs and concerns of their patients. This would be an excellent role for medical anthropologists.

Environmental issues

As intersecting international movements, such as School Strikes for Climate, are quickly spreading to most countries of the world, the environment has become an important global issue. Since this is a global phenomenon with unequal impacts, it is imperative that countries work together to address it. As we know, climate change has been studied by scientists who are experts in atmospheric and ecosystem sciences. There are in-depth studies of changes in levels of CO_2 and other greenhouse gases which have impacted the ecosystem with consequences such as rising sea levels, increased frequency and severity of natural events such as hurricanes and tornados and changing local conditions such as temperature and the frequency of precipitation (Parton et al. 2015).

The human practices contributing to climate change have been recognized: the use or overuse of fossil fuels by individuals, industries and governments; farming and grazing practices that are no longer sustainable; logging rainforests, thus upsetting the natural balance; and general land use change such as the conversion of agricultural lands to urban development. Anthropologists are well-trained to examine the way these practices are affecting the environment and contributing to climate change. The situation of environmental degradation thus creates a need for anthropologists to work with ecosystem scientists to examine cross-cultural factors associated with these activities, to address the different adaptations needed and to ultimately reduce the negative impacts of climate change.

In my own practice, I worked with ecosystem scientists in Africa (Bohren 1993; Swift et al. 1994) to develop interview techniques that helped with the understanding of local decision-making processes and the traditional use of fertilizers. I also interviewed farmers and ranchers in the US Great Plains to gain an understanding of their decision-making process in response to the changing environment (Bohren 1995). Historically, ranchers were seen as different decision-makers than farmers in general. An important finding of my study was that irrigation farmers, who had more control over their environment due to designated water supplies and were thus less dependent on local weather conditions, were less concerned with changing environmental conditions. On the other hand, since both dryland farmers and ranchers had to rely on local weather conditions to make their jobs successful, they were more concerned about the changing environment's effect on their operations. In other words, less predictable production patterns made the producers more sensitive towards the unfolding climate change.

In conclusion, the ability to examine cross-cultural factors associated with human activities puts anthropologists in an excellent position to address the different causes and adaptations needed to reduce negative impacts of climate change. The Intergovernmental Panel on Climate Change (IPCC), that was formed in the 1990s to coordinate an international effort to understand climate change, engages scientists from around the world. The majority of them are experts in understanding the ecosystems but not necessarily the humans that occupy and transform them. Personally, I would like to see us more engaged in this urgent task of working with ecosystem scientists to stop and reverse climate change. This is an excellent role for environmental anthropologists.

Pollution issues

Ever since the industrial revolution, the growing pollution of air, water and soil has become a major world problem. Being harmful to human and environmental health, industrial processes and mobile sources have been major contributors to the problem. Emissions standards for mobile sources and for industrial processes have become essential.

In the United States, Air Quality Inspection and Maintenance (I&M) programmes are the mechanism for measuring mobile source emissions. When emissions standards are exceeded, there are penalties to the companies and/or drivers, which can range from fines to temporary shutdowns that last until the necessary changes have been made. This has not been easy, because many programme administrators have only been interested in technical solutions to the problem such as the addition of catalytic converters to cars. It has taken a long time for administrators to recognize the behavioural part of the problem because issues such as driving behaviour are much harder to control. Basically, when I worked on this topic I had to remind administrators that *people* drive cars! One of the issues I worked with was the check engine light on the car's dashboard which was added as an indicator of emissions problems. When I conducted focus groups throughout the United States about drivers' knowledge of and response to the light, we found that very few drivers knew what it meant and how to respond to it (Bohren 2001). Our final report suggested that drivers need to be taught what each indicator on their dashboard means before they go out on the road. After all, we would never let pilots fly a plane without their knowing what all the devices were on their control board.

Another issue of importance is that of indoor air quality (IAQ). Poor IAQ is characterized by chemical, biological and physical contamination of indoor air that may result in adverse health effects. Bad IAQ has many causes, some of which originate from the construction materials, such as pressed board or glues for carpets, and everyday use, such as the location of Xerox machines or the incorrect spacing of offices. In 1989 I worked on an IAQ project in Washington, D.C., that studied the conditions of the Environmental Protection Agency (EPA) headquarters. The study revealed that employees were unable to continue working in these buildings without risking their health. It turns out that the conversion of a mall into offices created spaces with inadequate ventilation systems resulting in many symptoms of the Sick Building Syndrome, a medical condition where people in a building suffer from symptoms of illness or feel unwell for no apparent reason (Bohren 1989). A response to the Sick Building Syndrome was the green building movement which has become a major direction for new construction. A green building, in its design, construction or operation, reduces or eliminates the potential of negative impacts on its users. Over the years I have been involved with several inspiring projects such as Green Schools (Magzamen et al. 2017), improving IAQ for healthier learning environments; Green Walls (Bartczak, Dunbar and Bohren 2013), the introduction of walls with plants absorbing CO_2; and on Native American Reservations (Bohren 2005), fixing homes and schools with severe IAQ issues. Clearly, the importance of anthropologists in environmental assessments and new construction projects cannot be overstated. Again, an important role for environmental anthropologists.

As long as anthropologists keep doing fieldwork *with* and *among* various cultural groups, the unique relationship and knowledge it generates will always put them in an excellent position to research in concert with other scientists. Furthermore, there should be no reason for shying away from programmes and policies that can save lives, tame refugee and diversity challenges, and prevent the degradation of the environment at local, national and international levels. After all, without knowing and changing oneself, there can be no safe common ecologically friendly future for all.

FIGURE 2.1 Lenora Bohren presenting her work at *Why the World Needs Anthropologists* symposium in Ljubljana, Slovenia, 2015. Other participants of the panel discussion (from left): Thomas Hylland Eriksen, Joana Breidenbach, Lučka Kajfež Bogataj and Genevieve Bell. The discussion was moderated by Dan Podjed (sitting on the right). Courtesy Vishvas Pandey.

The world has become a much smaller place

The world's diverse populations have come into contact more often and have been forced to solve problems that become challenging due to the diversity of values. These challenges are numerous and interconnected: the displacement of large populations, climate change, technological advancements and air, soil and water pollution. Because of concepts such as holism and cultural relativism, anthropologists can be important players in decision-making and the formation of effective policies that are needed to address issues such as refugee crises, cultural hybridization and global environmental degradation.

I have spent most of my career working as an applied environmental anthropologist. If there was to be only one underlying reason why the world needs anthropologists, for me it would be this one: the world is still very diverse, yet it has become a much smaller place.

MY ROAD TO ANTHROPOLOGY

At nineteen, I took my first international trip with my father who was an engineer working with Bell Telephone Laboratories (Bell Labs) on the Telstar radar system. This was my first experience leaving the country. The trip was to Europe, where I was fascinated by the variety of ways people lived, their languages and the food they ate. I returned to the United States with a desire to travel and learn more. I enrolled in a study abroad programme in Spain during my junior year at Pennsylvania State University (Penn State). Penn State's programme was only three months long which was not enough time to learn the language or to really get to know Spanish cultures. I did, however, learn the importance of understanding non-verbal communication. Once, as I was leaving for class, I closed the door in my host family's face. I thought they were saying goodbye, but they were actually signalling for me to come back into the apartment. As you can imagine, they were not happy with my action.

After graduating from Penn State, I worked in New York City (NYC) saving money, intent on going back to Spain. It took me several years to earn enough to plan another trip. However, by the time I saved enough, my vision had changed. My curiosity to experience different cultures had expanded beyond Europe; I wanted to see more of the world. In 1968, I took a freighter from NYC to Morocco, not knowing how long I would be away. From Morocco, I took another freighter to France and then travelled on to Greece where I lived in a cave for a while. During this time, unknown to me, there was a six-day war in Israel; I decided to help with reconstruction and ended up working on a Kibbutz in Israel picking potatoes. After three months I was ready to head east. My first stop was in Iran where I stayed with several friends' families and had a first-hand view of the country of Shah Pahlavi and learned about Bhai and Muslim customs.

(Continued)

My later experiences in Afghanistan and Pakistan were real eye open-
ers. Middle Eastern cultures were so different from the United States. In
Afghanistan, I travelled across the country by bus, ate from a communal
bowl and slept on the floor at rest stops with the other Afghan passengers.
A woman travelling this way was very unusual, but I was treated with courtesy. In Pakistan, I met a young man on a bus and was invited to stay with
his family in Lahore. I learned that he was going home to marry his cousin
even though he was in love with another woman. While in Lahore I helped at
family planning clinics which were essential in a male dominated culture; the
women had to take the responsibility for birth control since the men wanted
as many children as possible to prove their worth as men. As I left, my friend
was just about to marry as tradition required, which left me wondering why
he was not free to make his own choices.

At the end, the trip lasted a year and a half. I learned more about the
diversity of ways people live than I could have imagined. I returned with
so many questions and felt the urge for answers. When I came back to the
United States, I worked again in NYC to save money for graduate school.
Being responsible for hiring new employees for a company and working with
personnel problems, now called human resources, one of the issues I found
was that many of our Latino employees had worse attendance records and
were often fired because of it. Why was this happening? I learned that the
problem was a cultural misunderstanding between the companies' priorities
and Latinos' values and priorities. Looking back on this experience, I could
have done a much better job with the knowledge I gained from anthropology, because my understanding of culture would have made me a better
mediator by helping the concerned parties understand each other. Nevertheless, the trip I made and the job I had when I came back contributed to my
new path. The challenges of life I witnessed made me realize that I wanted to
become an anthropologist in order to understand what I had seen and heard,
and to mediate between culturally diverse communities.

A CROSS-CULTURAL CAREER EXPERIENCE

While in graduate school, I realized that I did not want to be an academic
anthropologist, but I wanted to work towards solving real world problems,
especially environmental ones. Even though CSU did not have an applied
or practicing specialty in anthropology, I had the opportunity to work with
professor Jack Schultz who had an applied emphasis. After I finished my master's degree, I taught in anthropology and sociology departments at every
community college from Denver to Fort Collins, Colorado. I also taught an
anthropology class in a non-traditional setting to soldiers on the Air Force

Base in Cheyenne, Wyoming. Later I was hired to help design and administer a survey of diesel car owners for the National Center for Vehicle Emissions Control and Safety (NCVECS) at CSU. I had never been interested in cars, but as I looked at twentieth century America, I realized the impact the car had had. As an anthropologist, I looked at the car issue in terms of the interface between culture, technology and the environment, and found that I could play a very important role in addressing serious environmental crises. I also learned that I preferred doing research to teaching, although I continued to teach as needed. I spent over 30 years working with NCVECS and the United States Environmental Protection Agency (USEPA).

NCVECS was funded by the USEPA to address issues concerning mobile source impacts on air quality; I was initially hired to be in charge of their socio-economic programme conducting surveys and focus groups. The goal was to understand the human factors contributing to poor air quality resulting from mobile source air pollution. As the car took over from the horse and cities began to sprawl, it was quickly clear that America's love affair with the car had influenced the development of cities and transportation. With the advent of mass production, it fit so well into the American culture with its sense of individualism and adventure. Owning a car became the dream of American youth; teenagers couldn't wait to drive, yet they had no understanding of the negative effects of car emissions. Soon, the negative effects of auto emissions became a major health issue (Bohren 1996). Because of this, I helped develop a curriculum that was available for all US middle school students to help pre-drivers become aware of the environmental consequences of driving. It was called Cars, Cultures and Cures (Bohren 2001, 2009) and it looked at the history of the car driving, taught students how their driving habits contributed to air pollution and discussed the negative environmental effects. Unfortunately, the curriculum was not adopted by many schools because the school boards were not receptive to changes even though the teachers felt it was an important and needed change.

As I touched on above in the case of the check engine light, for many years my work was to help cities and states create I&M programmes that were acceptable to the local populations. When I was sent to Mexico City, one of the most polluted cities in the world, yet again, it was my anthropological background that helped with the cross-cultural dimensions of research and application. In Mexico my role was to assist the city with the adaptation of an I&M programme. Addressing the technical issue was relatively easy; we encouraged US companies to set up inspection stations which measured automobile tail pipe emissions in Mexico. As expected, the behavioural part was more difficult. The first problem was the scope of awareness. Although many drivers were knowledgeable and chose to buy newer cleaner cars, they often did not understand that it was essential to buy unleaded gas since the newer cars were equipped with catalytic converters which were designed to reduce emissions. The second issue was socio-economic. Those drivers who

(Continued)

could not afford to buy newer cars did not bring their cars into the I&M stations. Policy adaptation was the real issue.

When the Mexican government introduced the I&M programme they included the US air quality control policies such as the *no-drive day*, which prohibited the use of cars on certain days of the week according to their license plate numbers. When this policy was applied to Mexico City, citizens that could afford a second car bought old, inexpensive cars with license plate numbers that would allow them to drive on their "no-drive" days. Obviously, since the cleaner cars were left at home and the dirtier ones were driven on the restricted days, the result was more pollution. As an anthropologist I worked to help the Mexican policy makers adapt our policies in a more culturally relevant way. They did this by allowing citizens with cars that were clean, as determined by the inspection programme, to be exempt from the *no-drive day*. The focus on the interface between culture, technology and the environment allowed for comprehensive policy decisions in Mexico City to be made, which led to the reduction in the use of older cars and thus a reduction in the level of air pollution.

FIVE TIPS FROM LENORA BOHREN

1.   **Be an opportunist.** Job offers come when least expected.
2.   **Be flexible.** Adjust your expectations to opportunities that come your way, or you create for yourself.
3.   **Acquire a variety of skills.** It will prepare you for a diversity of options in the job market.
4.   **See the possibilities behind job scenarios.** Many employers, especially if they manage human problems, can benefit from anthropological knowledge. Explain it to them.
5.   **Utilize the anthropological holistic approach and the concept of cultural relativism to help solve real world problems.**

About the author

Lenora Bohren, PhD, a Senior Research Scientist and Director of the National Center for Vehicle Emissions Control and Safety (NCVECS) at Colorado State University (CSU), is an environmental anthropologist who has had extensive experience in project management, data handling and data analysis. She conducted Mobile Source Clean Air Conferences in the United States, Mexico and Europe for over 25 years and worked closely with the United States Environmental Protection Agency (USEPA) for many years managing indoor and outdoor air quality studies. She also consulted with numerous agencies and research organizations, both national and international, addressing the human dimensions of climate change. Currently, she is active in professional organizations such as the American Anthropological Association and is a fellow with the Society for Applied Anthropology. She has served as President of the National Association of Practicing Anthropologists (NAPA) and the High Plains Society for Applied Anthropology (HPSfAA).

References

Bartczak, C., B. Dunbar and L. Bohren (2013), 'Incorporating Biophilic Design through Living Walls: The Decision-making Process', in R. L. Henn and A. J. Hoffman (eds), *Constructing Green: The Social Structures of Sustainability,* 307–30, Cambridge (MA) and London: MIT Press.

Bohren, L. (1989), 'Indoor Air Quality and Work Environment Study, Library of Congress, Madison Building, Volume I: Employee Survey', National Institute for Occupational Safety and Health etc.

Bohren, L. (1993), 'Socioeconomic Components – Example of Rapid Rural Appraisal (RRA) Interview', in J. M. Anderson and J. S. I. Ingram (eds), *Tropical Soil Biology and Fertility: A Handbook of Methods,* 2nd edn, 105–8, Wallingford, Oxon: C-A-B International.

Bohren, L. (1995), 'Socio-cultural Factors in Land Use/Management Decisions', PhD diss., Colorado State University, Fort Collins.

Bohren, L. (1996), 'Car Culture: Society and Mobility', *International Clean Air Conference,* Munich, Germany, 5 March 1996.

Bohren, L. (2001), 'Cars, Cultures and Cures: Environmental Education for K-12', *Practicing Anthropology,* 23 (3): 38–41.

Bohren, L. (2005), 'Indoor Air Quality (IAQ) on the Pine Ridge Indian Reservation', *Healthy Buildings Conference,* University of Waterloo School of Architecture, Cambridge, Ontario, Canada, 6 May 2005.

Bohren, L. (2009), 'Car Culture and Decision Making: Choice and Climate Change', in S. A. Crate and M. Nuttal (eds), *Anthropology and Climate Change: From Encounter to Actions,* 370–79, Albuquerque: Left Coast Press.

Magzamen, S., A. P. Mayer, S. Barr, L. Bohren, B. Dunbar, D. Manning, S. J. Reynolds, J. W. Schaefer, J. Suter and J. E. Cross (2017), 'A Multidisciplinary Research Framework on School Occupant Health and Performance', *Journal of School Health,* 87 (5): 376–87.

Parton, W. J., M. P. Gutmann, E. R. Merchant, M. D. Hartman, P. R. Adler, F. M. McNeal and S. M. Lutz (2015), 'Measuring and Mitigating Agricultural Greenhouse Gas Production in the US Great Plains, 1870–2000', *Proceedings of the National Academy of Sciences of the United States of America,* 112 (34): E4681–88.

Swift, M. J., L. Bohren, S. Carter, A. M. Izac and P. L. Woomer (1994), 'Biological Management of Tropical Soils: Integrating Process Research and Farm Practice,' in P. L. Woomer and M. J. Swift (eds), *Biological Management of Tropical Soil Fertility,* 209–27, Chichester: John Wiley & Sons.

Van Arsdale, P. and J. A. Psarowicz (1980), *Processes of Transition: Vietnamese in Colorado,* Austin (TX): High Street Press.

Vertovec, S. (2007), 'Super-Diversity and Its Implications', *Ethnic and Racial Studies,* 30 (6): 1024–54.

3

WHAT IS IT LIKE TO BE AN ANTHROPOLOGIST?*

Joana Breidenbach

After the 2016 United States elections I tried to do what many others did: I wanted to understand why so many Americans had voted for Donald Trump. From my perspective, living in Berlin as a digital-social entrepreneur, it made no sense why those very same people who would most likely be harmed by his policies in the future had elected him into office. The analysis of most commentators in newspapers and blogs did not convince me. It was only after I read a book by Arlie Russell Hochschild, *Strangers in Their Own Land: Anger and Mourning on the American Right* (2016), that the penny dropped. Her ethnographic portrayal of Louisiana supporters of the Republican Tea Party movement enabled me to see current American politics through the eyes of a Trumpist. Hochschild's explicit aim with this book was to climb the 'empathy wall'. And there I was: suddenly on the other side. Given the cultural frames, life experiences, values and media narratives her interlocutors had been immersed in, I understood – not only with my intellect but also viscerally – why voting for Trump made sense for these people. The book also reminded me of why the world needs anthropologists.

Why? Multiperspectivity!

Hochschild is not an anthropologist but a professor of sociology at the University of California at Berkeley. Nevertheless, ever since I spent a year at Berkeley myself and read one of her early books which were published in the year of my visit, *The Second Shift* (1989), I have been a huge fan of her work, which has been very much informed by the ethnographic method. Like a good anthropologist, she

---

* Trying to explore the consciousness of one anthropologist, this essay takes its inspiration from Thomas Nagel's famous article 'What Is It Like to Be a Bat?'

manages to listen carefully, to tell the 'deep story', and to cultivate our capacity to see the world from a new and different perspective. Such a perspective change is possible, as anthropologists aim to access the point of view of the social group and subjects they are studying.

This capacity for multiperspectivity is one of anthropology's great gifts. Instead of being caught in a specific identification and viewpoint, anthropologists realize that

> there are many different ways that humans relate to the world, each with their own logic. More importantly, they also begin to re-examine their own assumptions, and to see that their own cultural logics are not as commonsensical as they might have presumed.
>
> *(Hasbrouck 2018: 30)*

Or, as I used to say to my kids when travelling around the world, 'there is no such thing as "normal". There is only "different."'

In the early twenty-first century, in an era characterized by exponential increase in complexity due to global interconnectedness and digitization, being able to grasp multiple perspectives simultaneously is a key capacity. Multiperspectivity allows us to navigate complexity. It enables us to integrate perspectives from many different stakeholders and communicate across sectors in order to design and implement strategies – and get work done. Being able to shift between perspectives enlarges the playing field of thought and action, and makes a much-needed global view of life possible.

Why? Suspended judgement!

Most people react to different norms and behaviours by instantaneously judging them as bad or wrong, inferior or (more seldom) superior. Contrast this with the anthropological stance of trying to approach new social settings with a value-neutral lens, to strive to see things as if we knew nothing about them. Of course, this is impossible. But by being as aware as one can be about our own biases and filters, and entering 'the field' with as open agenda as possible, anthropologists often manage to come up with surprising and counter-intuitive insights.

This requires the researcher to apply a culturally relativistic lens and suspend judgement. We open ourselves up to many sources of information and to a variety of different factors which shape the cultural logic of the social scene we are studying. We hold them all in 'mid-air', preventing ourselves from premature conclusions and easy interpretations. We need to be comfortable with not-knowing, with ambiguity and with ambivalence.

In fieldwork settings it is important to reach familiarity with complete strangers very quickly. Yet very often the encounters are full of uncertainty: What is the appropriate behaviour? What is happening? How to understand and respond to a particular reaction? All of this requires the ability to navigate the ambivalence, to pick up subtle clues and to go with the flow and intuition. In the open space of uncertainty, information can reassemble itself and new connections and correlations can become apparent. The familiar can become strange and the strange familiar. Insights appear seemingly out of nowhere. Suddenly, we see patterns and connections which were hidden before.

The ability to defer judgement and thus to make space for new patterns to emerge prevents us from jumping to easy, and potentially misleading, conclusions. During the last decade, for example, we have seen how the concepts of 'culture' and 'ethnicity' have become lazy shorthands for politicians, economists and the media to explain all kinds of phenomena, especially problems and conflicts. This is an example of what the philosopher Timothy Morton (2016) calls 'easy think substances' which lead to 'easy think ontologies'. Anthropologists seeking a deeper understanding and immersing themselves in specific settings have demonstrated over and over how alternative factors, such as 'communities of practice' (Wenger 1998), economic competition or (subtle) societal power hierarchies, are often much more relevant causes for conflict than 'cultural differences' or 'intercultural misunderstandings' (Breidenbach and Nyíri 2009).

The capacity to dwell effectively in the areas of grey – in the uncertainties of life – means that we are not dependent on a binary view of the world as black and white, good or bad. Instead, we are able to transcend those polarities, reaching a new, more inclusive and nuanced understanding of reality.

Why? Coming closer to the fluidity of life

Whereas earlier generations of anthropologists tried to depict 'a culture' as a whole, writing ethnographies about the life of an entire population, such as *The Argonauts of the Western Pacific* (Malinowski 1922) or *The Nuer* (Evans-Pritchard 1940), this has given way to a much more modest and realistic aim. Today, most anthropologists claim to grasp a holistic snapshot of a specific social setting, constellation or field. They question monolithic representations and truth claims, while instead giving voice to other, often marginalized perspectives. I still remember my excitement upon reading the work of the anthropologist Orvar Löfgren, who deconstructed 'Swedishness' by analysing how a very specific set of middle-class values had become the hegemonic Swedish 'national culture' (1989). Viewing the internal and external structures of life as constructed, as man-made, as contested, is to understand that life is dynamic and in constant movement.

With digitization, the view that reality is not something static and fixed but fluid and in a state of constant 'beta', becomes more ubiquitous. The internet is in a continuous process of change. Not only do thousands of new websites, platforms and services emerge every day, the existing ones are also constantly updated. We are surrounded by unstoppable streams of real-time content. This dynamic also takes place on another level: all information can be dissolved into the smallest components and combined in a new way. By reducing information to 0 and 1, the digital world is extremely divisible and changeable. In principle, anything can be exchanged for anything else; for example, reputation for money and knowledge for attention. This fluidity presents a challenge to people who seek security in a supposedly stable and fixed external world. The anthropological lens is much better suited to cope with the factual reality that the world is in constant motion.

But fluidity does not only pertain to the external world. Since at least the 're-flexive turn' of anthropology in the late 1980s, the years which were formative for my own anthropological thinking, we know that the situatedness, fluidity and movement also apply to the observer. I recently found a similar perspective in the works of a group of philosophers and artists calling themselves metamod-ernists, a school of thought mediating between aspects of both modernism and postmodernism. As the metamodern writer Keks Ackerman (2018), who studies technological innovations, writes,

> Innovations are not the only elements in motion … we … observers are also constantly changing. We look through our respective personal perspectives at innovations and contemporary change. We carry different filters that contribute to how many details and perspectives we can capture. […] As founders and funders, we need to be self-aware that some things are within our scope, while others are outside of our field of vision. Where are our blind spots, and how do we fill them?

With our understanding of context-dependency and changeability of all phe-nomena, anthropologists are well trained to understand the perspective that we are 'a movement studying movement'. This dizzying point of view was well captured in the movie *Interstellar* (2014), when the astronaut Cooper needs to spin his ship in order to dock the rotating orbital station. The scene gives viewers an almost visceral feeling of what it means to navigate in multidimensional, moving environments.

Why? Including inner and outer dimensions!

Anthropologists are equally, if not more, interested in the 'why?' as in the 'what?'. In our endeavour to understand life, we not only focus on the visible, external processes and structures but insist on the inclusion of the invisible, internal pro-cesses, subjectivities, human needs and values. While many scientific disciplines increasingly focus on ever more specific and narrower areas of interests, anthro-pologists approach their subject areas with a more systemic view of life. This perspective looks less at isolated phenomena and more at the connections and interrelations between different parts of life.

In order to systematize this multi-perspective holistic approach, I find Ken Wilber's AQAL concept useful (Figure 3.1). Different events can take place in different spheres or dimensions. On the left side of the model are the inner di-mensions, on the right the external phenomena. Above are the individual aspects,

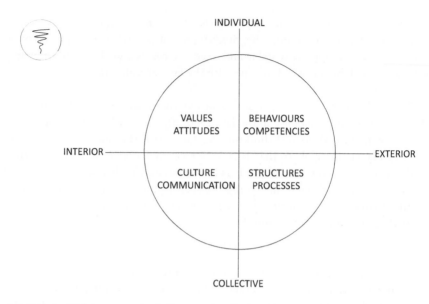

FIGURE 3.1   Multi-perspective holistic approach. Graphic adapted from Keks Ackerman (2018), based on Ken Wilber's AQAL.

below the collective aspects. With their immersive and open methodology anthropologists are in a unique position to empirically study how the quadrants influence each other; how attitude drives behaviour, behaviour drives attitude, culture drives processes and so forth.

The ability to see a bigger picture and the wider context of the phenomena studied – including those aspects of life which are not easily observable and quantifiable, such as inner subjectivities, emotions, physical sensations and so on – is a huge asset in a world dominated by an atomistic view of life. We all know how misinformed and detrimental the image of humans as 'Homo oeconomicus' was for the development of economic theories, policies and the world economy as evidenced by the 2007 crash. Humans are not rational, autonomous actors trying to maximize return but are deeply interdependent, embedded in nature and constantly being shaped and shaping culture. The latter understanding guides anthropology and the ethnographic approach and has recently fuelled the emergence of behavioural economics and a whole new generation of economists striving for a more nuanced economic thinking. In a similar way, the current trends of big data and machine learning desperately need to be informed by a much fuller and more realistic image of human agency and aspirations. Otherwise, we are likely to enter an age of 'tech solutionism' and 'dataism', as depicted by Yuval Noah Harari's *Homo Deus* (2016): we need to include the 'messiness of everyday life' in the design of our societal and economic systems, not some sanitized, quantified, reductionist cliché.

The insistence of anthropologists to put empirically documented human behaviour at the centre has already led to the popularity of new innovation technologies, such as design thinking and human/user-centred design. But the 'anthropological turn' of many disciplines, such as behavioural economics, geography or sociology, has often come with another bias: the vast majority of studies claiming to put human behaviour at the centre have consisted of looking at WEIRD – Western, Educated, Industrialized, Rich, and Democratic – subjects. If we jointly want to create a new operating system for a healthier, more inclusive and ecologically sustainable society, we will have to take much more diversity into account. Here, anthropologists can play a leading role by asking critical questions: What social dynamics are at play? What value systems drive behaviour? Who are the changemakers holding the keys? Which needs are expressed? To ask and answer questions like these is a key skill in contemporary life.

Why? Asking the big questions while studying the very concrete

Not only does the anthropological mindset encourage us to move back and forth between the four quadrants, but it also asks us to oscillate between the essential, big questions of life, and often utterly mundane everyday activities. It roots the concerns of philosophers and religious scholars about the deepest meanings and motives of human existence in the concrete lived lives. My favourite university teachers, László Vayda (Ludwig Maximilian University of Munich), Laura Nader (University of California at Berkeley) and Daniel Miller (University College London), excel(led) at this. Immersing themselves in the minute details of such phenomena as European witchcraft practices, arbitration cases in the United States (Nader 2002) or the use of Facebook in Trinidad (Miller 2011), they were able to make me see everyday actions as an expression of much larger and more significant phenomena. I deeply appreciate this perspective, as it stands opposed to a widespread attitude of cynicism or the view of modern life as shallow and superficial. Instead, it evokes a knowing caring for the world, a stance which metamodernists have called 'informed naivety' or 'ironic sincerity' and which we see in the books of David Foster Wallace or the artistic interventions of Shia LaBeouf.

With their feet on the ground, anthropologists are also uniquely positioned to observe the 'evolving edge of society'. By this I mean that they are often the early detectors of new trends, many of which originate in the so-called 'periphery' which is still the main location of anthropological knowledge production. Our quality of sensing the emergent has become an asset increasingly valued by companies, non-profits and other institutions who employ anthropologists as researchers, consultants or product designers.

Why? Listen to those stories!

Our contemporary, highly interconnected world is full of non-linear and exponential developments. These cannot be captured with linear, rational descriptions. We need to stand back to listen and observe the stories which emerge from the systems we are trying to understand. This analytical approach meets a deeply human propensity to learn through stories. As Mary Catherine Bateson wrote, 'Our species thinks in metaphors and learns through stories' (quoted in Hasbrouck 2018: 86). The anthropological tradition of 'thick description' (Geertz 1973) often verges on the literary and is ideally suited to transmit its insights through stories to a mainstream audience. It invites us to witness the complex, contradictory, fantastic fabric of life; to develop a mindset capable of grasping the fluidity and contradictions of reality.

Thus in the case of Louisiana's support for Trump, Arlie Russell Hochschild showed in the above-mentioned book *Strangers in Their Own Land* (2016), how deeply held values, such as pride in self-reliance, honesty and hard work and a very specific interpretation of societal changes, led a majority of citizens to vote against stronger environmental protection and social safety nets. In the view of largely white and male voters, liberal politics had helped women, minorities and immigrants to 'cut the line', preventing them from achieving the American dream. Culturally they felt more aligned with the Trump supporting petrochemical corporate establishment, even though their politics harmed them directly.

Complex thinking for complex times

Anthropology offers the potential for a much more world-centric world view adequate to tackle the most urgent contemporary challenges we face, which are all global in nature. At its best, anthropology opens up a new understanding of the mechanisms of the world, offering orientation in increasingly complex times. Its deep insights into human motivation, power dynamics and creative potential could inform a much broader set of policy makers, innovators and entrepreneurs, inspiring them to create healthier, more systemic and sustainable companies and policies. Personally, anthropology has encouraged me to dive into uncharted territory, experiment with new ideas, and look at the world with sustained awe.

LEARNING ABOUT CULTURE TO FREE MYSELF

Upon starting my studies at the Ludwig Maximilian University of Munich, I was pretty clueless. I felt I could study all kinds of subjects, from law to economics to philosophy. I initially enrolled in art history, mainly because I came from a family of art enthusiasts and some of my most peaceful and fond childhood memories had been of visits to the Prado, the Alte Pinakothek and the Uffizi Gallery. I also appreciated art as a lens through which we can explore history, my favourite subject at school. Looking back, I sense that art appealed to me also because it is an intense statement of humanity's drive for self-expression and societal exploration. Many artists living on the edge of society are seismographs of the future, and this resonated with my own drive to become 'someone'. On a more banal level, art history suited me because my fellow students were much more fashionably dressed than those of other departments and I did have a keen sense of style.

Besides my major, I had to choose two minors. Again, I tried out all sorts of courses: history, literature, archaeology. The idea to check out the anthropology department – or, as it was called at the time, the *Institute für Völkerkunde und Afrikanistik* (Institute of Ethnology and African Studies) – came from Stephan, a law student and flatmate in my first apartment in Munich Schwabing. (He would soon become my partner and has remained ever since.) Stephan raved about a Hungarian professor named László Vajda, whose lectures he had recently attended. Next term, I enrolled in a seminar Vajda gave on European witchcraft. I was immediately hooked; by the way he vividly described the details of everyday life and subjectivities in the seventeenth and eighteenth centuries, while at the same time connected them to larger social and cultural patterns, thus making sense of the internal logic behind these horrific acts. By the end of the term I had switched my major to anthropology. This meant that most of my time was spent amongst a much frumpier crowd. But I never regretted the move.

Vajda took me under his wing and tried (only half-successfully) to inspire me with his methodology, which consisted of an encyclopaedic index of excerpts from all areas of anthropology. The walls of his study were covered in slip boxes, categorized into hundreds of cultural practices and containing examples of these from around the world to be used for the purposes of comparative anthropology. Even though I later abandoned Vajda's encyclopaedic approach, the importance he assigned to history and social construction left a fundamental mark on my thinking. What fascinated me most in those early years was the revelation that everything we took for granted and saw as 'natural' was socially constructed. This applied not only to kinship patterns but also to deep emotions such as motherly love. I found the empirically documented diversity of human life and the intricate relations between cultural norms and inner subjectivities liberating. They opened up an existential space in me: if lifestyles, values and practices were constructed and relative, I had the freedom to distance myself from my upbringing and surroundings. I could follow my own needs, motivations and intuition, trying to become more and more myself.

My interest in anthropology further deepened during my year at the University of California at Berkeley where I was enrolled in seminars and lectures given by Laura Nader. Nader taught courses on law and conflict resolution, energy science and Occidentalism, always focussing on how central dogmas were constructed and identifying the power relations behind them. Later, while writing my doctoral thesis, I attended University College London and

(*Continued*)

became a huge fan of Daniel Miller's work on mass consumption. Whereas my education in Munich had been historically and comparatively oriented, at Berkeley and London I saw that the anthropological lens and ethnographic method were powerful tools to understand contemporary topics, including power dynamics and hegemonies. But they were also useful to bust widespread myths, regarding for example the supposed superficiality of consumer culture or the underpinnings of governing economic theory. Beyond these specifics, the critically informed, yet compassionate (instead of instrumental or cynical), portrayal of human endeavours, our vulnerabilities, the struggles to make meaning, express ourselves and create various versions of the good life, resonated deeply with me. Finally, I loved how fieldwork – of which I had only done short spells – allowed me to move close to people instantaneously and enabled me to very quickly become psychologically intimate with strangers.

Recently, one of my oldest friends from university days, who himself had studied law, remarked that he had always envied my choice of anthropology: 'It is so obvious that you studied something which really provided you with a lens and a whole tool kit to look at the world, make sense of it and find your place in it'. I think he was right.

FIGURE 3.2 Joana Breidenbach presenting her story of how anthropological perspectives on the society and a trip around the world inspired her to become a social entrepreneur. *Why the World Needs Anthropologists* symposium, Ljubljana, Slovenia, 2015. Courtesy Vishvas Pandey.

FROM POPULARIZING ANTHROPOLOGY TO SOCIAL ENTREPRENEURSHIP

Using the anthropological lens to make sense of the world for myself and others has served me well over 25 years. So far, I have had two different careers and I am currently embarking on a third one. I will briefly write about all of them, as I tapped into the anthropological mindset throughout my professional life.

My thirties – popularizing anthropology

Midway through writing my doctoral thesis I discovered a topic I felt passionate about: the globalization of culture. I was reading ethnographic case studies demonstrating how local societies adapted to and changed global goods, ideas and institutions. But this knowledge was not entering the mainstream discourse in Germany, where everyone was very concerned about stereotypical views of globalization as either unabated Americanization or dystopian fragmentation. Together with my friend from the anthropology department in Munich, Ina Zukrigl, I wrote an academic article for the most respected – yet also the most outdated – German anthropology journal about the new cultural diversity anthropologists were documenting in their encounters at the intersection between what was then referred to as 'the global and the local' (Breidenbach and Zukrigl 1995). Later, while I was busy raising two small kids, we turned this into a book called *Tanz der Kulturen* (*The Dance of Cultures*, Breidenbach and Zukrigl 1998), a pun on Samuel Huntington's *The Clash of Civilizations* (1996). This counter-narrative consisting of many ethnographic examples became popular and meant that Ina and I spent the next years spreading our message in numerous talks and articles for mainstream German-speaking audiences. Among the most effective outlets was a monthly column in the German business magazine *brand eins*.

I then turned my attention to other topics, which I researched with a new collaborator, the anthropologist Pál Nyíri. One of them was the new domestic mass tourism developing in China and Russia, about which Pál and I published a number of articles in diverse publications ranging from *Current Anthropology* (Breidenbach and Nyíri 2007) to the German travel magazine *Geo*. Our next publications, *Seeing Culture Everywhere* (Breidenbach and Nyíri 2009) and *Maxikulti* (Breidenbach and Nyíri 2008) critically questioned the sudden ubiquity of 'culture' as a concept that was to help us understand the tensions, conflicts and uneven developments of our world. Anthropological concepts, ethnographic case studies and our own fieldwork were the backbone of all of these writings and managed to attract a broad audience because of the inherent storytelling qualities of our material and our clear writing style that

(Continued)

avoided technical jargon. In retrospect, I would say that the main impact of all of these works was to popularize anthropological approaches and methods while at the same time the books, articles and talks contributed to a more differentiated, empirically based and potential-oriented discourse about globalization and Germany's place in the current cultural transformation.

My forties – kickstarting digital-social innovations

In 2007 I co-founded betterplace.org and in 2010 the accompanying Think-and-Do Tank, the betterplace lab. My main motivation to start an online platform enabling small grassroots initiatives from around the world to finance their projects was the insight – gained from decades of anthropological research – that the international aid industry might be creating as much harm as it does good. The idea of an 'eBay for help' seemed like a great way to give voice and visibility to local changemakers who often lack sufficient funds to turn their ideas into reality – and thus to democratize aid. Throughout the development of betterplace.org, which is now Germany's largest crowdfunding platform for non-governmental organizations and annually collects millions of euros in donations for social projects, we have applied a user-centric perspective, grounded in empirical data and guided by a vision to enable more effective support for the poor and marginalized.

With the betterplace lab, I was again able to reconnect much more to my fascination with broader cultural dynamics and empirical research. Having spent a few years trying to understand online fundraising, I became aware that digitization was to fundamentally change not only everyday communication styles, economic value chains and business models but also the way civil society will organize in the future. Thus, in our Think-and-Do Tank, we aimed at grasping the bigger picture of the digital transformation. To this end, not only did we do a lot of desk-based trend research, which resulted in the publication of over 30 digital-social trends, but we also started the Lab Around the World, a series of fieldwork in (until now) 27 countries, looking at the emergence of a global ecosystem of digital-social innovations. Our aim is to scout, curate and distribute the knowledge of an 'internet for good' to the German social sector and other mission-driven institutions, enabling them to use digital technologies for their own goals. Currently the betterplace lab is consulting a number of German ministries, companies and non-governmental organizations in their approaches to digitization, ranging from the integration of refugees with the help of digital platforms to strengthening online counterspeech and the new generation of digital democratic changemakers. At the same time the lab is experimenting with new – networked, rather than hierarchical – organizational and leadership models, in the course of which I stepped down as LaBoss and became the Godmother.

FIGURE 3.3   The betterplace lab at a team retreat. Working self-organized, without a boss or managers, involves new communication skills and a
lot of experimentation. France, 2019. Courtesy Joana Breidenbach.

My fifties – towards a new operating system for society and the economy

After the operative management of betterplace has been successfully handed over to the next generation, I have embarked on a new project called Das Dach (The Roof). This is, first, a space in Berlin which hosts a number of innovative people and companies, all working towards a world that serves humanity's highest potential. Das Dach also has its own research branch, investigating the connections between social systems change and inner transformation. One of the first outputs has been the book *New Work Needs Inner Work: A Handbook for Companies Moving Towards Self-organisation*, in which we describe new fluid ways to lead and collaborate (Breidenbach and Rollow 2019).

In line with the anthropological imperative to be comfortable with ambiguity and insecurity, Das Dach's founding team has given itself time to sense who exactly we were, what needs we can meet and where we can make a difference. Whatever we will do, I am pretty sure it will be aligned with some cornerstones of the anthropological mindset: looking at phenomena in their wider systemic context, revelling in messy empirical encounters and taking multiperspectivity seriously while embracing the fluidity of life. Were I to start my career all over again, I would enrol in an anthropology course at a good university anytime.

FIVE TIPS FROM JOANA BREIDENBACH

1. **Develop a public voice.** Engage in policy debates, organizational and company strategies as well as in the broader media discourse. Challenge the establishment with your constructive anthropological perspective. Don't stop at deconstruction. Prioritize which message to spread. If you want your message to be heard by a broader audience, you will need to focus on a few key statements, sacrificing some nuances.

2. **Study up.** While giving voice to marginalized populations is a very important anthropological task, Laura Nader's call to 'study up' – to analyse relations of power and those in positions of power – is as relevant today as it was in 1969 when Laura Nader's article Up the Anthropologist was first published.

3. **Dare to evaluate and acknowledge healthy hierarchies.** Anthropologists are deeply suspicious of declaring certain values and behaviours as more advanced and evolved than others. While this is important, I believe there are hierarchical differences; between less and more complex values and goals, wider and narrower perspectives, deeper and more superficial feelings. Dare to call a spade a spade and don't get stuck in postmodern nihilism.

4. **Take your kids, friends and mentees along your own intellectual and emotional journey.** Having experienced my enthusiasm for anthropology throughout her childhood, my daughter decided to study anthropology. In his college application essay, my son wrote about his early childhood realization during our many travels around the world: that there was 'no such thing as normal, only different'. Sharing what you love can make a lot of impact.

5. **Start meditating.** Ever since I started meditating, I have been amazed by the parallels between the anthropological mindset and the practice of mindfulness. Both aim to rest in 'open space' in order to observe life's movement: the meditator on the micro-level (inner thoughts, emotions, physical sensations), the anthropologist on the macro-level (social connections, power dynamics, cultural meanings). Meditation frees you from looking at the world with your habitual filters and shows you new, emerging patterns. Thus, ultimately, both meditation and anthropology can help us facilitate creating the kind of world we want to live in.

About the author

Joana Breidenbach has a PhD in cultural anthropology and is the author of numerous books on the cultural effects of globalization, migration and tourism. In 2007 she co-founded betterplace.org, Germany's largest crowdfunding platform for social projects, followed by the betterplace lab, a Think-and-Do Tank researching digital-social innovation. Recently Joana Breidenbach co-founded Das Dach, devoted to 'building a world that serves humanity's highest potential'. In line with her interests in impactful innovations she supports numerous initiatives such as the ReDI School for Digital Integration and CRCLR, and is a (mini)-investor in mission-driven start-ups such as Stadtfarm, Clue, DeepL and Nebenan.de.

References

Ackerman, K. (2018), *Future Sensor*. Available online: https://medium.com/future-sensor (accessed 15 October 2019).

Breidenbach, J. and I. Zukrigl (1995), 'Ethnologische Perspektiven auf die Beziehungen zwischen globaler und lokaler Ebene', *Zeitschrift für Ethnologie*, 120: 15–29.

Breidenbach, J. and I. Zukrigl (1998), *Tanz der Kulturen: Kulturelle Identität in einer globalisierten Welt*, Munich: Verlag Antje Kunstmann.

Breidenbach, J. and P. Nyíri (2007), '"Our Common Heritage": New Tourist Nations, Post-"Socialist" Pedagogy, and the Globalization of Nature', *Current Anthropology*, 48 (2): 322–30.

Breidenbach, J. and P. Nyíri (2008), *Maxikulti: Der Kampf der Kulturen ist das Problem – zeigt die Wirtschaft uns die Lösung?*, Frankfurt: Campus-Verlag.

Breidenbach, J. and P. Nyíri (2009), *Seeing Culture Everywhere*, Seattle and London: University of Washington Press.

Breidenbach, J. and B. Rollow (2019), *New Work Needs Inner Work: Ein Handbuch für Unternehmen auf dem Weg zur Selbstorganisation*, München: Vahlen Verlag.

Evans-Pritchard, E. E. (1940), *The Nuer: A Description of the Modes of Livelihood and Political Institutions of a Nilotic People*, Oxford: Clarendon Press.

Geertz, C. (1973), *The Interpretation of Cultures: Selected Essays*, New York: Basic Books.

Harari, Y. N. (2016), *Homo Deus: A Brief History of Tomorrow*, London: Harvill Secker.

Hasbrouck, J. (2018), *Ethnographic Thinking: From Method to Mindset*, New York and Abingdon: Routledge.

Hochschild, A. (1989), *The Second Shift: Working Families and the Revolution at Home*, New York: Viking Penguin.

Hochschild, A. R. (2016), *Strangers in Their Own Land: Anger and Mourning on the American Right*, New York: The New Press.

Huntington, S. (1996), *The Clash of Civilizations and the Remaking of World Order*, New York: Simon & Schuster.

Interstellar (2014), [Film] Dir. Christopher Nolan, USA: Paramount Pictures and Warner Bros Pictures.

Löfgren, O. (1989), 'The Nationalisation of Culture', *Ethnologia Europaea*, 19: 5–23.

Malinowski, B. (1922), *Argonauts of the Western Pacific: An Account of Native Enterprise and Adventure in the Archipelagoes of Melanesian New Guinea*, London: Routledge and Kegan Paul.

Miller, D. (2011), *Tales from Facebook*, Cambridge and Malden (MA): Polity Press.

Morton, T. (2016), *Dark Ecology: For a Logic of Future Coexistence*, New York: Columbia University Press.

Nader, L. (1969), 'Up the Anthropologist: Perspectives Gained from "Studying Up"', in Dell Hyms (ed), *Reinventing Anthropology*, 284–311, New York: Random House.

Nader, L. (2002), *The Life of the Law: Anthropological Projects*, Berkley, Los Angeles and London: University of California Press.

Wenger, E. (1998), *Communities of Practice: Learning, Meaning, and Identity*, Cambridge: Cambridge University Press.

4

ANTHROPOLOGY IN AN UNCERTAIN WORLD

Sarah Pink

The world needs anthropologists because it is a site of inevitable uncertainties, riddled with all types of inequalities, and inhabited by problems that cannot be solved and by solutions to problems that do not exist. In the near future it will moreover face what are being touted in business and technology news as a series of utopian or dystopian technological complexities. These are associated with a new wave of automation and machine intelligence, and corresponding uses of personal and other data, that have been predicted to change the ways we experience many aspects of our lives. In short, the world is not only in a mess but also needs to work out how to prepare for and engage with its technological futures.

Unfortunately, the existing modes of doing so are not tenable. One is what has been called 'solutionism' whereby technological solutions are continually developed and strived for, typical of globally influential sites such as Silicon Valley in the United States (Morozov 2013). Such thinking tends to assume that technological innovation will solve social and economic problems, yet does not necessarily have appropriate understanding of the social to be able to adequately formulate what the 'problem' is. Moreover, it represents a technological determinism that anthropologists have long since demonstrated to be naïve.

Another way many modern governments and institutions have sought to deal with such moments of present or possible future crisis has been to put into place anticipatory risk mitigation strategies based on predictive scenarios (Anderson 2010; Anderson and Adey 2011). Such anticipatory logics of risk mitigation permeate many contemporary societal institutions in the forms of insurance, health and safety regulations, and ethical approval committees, all too familiar to anthropologists (Pink 2017). Regulatory bodies are increasingly empowered to pursue such strategies through the use of predictive 'big data' analytics, whereby potentially massive amounts of data are harvested and analysed, often with little or no attention to the nuances of the everyday realities from which they have been produced. This has the worrying consequences of imposing governance measures on the basis of data that can never give a 'true' account of what people actually do in everyday life. Such measures often only exacerbate the inequalities that already existed (Chan and Bennett Moses 2017; Smith and O'Malley 2017) and therefore create new problems while doing nothing to change the irrevocable fact that the future is uncertain and we have no way of predicting what will happen next.

Indeed, there is not only a need to prepare for new technological futures but to participate in creating ethical and responsible data and machine intelligence futures, which are likely to be much more boring than the utopias and dystopias that are currently voiced. Without understanding how people really live in the world, their hopes, anxieties, aspirations and the improvisatory modes of action through which they weave their ways through the world, we stand very little chance of designing a future world in which our relationships to technology will change.

An anthropology of emerging technologies

For these (and other) reasons the world needs anthropologists. In particular, at this contemporary moment the world needs an interdisciplinary and interventional anthropology of our relationships with the emerging technologies that have been predicted to impact our lives.

The Anthropology of Emerging Technologies that I propose would push forward a new way of understanding technological change and its relationship to people, society, institutions and places. Such an anthropology is theoretically informed, ethnographically rooted and interventionally focussed. It goes beyond research about human–machine and socio-technical relations, which have dominated disciplines such as human–computer interaction (HCI), sociology, science and technology studies (STS) and human geography, to, instead, understand emerging technologies as part of an emergent world. As such it considers how technologies and people are part of constantly shifting configurations, which are also contingent on multiple other things and processes of different qualities and affordances. This includes accounting for what Ingold has called the 'weather world' (Ingold 2010) and more broadly the environments of which we and technologies are part.

Based in an interventional design anthropology agenda, which puts a processual theory of emergence at its core and seeks to participate in processes as they play out (Akama, Pink and Sumartojo 2018; Pink, Ardevol and Lanzeni 2016; Smith and Otto 2016), it would not simply critically review what is wrong with the world. Rather it would make interventions in government, industry, the public sphere and everyday life that would lead to shifts away from the solutionism associated with technological advancement and replace it with an understanding of technology as creating possibilities. It would militate for replacing the predictive uses of big data in governance and anticipatory cultures of risk mitigation with transparent cultures of responsibility and anticipatory concepts of trust and hope. In doing so it would bring closer together processes of technology design, making, markets and users and, in some cases, dissolve the distinctions between them (Pink, Lanzeni and Horst 2018). Overall, it would make visible the interests of all stakeholders in our technological futures, and seek to enable them to create a shared imagination and agenda for how these futures should play out.

Anthropology in a world of possibilities

As this implies, fixing the world is not the work of a single anthropologist or a single discipline. Moreover, rather than crafting closed solutions, the role of anthropology in such a project is to demonstrate how processes of opening productive possibilities are compatible with the way life is already lived. A design anthropology focus on possibilities rather than solutions (Halse 2013) offers a way of understanding the world as ongoingly emergent and continually reconfiguring to open up new possibilities for what might happen next (Akama, Pink and Sumartojo 2018). Such an approach is most usefully situated within an interdisciplinary anthropological agenda that seeks to participate and intervene in the design of, and preparation for, emerging technologies. It differs from traditional anthropology in three ways.

First, it accounts for the detail of locality and cultural specificity. Yet, in doing so, it seeks to address bigger questions and to think not only through anthropological theory. By bringing the critical perspective of anthropological ethnography, that is, the ethnography informed by anthropological theory and principles, to practice and theoretical debates in the fields of design (Pink et al. 2013), human geography (Pink and Fors 2017) and sociology (Pink 2012), I have developed this focus in my own work. However, I have also engaged with debates in interdisciplinary fields including material culture (Pink, Morgan and Dainty 2014), cultural studies (Pink, Leder Mackley and Morosanu 2015) and construction management (Pink, Lingard and Harley 2017). In doing so, I have likewise sought to rethink certain questions that scholars and researchers address in those fields through an interdisciplinary anthropological approach.

Second, it disregards the old model of the lone anthropologist to instead perform various configurations of teamwork and traverse a journey through different collaborative research projects. By taking this approach in my own research I have learned progressively through a series of research sites and projects that to be effective in the world anthropology needs to be much more than a discipline that bases its reputation in doing long-term ethnography and engaging the ensuing ethnographic knowledge in a dialogue with theory. My research has developed across projects focussing on homes, energy, sustainability, health, safety and wellbeing, and digital and emerging technology. My research sites are in urban and rural contexts, in homes, organizations and public spaces. In the last 20 years, I have developed collaborative ethnographic projects in the UK, Spain, Sweden, Australia, Brazil and Chile, working in often interdisciplinary research teams and with non-academic partners. I have no doubt that this has impinged on my capacity to create a deep resource of ethnographic knowledge about one particular site, and that it diminishes my capacity to be an 'expert' on one particular site. Yet, as Paul Sillitoe (2007) has pointed out, we as anthropologists never had the right to pretend that we were the experts on other people's cultures; rather it is our role to enable people who are the experts on their own culture to engage their local knowledge in ways that are empowering for them. Although anthropologists might have problems with calling themselves experts in this sense, I argue that, in order to be able to participate in debates that matter for the world, they, nonetheless, need to take on the role of expert in a different sense. What is more fitting for the anthropologist is a form of meta-expertise that does not claim to speak for a particular group but that, instead, seeks to navigate the uncertain and often indeterminate space between groups in ways that are informed by an ethics of responsibility. To occupy this space entails a shift towards a new anthropology that is not guided solely by the principles and practice of traditional anthropological lone researcher long-term fieldwork through modes of deep immersion and cultural contextualization.

Third, it involves methodological creativity. My work has also involved the development of visual, sensory, digital and design ethnographic methodologies, which are collaborative, experimental and, again, exceed the anthropology that I was taught as an undergraduate. In proposing that the kind of anthropology that the world needs the most should have a methodological core, I am also calling for a methodology rooted in a design anthropological theory of emerging technologies. This approach, which draws on anthropological and design practices, transcends conventional anthropology in a number of ways: it is interventional, future-focussed in that it seeks to make change happen, does not take ethical or other refuge in the past and, instead, takes responsibility for voicing possible ways forward into an uncertain future. It seeks to engage not with what is already knowable but with what is not known, including the speculative, the imagined, what is feared and what is hoped for.

The world therefore needs an anthropology that is methodologically coherent, that can engage with the overview, and which is collaborative and team-based. This is not to say that ethnographic research should not be local. As described below, in my projects it always is. However, anthropologists need to be able to engage with the local and the global, with industry and stakeholders from other sectors, and with the everyday worlds of individuals. The lone anthropologist might be able to achieve this over a long period of time and of relationship forming. In contrast, an effective team, who can constitute the relevant relationships and knowledge by working together in different locations, with different stakeholders and with different degrees of skill and experience, can achieve more. Such teams can also be the places and groupings where new interdisciplinary and interventional anthropologists are trained.

New directions for anthropology

Anthropologists, such as Henrietta Moore, Thomas Hylland Eriksen, Tim Ingold and others, whose work has had enduring relevance outside the discipline have been those who have either confronted interdisciplinary questions, and thus contributed to interdisciplinary theory building, or advanced their own universal theories. Such anthropologists have developed modes of pulling together things that might appear globally disparate into conceptual dialogues, so as to create understandings that span the world and not just the local. For instance, think of Henrietta Moore's advancement of concept-metaphors (e.g. Moore 2004). The discipline of anthropology needs internal debate and detailed ethnographic knowledge of specific sites and subjects, but the world also needs bold anthropologists who are prepared to advance views that are general, while remaining attached to the particular. This involves transcending the immediate concerns of the discipline in both their theoretical explorations and arguments and in their practical interests and applications. This is not to say that the world does not need the local epistemologies, ways of knowing, being and imagining of the people who live in it. Indeed, the need and value of this is demonstrated most vividly through the work of anthropologists such as Paul Stoller and Andrew Irving, whose theoretical and empirical work engages with publics on a range of levels and, in doing so, urges us towards responsible forms of engagement. However, the world also needs something else: it requires anthropological teamwork, commitment to a shared agenda and a movement towards change that can engage not only other anthropologists. Instead, such an agenda needs to also engage and partner with industry, government, the public sphere and the many other institutions that impact, impinge on or support how everyday life is lived. Anthropologists have the ideal training to be able to be implicated in such an agenda because we have been taught right from the outset to appreciate how different cultures think, how different societies and institutions work, how to create relationships and how to sense the resonances between things that might at first glance appear to be completely different. But, again, anthropologists cannot do this alone.

Finally, the world needs a future-focussed anthropology, which constitutes another way of advancing beyond traditional anthropological practice (Pink and Salazar 2017). The Future Anthropologies Network (FAN) of the European Association of Social Anthropologists, which I founded with Juan Salazar in 2014, has created a collective manifesto that calls for new modes of anthropological engagement with futures (Salazar et al. 2017, Chapter 1). The manifesto has ten points, which, amongst other things, emphasize intervention, interdisciplinarity, internationalization, uncertainty, responsibility, ethics, the wider ecological and technological environment and the need to form a community of practice.

The Future Anthropologies manifesto also acknowledges the past. For the agenda of an Anthropology of Emerging Technologies that I propose here, we might take with us two things from past anthropologies. They are demonstrated in David Mills' (2005) discussion of how in the mid-twentieth century, when confronted with the possibility of collaborating with industry the leading anthropologists of the time proffered that anthropology was not a problem-solving discipline (even if for reasons different to those advanced here); and in Tim Ingold's emphasis that anthropology involves doing research *with* rather than *about* people (2008). If we add to this Anusas and Harkness's more recent (2016) argument for likewise making design anthropology interventions *with* research partners, a mode of anthropological practice emerges whereby anthropology keeps its principles of doing research *with* the different stakeholders in our projects, and of creating possibilities rather than solving problems.

To sum up, the world needs anthropologists because it confronts a series of complex challenges, one of which concerns its future relationship with technology. As I have argued, the kind of anthropologists that are needed should be committed to a future-focussed interdisciplinary mode of theory and practice. They should be generalists as well as focussing on the specific and the local, and they should work in teams. However, the need is mutual. As the world drifts into new technological futures, the movement towards interventional anthropology needs to unleash within the discipline. Otherwise anthropologists will not be able to assist and engage with the changes productively.

COLLABORATIVE, RESPONSIBLE AND ETHICAL INTERVENTIONS IN THE WORLD

I first became fascinated by anthropology when I took a first-year undergraduate course in the 1980s. Starting my studies in the UK at that time, anthropology was exciting for me because it accounted for other people's perspectives and was a critical discipline. Anthropological ethnography went under the surface to tell different stories about what was happening, which were not immediately apparent or that were not represented in dominant discourses. I changed my degree program to anthropology, and then continued to do a master's in visual anthropology and a doctorate in social anthropology. However, throughout my career the way I have learned and practiced anthropology has always gone beyond the boundaries of the discipline.

During my bachelor's I was taught by sociologists, as well as anthropologists, and their thinking was another of the stands that attracted me to academia. After completing my bachelor's in anthropology, I worked as an applied researcher and considered a career outside academia but found that this environment lacked the theoretical, critical and exploratory dimension that had first attracted me to anthropology. I also wanted to take further my interest in bringing together anthropology with audio-visual practice.

The next step, a master's in visual anthropology, was formative, both in determining how I would work as an anthropologist and in my understanding

(Continued)

of the purpose of anthropology beyond academia. Visual anthropology both brought me closer to film, photography and media theory, and practically enabled me to learn with research participants and to understand the world through the camera, in ways that were collaborative and beyond the conventions of the time. It was at this point in my career that I began to define my approach to ethnographic practice through photography and video. I followed this through during my doctoral studies which resulted in *Women and Bullfighting* (adapted for publication as Pink 1997).

During my doctoral research, I kept anthropology at the centre of my work but connected it with sociology and media studies to be able to critically explore areas related to embodiment and media, which I believed needed to be addressed as part of an ethnographic study. I also realized that to understand the contemporary social and cultural phenomena of my fieldwork site I also needed to engage with the role that technology and media – at the time, video, photography, television and print media – were playing in the lives of the research participants. While this topic was far from applied anthropology, its popularity gave me my first taste of public scholarship as during my doctoral research and later I was interviewed for radio in three countries, participated in the local media culture in Andalusia where I undertook my ethnographic research and had my photography published in non-academic outlets.

FIGURE 4.1 The Bullfighter's Braid. A photograph from Sarah Pink's doctoral research which won two awards and was published in several outlets. Courtesy Sarah Pink.

After I completed my doctorate, I worked in sociology groups in the UK for the next seventeen years before moving to Australia. There I first took up a position at the Design Research Institute and School of Media and Communication at RMIT University, before becoming the Director of the Digital Ethnography Research Centre at RMIT. I then moved to Monash University to establish an Emerging Technologies Lab across the Faculties of Information Technology and of Art, Design and Architecture. I have held Professorships in departments, schools or centres of Social Science, Design, Information Technology, and Media and Communication. I have had Guest, Visiting and Adjunct Professorships in areas including Public Culture and Ideas, Civil and Building Engineering, and Design as well as in Anthropology. Although anthropology has remained at the core of my practice throughout my career I have never had a full academic position in an anthropology department.

During the earlier years of my career, I considered leaving academia to pursue a research career in industry. However, because the relationship between theoretical scholarship and applied practice was central to my practice as an anthropologist and subsequently also to the contribution I wished to make to academia and applied research, I determined that a University would be the better site to develop this. I believe that the anthropological 'community of critics' (Strathern 2006) plays an important role in constituting the theoretical commitments that the discipline bases its arguments in and presents to other disciplines. Indeed, some of my publications directly address anthropology and I have participated in anthropological debates. Nevertheless, from the outset, based on my experience from my bachelor's onwards, I realized that in order to be mobilized in the world and across academia anthropology needs to be connected with the expertise and approaches of other disciplines. For me this has involved creating an interdisciplinary anthropological practice, which is based in dialogue between ethnography and theory.

My main interest has been in developing a mode of doing anthropology that speaks to other disciplines, engages with interdisciplinary theory-building (Akama, Pink and Sumartojo 2018), can speak to interdisciplinary and non-academic audiences (Pink 2007) and can cope with future temporalities (Pink and Salazar 2017). My practice is thus, simultaneously, open to other disciplines and the theory and practice they bring with them, it is able to experiment, and goes beyond the defence and definition of the discipline itself. In seeking not only to study and criticize the social world, and the responses to it proposed by others, the version of anthropology I advocate for strives to collaboratively, responsibly and ethically intervene in the world.

In the next section, I discuss a composite example based on my collaborative research into emerging technologies and technological futures. I do so to demonstrate my argument for an anthropological vision that necessarily

(Continued)

travels and learns across and between different but related projects and with multiple stakeholders. In doing so I draw from a set of existing co-authored publications in which the findings and methodological advances of our work are presented in more detail. Anthropological teamwork I propose is part of the future of an anthropology that can better draw together the collective expertise of diverse researchers to create new knowledge and interventions.

BEING AN ANTHROPOLOGIST IN AN UNCERTAIN WORLD

In a contemporary world, the practical use of anthropology manifests itself in various ways, most often in project-based research. Such projects form the basis of many of our engagements with different academic and non-academic research partners, yet there needs to be a bigger agenda for anthropology to become relevant to the world. As I argued above, we should go beyond the single project that helps a client, organization or group of people to achieve a set of aims and reach a particular 'impact'.

Over the last 20 or so years, I have moved between different research projects, sites, partners and modes of industry, public sector or research council funding, learning from different projects and sectors in ways that shaped my work with others. Through this trajectory I have developed, honed and understood the relevance of a core methodology for my anthropological practice (Pink and Leder Mackley 2012). In this section I discuss how this methodology has played out by bringing together selected projects to create a collective example. My research is always collaborative; therefore, I discuss not just my own skills but what my skills become once they start to be put into practice in collaboration with others.

My practical use of anthropology began in earnest when I started to develop research projects with Unilever in the UK in 1999, working across three projects, sometimes in collaboration with other academic colleagues. The first practical application of this body of research was in its business uses. However, a second significant practical application was the projects' impact on the trajectory of my methodological research, leading to my development of video-based methodologies including video re-enactment methodologies (Pink and Leder Mackley 2014). Using them subsequently across a range of projects, they were advanced further. The latter project led to the *Laundry Lives* (2015), ethnographic film co-directed with Nadia Astari. The *Laundry Lives* has been selected for several ethnographic film festival screenings, and used for teaching in universities and in industry contexts.

The clothes may get damaged quicker, especially the ones with prints on them.

FIGURE 4.2   A still from *Laundry Lives* ethnographic film, representing a clip that Sarah Pink often shows to audiences outside academia to demonstrate how people improvise with technologies. Courtesy Sarah Pink and Nadia Astari.

The first practical application of the advanced methodology was used as part of the UK-based interdisciplinary project Low Effort Energy Demand Reduction (LEEDR), prior to the *Laundry Lives* film. Here the video ethnographies produced insights that informed the design of prototype digital interventions for energy demand reduction (Pink, Leder Mackley et al. 2017). Simultaneously, I led the ethnographic strand of another interdisciplinary research project, where we researched how construction worker safety was differently constituted through worker improvisation and regulatory frameworks. Based on our ethnography I have argued that more attention needed to be paid to how workers really keep safe, in the devising of new safety policies, both in our academic work (Pink, Morgan and Dainty 2014) and at the Institution for Occupational Safety and Health. It was apparent that safety was structured and framed by similar societal risk mitigation narratives to those that also shaped the discourses around energy demand reduction in relation to climate change. The further interventions involve seeking to shift thinking and approaches within institutions. This might, for instance, involve convincing stakeholders – whether householders or safety regulators – of the benefits that might be accrued from new policies or practices.

During 2017 and 2018, I worked across several projects focussed on how emerging technologies were experienced, imagined and designed. Some

(Continued)

projects were with industry partners including research about autonomous driving (AD) cars in Sweden; screenless technologies in Brazil; motorway noise transformation technologies in Australia; and digital assets in Australia. While each project had a different brief, partner organization and research team, they have one important element in common: they are all about technologies that do not exist in everyday life. These technologies have imagined future users and market values. Yet, they differ from the ordinary objects of anthropological research precisely because they are emerging and because they required us to research in spheres of uncertainty that are different from how anthropologists usually characterize the uncertainty of what they will find out (Pink, Akama and participants 2015). For instance, since our object of study was dispersed and did not exist in either one singular form or imagined thing (Pink, Lanzeni and Horst 2018), our research into digital assets provided a new challenge. We solved the issue doing research through anticipatory modes, including those of regulation and risk mitigation mentioned above, but with particular attention to hope, trust, anxiety and aspiration, which are associated with human improvisation and learning (Pink, Lanzeni and Horst 2018).

To research anticipated or possible experiences involves future-focussed methods; using existing and prototype technologies of different kinds to invite participants to consider how they might feel in environments where these technologies were part of their future lives. For example, during our research into AD cars, our team investigated participants' experiences on test sites (Pink et al. forthcoming), how they already experience and use AD features in their own cars (e.g. auto brake features) and how they imagined their AD futures (Pink, Fors and Glöss 2018). We accompanied families testing AD features on the roads, and investigated how people imagine and communicate the arrival of their new Tesla cars in online forums (Lindgren et al. 2018). Our research into people's experience of motorway noise transformation was undertaken with a team of sound artists, designers and engineers. We used sensory ethnography to investigate how people experienced an innovative technology that transformed noise into pleasant sounds and we considered how such transformation technologies might play a role in public space in the future (Lacey et al. 2017).

Each project created new insights that have practical applications. However, while the individual projects we work on can be interventional in technology design and in shifting understandings in industry, there is a wider challenge – social change is not achievable in short term projects or by one anthropologist alone. My response to this is to work in teams and to work across projects, bringing my insights to the attention of others through public speaking at academic and industry conferences and

FIGURE 4.3 Listening to motorway noise transformation during fieldwork in Melbourne, Australia. The ethnographers experienced the transformations, which were designed by the sound artists, designers and acoustic engineers, auto-ethnographically as well as engaging with others to understand their experiences. Courtesy Shanti Sumartojo.

seminars. The issues, theory and methodology created through these earlier projects and more recent work have informed my call for a new design anthropology approach to emerging technologies. The ultimate practical application should be a collective agenda in seeking to change how technology design, use and regulation are conceptualized.

FIVE TIPS FROM SARAH PINK

1. **Define what anthropology can be for you as a contemporary practice.** Build on definitions from the past, but do not let them limit you.
2. **Train in other disciplines as well as in anthropology.** While it is difficult to simultaneously practice and excel in more than one discipline, being able to engage with the thinking and practice of other disciplines and practices is an essential skill for changing the world. In addition, anthropology can always remain your core discipline.

(Continued)

3. **Be open to other people's way of working, thinking and under-standing the world.** Seek to create correspondences and find points of collaboration. You will be more able to create an applied practice in the world if you collaborate with others.
4. **Contribute to both academic scholarship and applied practice.** Use your theoretical and methodological skills in both domains to mutually nurture each other.
5. **Put an ethics of responsibility at the core of all of your research.** Demonstrate why this is important to others.

About the author

Sarah Pink is Professor and Director of the Emerging Technologies Lab in the Faculties of Information Technology and of Art, Design and Architecture at Monash University, Melbourne, Australia. Prior to this she was Distinguished Professor in the School of Media and Communication and Director of the Digital Ethnography Research Centre at RMIT University, Australia. She is also International Guest Professor in the Department of Information Technology at Halmstad University, Sweden. Her research is interdisciplinary, international and interventional, and involves collaborations with academics from a range of disciplines and non-academic partners. Her most recent works include the co-authored and co-edited books *Uncertainty and Possibility* (2018), *Anthropologies and Futures* (2017), *Making Homes* (2017) and *Theoretical Scholarship and Applied Practice* (2017). She co-directed the ethnographic documentary *Laundry Lives* (2015).

References

Akama, Y., S. Pink and S. Sumartojo (2018), *Uncertainty and Possibility: New Approaches to Future Making*, London: Bloomsbury.

Anderson, B. (2010), 'Preemption, Precaution, Preparedness: Anticipatory Action and Future Geographies', *Progress in Human Geography*, 34 (6): 777–98.

Anderson, B. and P. Adey (2011), 'Affect and Security: Exercising Emergency in "UK Civil Contingencies"', *Environment and Planning D: Society and Space*, 29 (6): 1092–1109.

Anusas, M. and R. Harkness (2016), 'Different Presents in the Making', in R. C. Smith, K. T. Vangkilde, M. G. Kjærsgaard, T. Otto, J. Halse and T. Binder (eds), *Design Anthropological Futures*, 55–70, London: Bloomsbury Academic.

Chan, J. and L. Bennett Moses (2017), 'Making Sense of Big Data for Security', *The British Journal of Criminology*, 57 (2): 299–319.

Halse, J. (2013), 'Ethnographies of the Possible', in W. Gunn, T. Otto and R. C. Smith (eds), *Design Anthropology: Theory and Practice*, 180–96, London and New York: Bloomsbury.

Ingold, T. (2008), 'Anthropology Is Not Ethnography', *Proceedings of the British Academy*, 154 (11): 69–92.

Ingold, T. (2010), 'Footprints through the Weather-world: Walking, Breathing, Knowing', *Journal of the Royal Anthropological Institute*, 16: S121–S139.

Lacey, J., S. Pink, L. Harvey, X. Qiu, S. Sumartojo, S. Zhao, S. Moore and M. Duque (2017), 'Acoustic Design Innovations for Managing Motorway Traffic Noise by Cancellation and Transformation', *Transurban Innovation Grant Report*. Available online: https://research.monash.edu/en/publications/transurban-innovation-grant-acoustic-design-innovations-for-manag (accessed 29 October 2019).

Lindgren, T., M. Bergquist, S. Pink, M. Berg and V. Fors (2018), 'Experiencing Expectations: Extending the Concept of UX Anticipation', in S. Müller and J. Nielsen (eds), *Nordic Contributions in IS Research*, SCIS 2018, Lecture Notes in Business Information Processing, vol. 326, 1–13, Cham: Springer.

Laundry Lives (2015), [Documentary video] Dir. Sarah Pink and Nadia Astari, Australia: Digital Ethnography Research Centre, RMIT University.

Mills, D. (2005), 'Dinner at Claridges? Anthropology and the "Captains of Industry", 1947–1955', in S. Pink (ed), *Applications of Anthropology: Professional Anthropology in the Twenty-first Century*, 55–70, New York: Berghahn Books.

Moore, H. L. (2004), 'Global Anxieties: Concept-metaphors and Pre-theoretical Commitments in Anthropology', *Anthropological Theory*, 4 (1): 71–88.

Morozov, E. (2013), *To Save Everything, Click Here: Technology, Solutionism, and the Urge to Fix Problems that Don't Exist*, London: Penguin Books.

Pink, S. (1997), *Women and Bullfighting: Gender, Sex and the Consumption of Tradition*, Oxford and New York: Berg.

Pink, S. (2007), *Visual Interventions: Applied Visual Anthropology*, Oxford: Berghahn.

Pink, S. (2012), *Situating Everyday Life: Practices and Places*, London: Sage.

Pink, S. (2017), 'Ethics in a Changing World: Embracing Uncertainty, Understanding Futures, and Making Responsible Interventions', in S. Pink, V. Fors and T. O'Dell (eds), *Theoretical Scholarship and Applied Practice*, 29–51, Oxford: Berghahn.

Pink, S. and V. Fors (2017), 'Being in a Mediated World: Self-tracking and the Mind-body-environment', *Cultural Geographies*, 24 (3): 375–88.

Pink, S. and K. Leder Mackley (2012), 'Video as a Route to Sensing Invisible Energy: Approaching Domestic Energy Consumption through the Sensory Home', *Sociological Research Online*, 17 (1). Available online: http://www.socresonline.org.uk/17/1/3.html (accessed 29 October 2019).

Pink, S. and K. Leder Mackley (2014), 'Reenactment Methodologies for Everyday Life Research: Art Therapy Insights for Video Ethnography', *Visual Studies*, 29 (2): 146–54.

Pink, S. and J. F. Salazar (2017), 'Anthropologies and Futures: Setting the Agenda', in J. F. Salazar, S. Pink, A. Irving and J. Sjoberg (eds), *Future Anthropologies*, 3–22, Oxford: Bloomsbury.

Pink, S., K. Leder Mackley, V. Mitchell, C. Escobar-Tello, M. Hanratty, T. Bhamra and R. Morosanu (2013), 'Applying the Lens of Sensory Ethnography to Sustainable HCI', *Transactions on Computer-Human Interaction*, 20 (4). Available online: http://dl.acm.org/citation.cfm?doid=2494261 (accessed 28 October 2019).

Pink, S., J. Morgan and A. Dainty (2014), 'The Safe Hand: Gels, Water, Gloves and the Materiality of Tactile Knowing', *Journal of Material Culture*, 19 (4): 425–42.

Pink, S., Y. Akama and participants (2015), *Un/Certainty*. Available online: http://d-e-futures.com/projects/uncertainty/ (accessed 29 October 2019).

Pink, S., K. Leder Mackley and R. Morosanu (2015), 'Hanging Out at Home: Laundry as a Thread and Texture of Everyday Life', *International Journal of Cultural Studies*, 18 (2): 209–24.

Pink, S., E. Ardevol and D. Lanzeni, (2016), 'Digital Materiality: Configuring a Field of Anthropology/Design?', in S. Pink, E. Ardevol and D. Lanzeni (eds), *Digital Materialities: Anthropology and Design*, 1–26, Oxford: Bloomsbury.

Pink, S., K. Leder Mackley, R. Morosanu, V. Mitchell and T. Bhamra (2017), *Making Homes: Ethnographies and Designs*, Oxford: Bloomsbury.

Pink, S., H. Lingard and J. Harley (2017), 'Refiguring Creativity in Virtual Work: The Digital-material Construction Site', *New Technology, Work and Employment*, 32 (1): 12–27.

Pink, S., V. Fors and M. Glöss (2018), 'The Contingent Futures of the Mobile Present: Beyond Automation as Innovation', *Mobilities*, 13 (5): 615–31.

Pink, S., D. Lanzeni and H. Horst (2018), 'Data Anxieties: Finding Trust and Hope in Digital Mess', *Big Data and Society*, 5 (1): 1–14.

Pink, S., K. Osz, V. Fors and D. Lanzeni (forthcoming), 'Simulating and Trusting in Automated Futures: Anthropology and the Wizard of Oz', in M. Kazubowski-Houston and M. Auslander (eds), *Unimaginable Worlds*, London: Bloomsbury.

Salazar, J. F., S. Pink, A. Irving and J. Sjoberg (2017), *Anthropologies and Futures: Techniques for Researching an Uncertain World*, Oxford: Bloomsbury.

Sillitoe, P. (2007), 'Anthropologists Only Need Apply: Challenges of Applied Anthropology', *Journal of the Royal Anthropological Institute*, 13 (1): 147–65.

Smith, G. J. D. and P. O'Malley (2017), 'Driving Politics: Data-driven Governance and Resistance', *The British Journal of Criminology*, 57 (2): 275–98.

Smith, R. C. and T. Otto (2016), 'Cultures of the Future: Emergence and Intervention in Design Anthropology', in R. C. Smith, K. T. Vangkilde, M. G. Kjærsgaard, T. Otto, J. Halse and T. Binder (eds), *Design Anthropological Futures*, 19–36, London: Bloomsbury Academic.

Strathern, M. (2006), 'A Community of Critics? Thoughts on New Knowledge', *Journal of the Royal Anthropological Institute*, 12: 191–209.

5

MAKING ANTHROPOLOGY RELEVANT TO OTHER PEOPLE'S PROBLEMS

Steffen Jöhncke

The editors of this volume have asked contributors to reflect on 'why the world needs anthropologists'. I must admit that sometimes I think the real challenge is to remind anthropologists that *they* need the world. In much anthropological writing and debate I find a certain complacent and self-gratulatory tone, assured of the marvels of the discipline and of the enormous difference anthropology *could* make, if only the world would listen. I like to call this approach 'the Church of Anthropology', as a parallel to the Roman Catholic church's response to critics who want it to modernize: it is the world that should follow the Church, not the other way around. I am uncomfortable if a similar notion is implied in the question 'why the world needs anthropologists', because today the task of anthropology is less to preach than to humbly listen and critically explore the big and small problems that humanity faces. The world does not *need* anthropologists per se, unless they are willing to contribute to the collaborative effort of saving the planet, creating a more just world, or whatever fair cause we choose. Or perhaps we want to contribute to the rather more mundane task of helping private and public organizations succeed, which is how most anthropologists today make a living. To me, anthropology does not *in itself* hold a particular message to the world, beyond the promise of enlightenment. Anthropology is a professional, analytical tool that we need to keep sharp and relevant.

AnthroAnalysis: breaking new ground through collaborative projects

My approach to anthropology that makes a practical difference starts with an interest in problems that are initially defined *outside* of the discipline, by the practical and political concerns of people – professionals and citizens – in public institutions, private companies and civil organizations. AnthroAnalysis – Centre for

Applied Anthropology, the research unit that I headed for just over ten years in the Department of Anthropology at the University of Copenhagen in Denmark, explicitly aims to take anthropology into new fields and forms of application. Since 2005, the staff at AnthroAnalysis have been using anthropological skills and competences to help solve practical problems in collaboration with partners in society. This work has been done in a deliberate attempt to demonstrate how and why we need to do away with the unproductive split between academic and non-academic anthropology. In the process, it has become clear that in this work we do not so much 'apply' anthropology as a finished package of knowledge that is 'put to use'. Rather, we explore and develop new formats and adaptations of anthropological university-based research through on-going exchanges with collaborative partners in potentially all sectors of society.

Around 2005, Kirsten Becker, a visionary young anthropologist in the department, noticed the growing interest in the use of ethnographic methods in fields like industrial and service design in Denmark, as well as the effort to use anthropology in 'user-driven innovation' as an approach to technological and commercial development. In order to pursue and study at close sight these emerging trends and their implications for the discipline, Kirsten raised funding and established collaborative projects, particularly between start-up companies and young anthropology graduates who were keen to use their skills in practice. One example was a project with a medico-technology company that was developing an early-warning fit alarm for young people with epilepsy. The company needed a better understanding of what daily life with epilepsy means to children and teens. The project is an example of the anthropological approach that focusses on living with a chronic disease (Wahlberg 2009) and it gave the company key insights into the conditions under which their new product should function. The study revealed how developers' ideas about their potential product did not match the reality and needs of families dealing with the disease in their everyday life. This and other projects drew on the vast expertise within medical anthropology that has been developed in the department since the 1980s, not least through the efforts of professor Susan Reynolds Whyte. Later, Kirsten – then with the new surname Lauritsen – moved to Ida Institute to work with hearing loss and afterwards to the large pharmaceutical company Novo Nordisk. There, she is currently employed as a specialist in user insights, translating ethnographic knowledge about daily life with diabetes, haemophilia and obesity to engineers in device development, and generally sensitizing the organization to the value of understanding the social and cultural circumstances in which chronic conditions are treated.

Laying new tracks in academia

While working in the Department of Anthropology, Kirsten realized that activities she was developing needed an identity, a name of its own. She came up with Antropologisk Analyse, which was later anglicized by me to AnthroAnalysis. In 2008, I had the good fortune to take over the management of the unit. Since then, and particularly since 2015 with my close colleague Bettina Skårup, we have continued to explore new formats, themes and fields for projects at the interface between academia and practical problems. In this work we have found no obvious models to follow within our own or other universities, so we are laying the tracks while the train is moving. Consequently, a considerable amount of time and effort is going into agile project management and leadership. The challenge is to negotiate the administrative, legal and budgetary requirements of the university while we develop project contents, frameworks and contracts with external partners, secure funding and recruit research workforce among department staff or recent master or doctoral graduates – all at the same time. Projects are funded by our partners or by grants from private companies or foundations, or from public sources at the local or national level. Once a project is agreed on, the research process must be implemented and supervised. Afterwards, the dissemination of results – usually through presentations, a published report and academic articles – must be completed. Projects are also used as case material in the training of anthropology students in the department. Thus – unlike the common practice of consultancy companies – it is essential for AnthroAnalysis not to renounce rights to data material, analyses and reports; we need to retain these as accessible contributions to the development of anthropology as a practically oriented professional activity.

Over the years, we have completed over 30 small and large projects in the most diverse collaborative arrangements; space allows for just a few examples here. We have done a number of evaluation studies of projects and services. Among those was a project with the Danish Board of Health on the experience of care among people with diabetic foot ulcers (Andersen, Pedersen and Steffen 2017), which pointed to the inconsistency and incoherence of services as a central concern. We have done a study with the Danish Cancer Society in relation to counselling and support services for people with cancer (Tonnesen, Jöhncke and Steffen 2011). There, we discussed, among other things, the sometimes-hidden mechanisms of inclusion and exclusion of social groups in the way that services were presented. In an entirely different field, in collaboration with the Rockwool Foundation, we have studied the effects and implications of a large agricultural development project in northern Tanzania as seen from the perspective of local farmers (Lilleør and Lund-Sørensen 2013). In this study, we shed light on how different new techniques and crops affected individual households in various ways, thus helping to explain the overall outcomes of the development project. We have done studies of how Danish fire-fighting services may improve recruitment and retaining of part-time staff (Weisdorf 2017) by exploring what really motivates fire-fighters to do this low-paid and risky work. We have studied how staff of nursing homes deal with requirements of documentation in their work (Christensen 2014) as well as how they handle professional learning and skills development (Felding et al. 2017) amidst the complex and sometimes conflicting requirements of care work.

It may be taken as an illustration of the fast-growing interest in anthropological perspectives in Danish society that increasingly projects have been initiated by external partners who call on us. But it is also clear that collaborative projects rely first of all on our active and continuous networking and long-term relationship building. Many large engagements commence with short pilot projects. An example is a current three-year industrial postdoctoral project with the company Exruptive on new security and information technologies for airports (Ilkjær 2019). Another one is a project on the management of innovation in the Danish postal services (Lex 2016). In fact, new technologies have been the focus of several projects in recent years. In particular, they concern the challenges that developers and organizations experience with implementation and daily use of new technologies. Here anthropology helps to shed light on what happens in practice when technologies travel from the drawing – and management – boards to the everyday working conditions of practitioners. We can offer insights into how and why technologies are always assessed, adapted and used differently than anticipated. In this line of work, we have worked with a wide range of professionals: craftsmen on the job who use cell phone apps to order spare parts (Karsten 2019), captains on ships of the DFDS shipping company who use (or do not use) navigational decision support systems (Jakobsen, Skårup and Jöhncke 2017), nursing home staff who use welfare technologies in care work for people with dementia (Felding 2018), as well as builders, engineers and developers who negotiate the potentials of using robots on building sites (Leeson 2017).

Recasting problems anthropologically

A crucial element of our work is the critical interpretation and translation of organizational needs and collaborator organizations' understanding of problems into anthropological research questions. In this, we use the capacity of anthropology – theoretical and methodological – to account for good reasons people have for doing what they do. However strange, problematic or unknown a field might seem from the outside, anthropologists will assume that there is an abstract systematicity to it. We can refer to it as culture – something that we know how to study, understand and explain. It is no coincidence that in many of the projects mentioned, we are initially called in to study staff, users, patients, customers, project recipients or other 'groups' who are the target audiences of some form of intervention; be it in the form of medical treatment, a training or support system or the introduction of a new technology. It is usually a powerful and high-ranking group of professionals who call on the anthropologists to help them explain the thoughts and behaviour of some 'others', namely, the target groups of their professional intervention.

However, as anthropologists, we can do more than just explain the experiences and life worlds of these 'target audiences'. We can use these insights to challenge the assumptions and perspectives of the professionals, managers, policy makers and technology developers who defined the interventions in the first place. These groups may not realize (or understand) this at first, but, in fact, they are as much a part of the ethnographic field that we account for as are the target groups of their endeavours. In the end, the professional groups that we collaborate with are very much the objects of our critical examination as the limitations of their assumptions are exposed. It is then an essential part of the anthropological task to disseminate this critique to them in such a way that they may actually understand and appreciate it – and act on it appropriately. Findings are also made available to the professionals' target groups that we study, so that they too may take their own course of action. We strive to make our reports available and accessible for non-academic audiences, which is one more reason why keeping our publication rights is essential.

The general purpose of AnthroAnalysis is to be part of the ever-evolving ways in which anthropology is being put to work in Danish (and global) contexts and to organize and develop innovative ways of incorporating this knowledge and experience *into* the practices of teaching and research taking place in the Department of Anthropology in Copenhagen and elsewhere. The point is thus to *expand* the field of possibilities of anthropological research by giving researchers *access* to new sites and new problematics that they might not otherwise have thought of as accessible or even interesting. In this way, we hope to give rise to new forms of engagement and interaction. In addition, we have strived to find ways to further increase the short or long-term participation of faculty members in our projects, in order for more of them to gain additional first-hand experience with practically oriented work. This should also develop their understanding of the skills and competencies that it requires, not least in terms of collaboration with external, professional partners.

FIGURE 5.1 Steffen Jöhncke and Bettina Skårup of AnthroAnalysis facilitated a workshop on collaborative projects at *Why the World Needs Anthropologists* symposium in Tartu, Estonia, 2016. Courtesy Aivo Pölluäär.

Collaboration is key

Probably 'collaboration' remains the best shorthand term available for the core characteristic of the work that we do. Collaboration means working together to take the interests and perspectives of all concerned into consideration. I notice that it has become common among some anthropologists to employ the term 'collaboration' for any kind of relationship with people during fieldwork so that 'collaborator' appears to be simply a new euphemism for people formerly known as 'informants' or 'interlocutors'. This is sometimes the case even when there does not seem to be any other purpose of the 'collaboration' than the production of data for the advancement of the anthropologist's analysis and, one may add, career.

In our work, 'collaboration' connotes something different and involves rather more mutual forms of obligation and consideration. First of all, it is based on the premise that we are dealing initially with a practical problem that our collaborator has identified. The definition of the problem has been made from a particular *perspective* within the collaborating organization – usually management – who has successfully claimed the right to speak for the organization as a whole. But the premise is also that this definition of the problem does not provide the answers, since a decision has been made to consult with university-based anthropologists in order to get the practical problem solved, or – which is often the case – to have the problem approached and explored in novel ways. As anthropologists in policy and practice, we have an obligation to take the collaborative partners' problems seriously – otherwise we should decline to work with them. However, and this is crucial, we are not obliged to adopt their definition or theory of the problem and in that sense, we never simply reply to a given question. Our collaborative partner must give us as anthropologists the liberty to explore the problem, the people who define it, as well as those who are affected by it in different ways.

For instance, in our project with the DFDS shipping company mentioned earlier (Jakobsen, Skårup and Jöhncke 2017), the initial question was why particular technologies that were designed to assist navigational decision-making, save fuel and reduce CO_2 emissions, were being used differently by identical ships. Did this have anything to do with differences between ships in terms of the local management culture on board? What we found during fieldwork on board four ships at sea was that the notion of 'identical ships' was misleading. One of the main problems was miscommunication between the shore and the ship in the introduction of new technologies as well as some lack of appreciation within the company for the decisive role of professional experience, discretion and the strong sense of responsibility that is essential for navigation. Consequently, the solution suggested was not to strengthen management tools, as was probably expected by the company, but a more careful implementation of new technologies on board the company's ships. Definitely the problem had to do with social relations, as the company management had anticipated, which is probably also why they had approached anthropologists in the first place. But the challenge was in no way limited to on-ship conditions. Rather, it was a question of relations between land and sea sections of the company, which became clear when we saw the company as a whole from the perspective of the ships' crews. As it happens, the company later reported that our study has helped to increase general attention to how route optimization tools are designed, implemented and used, thus substantially helping to save fuel and reduce CO_2 emissions from DFDS ships.

So, in this manner, to us in AnthroAnalysis, 'collaboration' implies the meeting of practical challenges with the expertise of anthropologists to conceptually recast problems based on empirical observation and critical analysis. What is being 'applied' here is less an existing body of anthropological knowledge (though that may play a role, too) and more the ability to reframe problems and therefore recommendations and possible solutions. Often it has to do with fundamental anthropological epistemology: what may be known about the world and how it may be known. Frequently we get the response from collaborators that not only are our insights as such new to them, but that they also did not know that this *kind* of knowledge could be produced.

From discipline to profession

This idea of collaboration – in the sense of a mutual and professionally based obligation – as a crucial aspect of contemporary anthropology is akin to what American anthropologists Les Field and Richard Fox (2007) argued already more than ten years ago in their book *Anthropology Put to Work*. Based on evidence from a range of anthropologists working in and outside the academia, they explain that the ability to collaborate across disciplinary and professional boundaries amounts to a new paradigm of anthropology. They suggest that approaches to social relations in fieldwork focus less on the often self-absorbed and emotionally laden ideas of 'rapport' and 'reflexivity', and increasingly more on collaborations as forms of professional and responsible engagements with the field. Building on this, I would argue that this shift of emphasis is but one expression of a more general development in the status of anthropology from being a *discipline* to becoming a *profession*: that is, from a discipline with its centre of gravity in academia as the obvious and undisputed source of legitimacy, to a profession with a broader set of potential criteria for relevance and competence, not to speak of a broader set of legitimate career patterns and experiences. The ability to professionally handle collaborative relationships of a multitude of types has always been essential for anthropologists working in policy and practice – a format of work that parts of academic anthropology are now beginning to catch up with and that is essential for the training of future generations of anthropologists.

FINDING MY PLACE IN ANTHROPOLOGY

I was only eighteen years old when anthropology became my vocation of choice. Towards the end of high school in 1981, I had convinced myself that I wanted to go to university and that anthropology should be my subject of study. After a year of travel in Iceland and Israel/Palestine, I started as the youngest student out of a group of only 25 – and with a seemingly endless and foggy road ahead of me. Traditionally, university programmes in Denmark are long and monodisciplinary, which was even truer 40 years ago than it is today. In anthropology, there was one degree only, the 'magisterkonferens', roughly corresponding to a Master of Philosophy, which was awarded after seven years of studies. If you stopped before that, you left with nothing. In Denmark, anthropology is still taught in predominantly monodisciplinary programmes, but at least it is now possible to leave with either a bachelor's or a master's degree – and to combine anthropology with courses or degrees in other disciplines. Today I find it difficult to recall what exactly made me embark on such a project: seven years of studies in a virtually unknown subject and with absolutely no idea of employment prospects at the end of it. Still, anthropology seemed to combine arts and social science in an attractive way, and most of all, it allowed me to postpone the decision about what I really wanted to do for a living. As it turned out, anthropology proved flexible enough to be adapted to the many different interests and phases of my life. In fact, I have chosen and re-chosen anthropology several times.

I come from a working-class family that was highly devoted to learning, social commitment and cultural outlook. My parents were not wealthy at all, but they prioritized sending us three kids to a private, Catholic school – exactly because we were *not* Catholics and my parents thought it would be good for us to meet a different culture in addition to what we knew already. As a family, we travelled as much as the budget allowed. This did not include aeroplanes, but holidays in the car enabled us to see the mountains of Norway and Austria as well as the war cemeteries of Verdun in France and the cathedral of Aachen in Germany; no reason why a summer vacation could not be educational. Travelling and meeting people in other countries were passions of mine as far back as I can recall, and I am sure this formed a crucial part of my decision to study anthropology. (What other subject could provide better excuses for global travel?) Still, I am not sure how exactly I first became acquainted with the existence of the discipline. It might well have been through the Ethnographic Collection in the National Museum of Denmark, which I loved, or through reading about the peoples of Amazonia and the Andes in high school.

FIGURE 5.2 Steffen Jöhncke and Peter have been partners and comrades in arms since 1983. Here they are in 1988. Private archive of Steffen Jöhncke.

At any rate, anthropology caught me. Anything could be treated anthropologically, I realized. When I came out as a gay man in my second year of studies, I wrote a major assignment about accounts of same-sex relationships in historical ethnographies from practically everywhere. As friends of mine started to succumb to a new disease – what we found out only later was HIV – I took courses in anthropology of health and analysed public media reactions to AIDS and my own observations of fear and stigma in the community. Reading Foucault was a revelation in the 1980s and the Copenhagen Department of Anthropology allowed me to thrive. Although I spent long periods of time away from my studies as a writer and activist in the LGBT movement, I still felt at home in the discipline and involved myself in the running of the Danish Association of Anthropologists. In 1987, Anders Dahl, a fellow student with a background in social work, invited me to join a group of social workers and anthropologists who were setting up a study of male-to-male sex work in Copenhagen – a theme of particular interest due to the HIV epidemic. The National Board of Health and the Copenhagen city council decided to fund us for a year, during which we conducted fieldwork with sex workers as we tried to understand the rapidly changing scene and the possibility of supportive interventions. Authorities regarded the sex workers mainly as *a risk* in terms of spreading HIV to 'the general population' whereas our approach acknowledged that sex workers were *at risk* themselves. Based on this, we

(Continued)

called for health and counselling interventions to take account of that. As it turned out, my part of the study of male sex work became the basis of my 'magisterkonferens' thesis in 1991, after a very inspirational year studying social anthropology and social policy with Susan Wright at the University of Sussex in the United Kingdom.

After working in practice for ten years – mainly in the field of social work, and particularly in relation to services for drug users (described in the next section) – I was fortunate enough to be able to choose to study anthropology yet again in 2001. This time I joined the Copenhagen Department of Anthropology as a doctoral student. I partly worked with the material that I had collected as a practitioner and my doctoral thesis thus combined my interest in critical anthropology with making a practical difference beyond the discipline. My supervisor, professor Susan Reynolds Whyte, whom I have known since my first days in the department in 1982, reminded me that this had been my sceptical approach from the start: 'Anthropology is *interesting*, yes ... but I need to see how it makes a *difference* to the world'. I must admit: that still drives me.

APPLIED ANTHROPOLOGY IN SOCIAL WORK

A leitmotif in a life course is usually a reconstruction of apparent coherence that might not have been clear at the time, and least of all the result of a strategy. At any rate, applying anthropology to social work has been a recurrent theme in my trajectory. The work with HIV that I began in relation to male sex workers in the project described above continued with an evaluation of information and support work directed to men who have sex with men (Jöhncke, Jørgensen and Hald 1993), in collaboration with a psychologist and a fellow anthropologist. This further led to a European Union funded project on services to immigrants living with HIV in three European cities, within which I was responsible for the Copenhagen study (Jöhncke 1996). The study was hosted by HIV Danmark, an organization founded and run by people affected by HIV in order to work for their rights and provide counselling. In this context, the project found a very welcoming and fertile ground for anthropological perspectives, in the sense that we analysed services 'bottom-up' with a focus on the experiences and predicaments of users and professionals alike.

Working with people living with HIV drew my attention to the situation of intravenous drug users as another highly vulnerable group. In 1996, the social services department of the Copenhagen city council advertised a one-year position to do an evaluation and user study of four public treatment centres for drug users in the city that had been set up a few years earlier. Their main tasks consisted of intake assessments of drug users seeking treatment and administering methadone treatment on a daily basis as an out-patient service. I applied for the job and got it; apparently, I successfully argued that if the department wanted an evaluation with an emphasis on users' experiences with treatment, they needed an anthropologist who would do participant observation in the centres in order to study the daily practices, interactions, and get to know the users and their lives. In practice, it was the handling of methadone that took centre stage in my fieldwork.

Methadone is a form of medication, ideally with a day-long effect, given as a substitute for other so-called opioids, usually heroin. If given in the right amount, methadone covers the tolerance to opioids that users have developed, thus preventing withdrawal symptoms and allowing users to live a steady life without illegal drugs; though for most users, methadone alone does not achieve this. As it turned out, conflicts and negotiations over methadone prescriptions and drug intake were major concerns for users as well as staff, and this dominated the relations between them. Many staff members were more or less openly opposed to the prescription of methadone that they handled on a daily basis. Conditions of methadone use were also the single most regulated element of treatment by the Danish health authorities and the local centres. Users' appearance, behaviour and drug habits were continuously monitored by staff, including compulsory urine testing. As a consequence, users felt constantly subjected to suspicion and the threat of expulsion for breaking the rules (even though this rarely happened in practice). Everybody's firm focus on the methadone use was in sharp contrast with the formally stated policies and intentions of treatment in which methadone was supposed to only be a 'supportive' means. 'The real treatment' was to be the social and psychological services that users were (ideally) to be offered – a never realized ambition about which users and staff actually agreed would be ideal.

My initial report to the social services department outlined the problems that I had observed and the criticisms and concerns raised by the users during our conversations and interviews (Jöhncke 1997). Some of my findings were met with scepticism: drug users were by some perceived as invariably disturbed and hence the real source of trouble. However, many staff members and certainly the department management accepted my point that the daily conflicts in the clinic should be regarded as expressions of underlying inconsistencies in the approaches and practices of methadone use in the treatment system. Despite the fact that many users clearly benefit from methadone, as also shown by numerous studies, the substance has never been fully accepted by a treatment system and by public opinion that fundamentally

(Continued)

values abstinence over everything else. Hence, this results in the reluctant and control-obsessed regime that surrounds it.

By way of conducting several other projects in the same field, while working as a research associate and an assistant professor, I eventually finished my doctoral thesis on the subject of drug use treatment in 2008. My initial observations of the evident contrasts between intentions and clinical realities sent me on a long journey into the cultural and political history of drug use treatment. I realized that my bewilderment about the many meanings and uses of the emic term 'treatment' was actually at the core of the issue. In short, 'treatment' in relation to drug use has no specific meaning or content. The floating notion of treatment represents a piece of political wishful thinking, the idea that the unfortunate and illegal behaviour of drug use may be eradicated, one individual at a time. Users are subjected to a series of institutionalizations and various forms of influence, often regarded and handled in isolation from users' general conditions of living. Closely related to this is the cultural misconstruction of drug use as a specific 'disease', which perfectly suits the idea of treatment as a form of cure.

In my eyes, anthropology is well suited to expose and critique the consequences of these harmful and irrational cultural notions of drug use, drug users and treatment (Jöhncke 2009). It is also an example, I think, of how social indignation can be an important driver of anthropology. At least for me, what started as the subject of a one-year job more than twenty years ago not only continues to be a source of outrage but has also worked in tandem with my attitude to anthropology: use anthropology as a tool for what you think is important and what you want to challenge, change or help improve – 'interesting' is not quite enough.

FIVE TIPS FROM STEFFEN JÖHNCKE

1. **Use your ethnographic skills to study and decipher each potential employer.** What is important for his or her organization and how would your anthropological approach support him or her?
2. **Anthropology is not just a set of methods, it is a theoretically informed approach** to understanding why people do as they do – practice explaining that in plain words.
3. **When you apply for a job, explain what you bring to the job**, not how the job will interest or develop you.
4. **Your competences are not recognized until you can explain that you have them** – know what you know and show it.
5. **Dare do with anthropology what *you* think is important** – the university will not teach you what that is.

About the author

Steffen Jöhncke, PhD, was trained in social anthropology at the University of Copenhagen (Denmark) and the University of Sussex (United Kingdom). Since his postgraduate studies, he has applied anthropological perspectives to social work and health issues, being employed as an evaluator, civil servant and independent scholar before returning to academia in 2001 for doctoral studies. From 2008 to 2018, he was manager of *AnthroAnalysis – Centre for Applied Anthropology* in the Department of Anthropology at the University of Copenhagen. In 2019/20 he was visiting professor in the Danish School of Education, University of Aarhus (Denmark), and from 2020 he is senior lecturer in social anthropology in the School of Global Studies at the University of Gothenburg (Sweden).

References

Andersen, S. L., M. Pedersen and V. Steffen (2017), 'Illness, Normality, and Self-management: Diabetic Foot Ulcers and the Logic of Choice', *European Wound Management Association Journal*, 16 (2): 23–30.

Christensen, L. K. T. (2014), *Barrierer for dokumentation: En undersøgelse af dokumentationspraksis i Distrikt Øst, Center for Ældre, Næstved Kommune*, Copenhagen: Antropologisk Analyse, University of Copenhagen.

Felding, S. (2018), *Demensteknologier i praksis: En antropologisk undersøgelse af hverdagspraksis og implementering af velfærdsteknologier til mennesker med demens på danske plejecentre*, Copenhagen: Antropologisk Analyse, University of Copenhagen.

Felding, S., A. S. G. Kristensen, N. Schwennesen, B. Skårup and S. Jöhncke (2017), *Hverdagslæring på kommunale plejecentre: En antropologisk analyse af oplevelser med kompetenceløft og læring i regi af Fremfærd Ældre/Demens*, Copenhagen: Antropologisk Analyse, University of Copenhagen.

Field, L. W. and R. G. Fox (2007), 'Introduction: How Does Anthropology Work Today?', in L. W. Field and R. G. Fox (eds), *Anthropology Put to Work*, 1–19, Oxford: Berg.

Ilkjær, H. (2019), 'The Future Airport – Experiments and Innovative Technologies', *Journal of Business Anthropology*, 8 (1): 86–107.

Jakobsen, C., B. Skårup and S. Jöhncke (2017), *Maritim beslutningsstøtte om bord: En antropologisk undersøgelse af, hvordan to digitale beslutningsstøttesystemer betragtes og bruges i praksis*, Copenhagen: Antropologisk Analyse, University of Copenhagen.

Jöhncke, S. (1996), 'Culture in the Clinic: Danish Service Providers' View of Immigrants with HIV', in M. Haour-Knipe and R. Rector (eds), *Crossing Borders: Migration, Ethnicity and AIDS*, 167–77, London: Taylor & Francis.

Jöhncke, S. (1997), *Brugererfaringer: Undersøgelse af brugernes erfaringer med behandling i de fire distriktscentre i Københavns Kommunes behandlingssystem for stofmisbrugere 1996–97*, Copenhagen: Socialdirektoratet, Copenhagen City Council.

Jöhncke, S. (2009), 'Treatmentality and the Governing of Drug Use', *Drugs and Alcohol Today*, 9 (4): 14–17.

Jöhncke, S., S. Jørgensen and J. Hald (1993), *Mere end blot 'sikker sex': Evaluering af STOP AIDS-kampagnen*, Copenhagen: Forlaget Pan.

Karsten, M. M. V. (2019), 'Short-Term Anthropology: Thoughts from a Fieldwork among Plumbers, Digitalisation, Cultural Assumptions and Marketing Strategies', *Journal of Business Anthropology*, 8 (1): 108–25.

Leeson, C. (2017), *Robotteknologi til byggebranchen: En antropologisk undersøgelse af robotteknologiens potentialer og begrænsninger i den danske byggebranche*, Copenhagen: Antropologisk Analyse, University of Copenhagen.

Lex, S. W. (2016), 'In Search of Innovation: Operating with the Future as a Working Imperative', *Human Organization*, 75 (3): 230–38.

Lilleør, H. B. and U. Lund-Sørensen, eds (2013), *Farmers' Choice: Evaluating an Approach to Agricultural Technology Adoption in Tanzania*, London: Practical Action Publishing.

Tonnesen, S., S. Jöhncke and V. Steffen (2011), *Evaluering af Hejmdal – Kræftpatienternes Hus*, Copenhagen: Antropologisk Analyse, University of Copenhagen.

Wahlberg, A. (2009), 'Serious Disease as Kinds of Living', in S. Baur and A. Wahlberg (eds), *Contested Categories: Life Sciences in Society*, 89–112, Newcastle-upon-Tyne: Ashgate.

Weisdorf, M. (2017), *Hvad motiverer brandfolk? En antropologisk analyse af rekruttering og fastholdelse af honorarlønnede brandmænd*, Copenhagen: Antropologisk Analyse, University of Copenhagen.

6

SEARCHING FOR VARIATION AND COMPLEXITY

Tanja Winther

To me, anthropology's mission is to search for and document variety in human experience. If the goal of religious leaders is to translate what established doctrines imply in terms of how people should live, anthropology has explored the organization, meanings and implications of religion in a given context. If economy as a science is about trying to optimize the production and use of resources in a given society, anthropology seeks to explore how material resources and representations, such as money and the use of light bulbs, are entangled in social relations and cultural values. If engineering is about developing energy efficient and technology smart solutions, anthropology is concerned with the ways different groups of people potentially start using these technologies, and the social implications thereof. (I am presuming here that sociologists and other academics affiliated with Science and Technology Studies continue to focus on developers and engineers as an important group for social analysis.)

Hence, in contrast to religious leaders, economics and engineering, anthropology is less normative in its purpose, and more explorative, rather than attuned towards finding solutions to pre-defined questions. We cherish and celebrate the complex and often surprising and intriguing aspects of human living. Clifford Geertz (1973: 30) referred to the mission of (interpretative) anthropology as being 'not to answer our deepest questions but to make available to us answers that others, guarding other sheep in other valleys, have given, and thus to include them in the consultable record of what man [sic] has said'.

Today, having moved from the mainly interpretative approach of the 1970s towards studying social practices (Ortner 2006), we do not only pay attention to what people say but also to what people do, what they do with things and the relations of power in which people and objects are entangled. (To keep up with the changes in language, we would also replace Geertz's term 'man' with people or human beings.) Otherwise, the anthropological purpose of being witness to the variation in human experience seems to stand.

In an ideal world without pressing challenges such as global warming and inequity, the distribution of work between these different disciplines might work well. The differences in perspectives, focus and knowledge production would simply be of 'academic interest' and perhaps even complementary. However, as I will return to in this essay to the energy dilemma and anthropology's role in powering the planet, we cannot neglect the need for collaboration between disciplines. Without focussing our attention on this, we risk delaying rather than enhancing solutions to the current challenges. Moreover, because finding solutions to pressing problems is a joint concern that involves global and local levels, a key mission for anthropology today is to disclose power relations.

Anthropologists studying development in the past

In the realm of development, in the past, anthropologists were often invited in the aftermath of a project to explain why it failed. Eduardo Archetti's (1997) study of guinea pigs in Ecuador is a classic, and another is Lauriston Sharp's (1952) article 'Steel Axes for Stone-Age Australians'. Underlying some of these studies was a sometimes-romanticizing idea of cultural practices and how the new technology was either unsuited to the given context or had unintended negative consequences. Surprisingly, given that anthropologists had often conducted fieldwork in poverty-ridden areas, Booth and colleagues (1999) observed that few anthropologists had actively treated the concept of poverty, though see Mary Douglas (1982) who conceptualized poverty as lack of dignity, which continues to yield relevance today.

Some anthropologists took a more proactive stance, explaining why technologies fail but also pointing to people's needs for new solutions. For example, Emma Crewe (1997) accounted for why improved cook stoves promoted in the 1960s and 1970s were not taken in use. In laboratories, white male engineers had developed stoves that did not fit the needs of the female cooks living in the South. Her underlying message is that knowledge about social practices ('silent traditions'), both amongst developers as well as target groups, is required ahead of interventions.

The energy dilemma

The energy dilemma concerns the double challenge we face globally at present. On the one hand, energy production and use account for two thirds of the world's greenhouse-gas emissions (IEA 2015). Rich countries need to reduce consumption and solely use renewable sources for production. On the other hand, there is an urgent need to provide access to electricity to all. Approximately one billion people are restricted from using electricity today. Electricity access, in Amartya Sen's (1999) terms, can be considered an 'essential freedom' because this technology and adhering equipment condition the use of phones, mobile banking, water provision, light, health services and a range of other services that people conceive as essential for living a good life. I have witnessed that this perception is shared in various contexts. In this picture of a need to provide more people with access, what role can anthropologists play and how can we work with other disciplines to formulate purposeful research agendas for sustainable energy? Rather than attempting to provide a general answer to how the energy dilemma should be addressed, I will give one example of my own work in an interdisciplinary team in a project promoting increased access in the South and another focussing on sustainable energy in the North.

In the first case, the project was initiated by a human geographer, Kirsten Ulsrud, who had observed that India was a leading country in the distribution of solar power to people living in remote, poor areas (Ulsrud 2015). Here, governmental agencies in several states had introduced village scale systems, such as solar PV (photovoltaic) electricity stations combined with mini-grids. Similar systems were absent in Kenya, where only the private sector promoted solar home systems in the market. Our project raised the overall question 'What can Kenya learn from India?' with respect to village scale solar power supply. An international team was established, involving people from the implicated countries in addition to Norway and Austria. We worked interdisciplinary in that people from various disciplines engaged in dialogue when formulating the research questions and conducting data collection jointly in the field. To ensure that various types of knowledge formed part of the project, practitioners also played a key role in the project, which was thereby also transdisciplinary. We anchored the research in socio-technical system theory (Rohracher 2003), where the socio-cultural aspects on the user side received due attention. Being the anthropologist in the team, my responsibility was primarily to focus on material and socio-cultural aspects in the selected contexts in rural India and Kenya.

With the ambition to establish a village scale electricity system in Ikisaya, Kenya, through action research (Herr and Anderson 2005), the team met some challenges. First, the programme that funded our social science research (Norwegian Research Council) did not accept expenditures on material objects; hence, we needed to find private donors for buying the necessary equipment. Thus, we met a structural barrier in the funding regime for conducting transdisciplinary action research on energy. Second, we discovered differences in 'interests' within the research team. After examining the local context, including the existing settlement and transport (walking!) patterns and the needs and aspirations of various groups (e.g. old, young, women, men, schoolchildren, administrators and farmers), we were ready to design the system of supply in close collaboration with local stakeholders (a community-based organization). Here, we needed to decide what kinds of services to offer (limited budget) and how much users should pay for each service. The economist in the team was concerned about the system's financial viability. Based on economic calculations, he noted that a photocopying machine would never become profitable for the Ikisaya Energy Centre. He was also concerned that the charges for services (lantern renting, mobile charging) should not be too low and that people should

FIGURE 6.1 The family uses solar light, which helps the children to do homework and Ms Rose to do the cooking. In addition, they have a lamp outside as a security light. Nyandiwa Trading Centre, Homabay County, Gwassi Division, Sori, Magunga, Kenya, 2018. Courtesy Sven Torfinn/ ENERGIA.

hand in the lanterns after two days of use only so that the Centre would be able to recharge them frequently and thus get more income. I and other social scientists argued for the copy machine because many groups had highlighted the importance of this to avoid spending time travelling elsewhere to obtain photocopies. We also argued that people should be able to keep the lanterns for more than two days because it would constitute a burden for them to walk the long distance to the Centre (to some, up to six kilometres). We had some very intense and engaged discussions![1]

Coming from different disciplines, we needed to negotiate the solutions. The balancing between purposeful services and affordability on the one hand and system viability on the other was not only required during the planning. It also turned out to be key to the system's survival in the years to come, when local staff have increasingly taken over the management. There are plenty of examples of local energy initiatives that have not survived. Moreover, the project leader and I forwarded the idea to invite women to apply for positions at the Centre. In the beginning, this was met by some resistance among men in the village but gradually became accepted. Today the Centre is run by a woman, Winnie, whom customers praise for her patience, politeness, trustworthiness and her flexible but firm way of handling issues regarding payment. Ultimately, the project's concern for gender equality from the start allowed for positive impacts along several development dimensions such as increased gender equality. This would not have been a likely outcome if only technical and economic considerations had informed the project.[2] At large, the Centre's systematic attention to social aspects was key to its gender inclusiveness, financial viability and long-term presence in the village (still in operation).

In the second case, we ran a sequence of projects on sustainable energy consumption in Norway. An interdisciplinary team (led by CICERO, Oslo) was established to examine the effects of various interventions that promote sustainability. Here we drew on political scientists to understand how national and European Union regulations shape markets, policy tools and technologies that in turn may affect people's energy consumption. For example, through empirical investigation (both quantitative and qualitative), we found that Guarantees of Origin, that is policy-informed market mechanisms to promote renewable sources, are rather meaningless in Norway because people perceive electricity produced by hydropower (98 per cent) to be renewable in the first place. Comparing some of these results with parallel studies in France and the United Kingdom, we gained more insights into how electricity cultures differ between countries. We argued that such knowledge is needed for understanding the potential effectiveness of policy instruments.

Later we invited an engineer to contribute to a pilot project testing out Energy Performance Contracting in a housing cooperative, which did not turn out to be successful (Winther and Gurigard 2017). We also studied the use of heat pumps and accounted for how rebound effects occur due to people's concern for time management and comfort. In a study on in-home displays we found that they are perceived as 'toys' among affluent groups while people who were struggling financially saw them as tools to get in control of their lives. A central part of this work was to show that the introduction of policies and technologies might have different effects in different cultural settings and amongst various social groups. Energy is socially conditioned and it may strengthen social differentiations.

To illustrate some of the challenges involved in this work, the economist, psychologist and anthropologist spent the first year just agreeing on an analytical framework. What did we mean by social norms? How do social structures affect what people do with energy? What is the relationship between 'social practices' and 'behaviour'? Having reached a common understanding, the successive work went smoothly and today we sometimes forget who has written what as we exchange draft papers and comment on each other's work. A positive indication in relation to the collaboration with the engineer is that we did not compete in worldviews but understood our roles as complementary and I did most of the job writing our joint article.

A need for anthropologists in interdisciplinary teams

Above, I recaptured anthropology's non-normative purpose and our search for variety in human experience. Due to the pressing global challenges in the realm of energy, which constitutes a dilemma because less and more are required at the same time, anthropologists are needed to widen the scope of the problem. We are thus invited to become normative in terms of the objectives of research, but this does not mean that we must employ normative methodological approaches. Rather, by continuing to openly explore, compare and understand how people think and live in and with the social, natural and material world – which is undoubtedly best achieved through long-term fieldwork – we can help expand the knowledge base for policy-making in a direction that enhances social sustainability and social justice.

To this aim, given the continued weight put on technological optimism, determinism and/or individualistic models, a first and conceptual task is to refine and promote alternative understandings of social change. A second challenge is how to move from contextualized findings towards generalizations and recommendations. For this purpose, I strongly believe in interdisciplinarity and mixed methods. I provided two examples from research with practitioners and people from other disciplines where I also illustrated some problems we faced in terms of the need to achieve conceptual clarity and resolve differences in priorities between people representing different disciplines. In both cases, these 'investments' proved to be beneficial to the projects over time. Playing a part in these teams was also personally rewarding.

In comparison with many other disciplines, anthropologists are trained to ask qualitative questions including how, who and why. In my experience (e.g. Winther 2015; Winther et al. 2017), this type of empirical data can help understand important gaps in development and sustainability studies by focussing on the *preconditions* (Kabeer 2001) for a given intervention or measure and the *mechanisms* that produce or do not produce the expected effect. In particular, anthropological research is suited for studying power relations which come into play in any process involving technological change.

The process towards finding solutions to the energy dilemma would be enhanced if anthropologists increased their participation in this field. Rather than leaving to economists and engineers to define problems and suggest solutions, anthropologists could make an important impact if they took a lead and engaged more closely in dialogue with other disciplines at an early stage of the research process. Such involvement would not exclude, but the quality of the results would depend on, anthropology's trademark in terms of searching for variety, cherishing complexity and conveying the views and experience of different groups.

PERSONAL MOTIVATION AND A DISAPPOINTING ENCOUNTER WITH ENGINEERING STUDIES

At seventeen, still in high school, I was determined to work with solar energy in Africa one day. I had learned about the lack of electricity in many countries. In social science classes and from watching television, the slave trade and the enduring impact of imperialism had made a deep impact on me. In particular, and searching for solutions (was I already an engineer?), I could not understand why development agencies such as Norad (Norwegian Agency for Development Cooperation) did not put emphasis on developing and providing solar energy. In Africa, the sun was always shining! I did A-levels in science at the time and I quite liked math and natural sciences. One day, as I wondered whether to select physics or chemistry in the final year (in addition to math), I went to see the school advisor to ask for his opinion. He was approaching retirement and it turned out that he had been an acquaintance of my grandfather who had died before I was born. I was therefore confident that the advisor had the best intentions when he told me: 'I think you should go for chemistry because it is a well-known fact that girls and physics do not go well together'.

It later turned out that physics was a requirement in power engineering at the technical university in Trondheim, so his advice in effect equipped me to enter this master's programme (of course I had selected physics). But there I discovered two things that disappointed me. First, there was no emphasis on solar power, but rather hydropower, which Norway has in abundance. Over four years, the only input we got on solar energy was through a tiny assignment. We were asked to calculate the distance a chain of connected solar panels (one meter wide) would have to be in order to feed a small Norwegian town with electric power. The correct answer was a distance of more than 2,000 kilometres, from Lindesnes to Nordkapp! 'How stupid to even think about solar power when we have plenty of hydro', the dominating Norwegian power paradigm until this day.

The second thing I learned was that the study programme was not designed for me. We were only ten per cent women in my cohort (ten out of 100 students), which was considered to be a relatively high share. To address this issue, during the first year, I was asked by a group of women activists to help improve the gender balance by going back to my college and speaking to younger women about the benefits of studying engineering. Therefore, during that first year I went back to my former high school and held a passionate speech to students doing A-levels about the need for women in engineering, stressing the advantages for society as well as for the individual students. In the second year, I did not want to promote the engineering programme any longer. The reasons? First, the syllabus did not include any perspectives on energy in society, which remained my main interest, but only purely technological and mathematical matters. We were not required to read any theory of science but were presented with equations on the very first day. In addition, I felt invisible. For example, in the lab I would ask a question to the scientific assistant, always a young man. When giving his reply he would address my male student colleague as if speaking only to him.

(Continued)

As a result, I spent most of my time in the student society (student radio, organizing public debates), which made the four years in the programme rewarding after all. This was also the point in time when I discovered social anthropology and started to take anthropology courses that were not part of my engineering curriculum. Overall, I felt that my expectations for studying engineering were not met. I had experienced prejudices and was often ignored as a woman, but I think, partly thanks to my confident female colleagues, this never made me doubt my own capabilities. What this experience did trigger was a strengthened interest in understanding energy from a social and gendered perspective. Later, in a doctoral course in philosophy of science, it resonated with me when we learned about Roy Bhaskar (1989) who forwarded, leaning on Marx: listening to the voices of suppressed groups provides an important path for understanding social structures and their impacts.

DISCOVERING A CULTURAL CLASH BETWEEN ENGINEERS AND ANTHROPOLOGISTS

Determined to pursue my interest in energy in developing contexts, the master's programme in power engineering eventually allowed me to select a research topic of my own interest. I found a project on rural electrification in Zanzibar, which I approached as a 'cultural meeting' implicating Norwegian engineers, Zanzibari staff in the electricity company and local residents (potential 'beneficiaries'). Responding to this choice, my supervisor at the technical university initially asked me if I believed I would ever get a job as an engineer, but he later became more positive towards my project. I also received invaluable guidance for my thesis, which included three months of fieldwork in Zanzibar, from a historian of technology, Professor Haakon With Andersen.

During this project I noticed a division of work, or even a cultural clash, between anthropologists and engineers. In an inspiring chapter on gender, culture and appropriate technology, anthropologist Marit Melhuus spelled out the socio-cultural and relational aspects of technologies when considered in their context of use. However, I was astonished when she declared: 'I have said very little about technology and nothing about appropriate technology. This is not a coincidence. I am not a technical expert' (Melhuus 1989: 154). As if people and the technologies they use could be separated. And what a humble stance, as if technology to an anthropologist was a mystery or a 'black box', following Latour (1988). In contrast, a Norwegian engineer working in Tanzania told me in 1991: 'People studying culture are sitting in their offices in Oslo, thinking they know people. But as engineers, we are the ones who are out in the field and know how things really are'. Therefore, from this engineer's point of view – which was definitely less humble than that of the anthropologist – he suspected anthropologists *claimed* to know people and realities, rather than *really* knowing them. Only engineers who had hands-on experience of technology in the field were the genuinely knowledgeable.

The engineer's mistrust in anthropology was striking – and it was one of the reasons I decided to first work for some years as an engineer to gain experience (and respect from engineers), before searching for an opportunity to do more anthropology. The engineer would probably need a very convincing answer to the question 'why the world needs anthropologists' before letting go of this scepticism. At the technical university, nobody asked the reflexive question 'why the world needs engineers', probably because the purpose of technological development appears obvious. In contrast, several articles in undergraduate anthropology courses were focussed on legitimizing anthropology as a social science discipline. I was a bit surprised to see this, puzzled by how this discipline – with such powerful tools to think about and study social life – seemed to have limited self-confidence. I later learned that reflexivity is key for making knowledge production transparent and conclusions robust – and today I think such exercises amongst engineers would be valuable (cf. failed projects such as the cook stoves studied by Crewe (1997) and the guinea pig project studied by Archetti (1997)).

Bringing engineering into anthropology

My work on the master thesis convinced me that anthropological methods were highly suited for studying electricity, and personally, the work in the field and engaging with Zanzibaris was so fulfilling that I could think of nothing else at the time. I felt obsessed. I later completed undergraduate anthropology courses while working as an engineer (reading anthropological articles was more intriguing than reading novels!) and the courses at the master's level in social anthropology in Oslo, subsequently getting the fortunate opportunity to embark on a doctoral project. I kept the social implications of the arrival of electricity in Zanzibar as the enduring focus of research. Having collected data at different points in time, this allowed me to do a longitudinal study of electricity's impact on all kinds of relationships, spanning from people with and without electricity access, generations, genders and to the relationship between human beings and occult forces and spirits. I spent ten new months in the field living in a village with my family.

I also collected material by engaging in dialogue with staff at the electricity company. Playing with technical data in my interpretations of social aspects was fun, for example by studying load curves on electricity consumption in

(Continued)

FIGURE 6.2 Street lights in Dikoni ward, Uroa village, Zanzibar, Tanzania, 2004. Courtesy Tanja Winther.

Zanzibar during the fasting month of Ramadhan as compared to ordinary days. (During Ramadhan there was more consumption and activity at night because more people were reading the Koran at night, and less activity during daytime because of shorter work days for industry and shops.) Some of these technical data (and recommendations) did not get space in the anthropological dissertation, as my wonderful supervisor, Professor Aud Talle, rightly advised. Nevertheless, technical data helped me analyse the social phenomena I studied (e.g. representing social data through load curves). I also put emphasis on including the utility and engineering perspective and focussing on the relationship between supplier and customer. I found it interesting to learn that the famous anthropologist Edmund Leach had initially been a mechanical engineer. He wrote that his engineering background made him focus on how societies actually work and function, rather than just describing social structures, as had previously been common in anthropology (Leach 1984).

Ethical challenges in the field

My intention as an anthropologist in the field was to approach people and material objects as openly as possible, for example by not presuming that access to electricity would mean 'development' to the women and men concerned. However, I soon discovered that my identity as an engineer was difficult to abandon and it sometimes affected how people related to me. At the electricity company, the staff referred to me as 'the engineer', and as we shared the 'tribal' language of engineers, this enhanced communication, relation building and hence data collection. However, on at least two occasions, my engineering

FIGURE 6.3   Tanja Winther as a PhD fellow doing fieldwork in Uroa village, Zanzibar, Tanzania, 2001. Courtesy Henrik Bentzen.

identity almost caused disaster, at least that is how I felt as an anthropologist. I wanted to be empathic, not impose my own views on people and cause absolutely no harm to the people helping me in the field. One day, after I had repeatedly asked utility staff how many customers they had in the villages, a senior officer finally gave me a concrete answer. He did not yet know the exact number, he said, but assured me that utility staff would soon make a tour to every village in Zanzibar to get a proper count of both legal and illegal connections. In that way they would also be able to punish people using illegal connections. I hurried to respond that the numbers were not that important to me and urged that they should not do this exercise to meet my research needs.

The other incident occurred in the electrified village where I lived. I was intrigued by observing a contradiction in what people said they did and what they actually did. During my first visit, many men had told me that when they were able to afford it, they would buy electric stoves which would help their wives. However, when I returned ten years later, there were only two stoves in the whole village (and they were not in use), while the uptake of television was massive. Women I spoke with often highlighted the benefits they would experience if cooking with electricity, signalling, at least in the meeting with a Western researcher used to electric stoves, an interest in pursuing their modern identities by cooking with electricity. Nevertheless, the number of

(Continued)

stoves remained low and I tried in various ways to understand the practice of cooking by exploring the issue of taste, finances, gender roles, fertility and so on. Given my expressed interest in this matter, a village leader approached me one day and said they were planning a general meeting the following week. The meeting would focus on stoves. Here I was, invited to explain to the entire village why they should cook with electricity. I certainly did not want to promote stoves, which would be a role that contradicted that of an empathic anthropologist, and I tried as politely as I could to decline the offer and the plans for the meeting were cancelled.

Electricity and anthropology matter

During fieldwork I also struggled with the fear that I might overestimate the significance of electricity and overlook other aspects of life in rural Zanzibar that mattered more to people themselves. If so, I would be treating electricity as a fetish, constructing an account that takes a relatively marginal technology as the basis of a superstructure within which everything else is considered (cf. Miller 1998: 3). However, as I discuss in the book that was later published on this material (Winther 2008), I concluded that electricity actually mattered.

Publishing this book on electricity in Zanzibar resulted in attention from development agencies as well as anthropologists. This kind of ethnography turned out to be original and I think the comment that made the most impact on me came from a senior economist in the World Bank. She told me through email that reading my book had changed her view on electrification processes in a fundamental way. I take this statement to express what anthropology in general may bring to fields of enquiry dominated by other disciplines such as economics and engineering: new perspectives, new topics for research, new ways of inquiry and new knowledge, potentially influencing policy and practice. Our key tool is trying to represent the world, including technologies, as closely to the way people themselves perceive and experience this world. As simple – and complex – as that.

FIVE TIPS FROM TANJA WINTHER

1. **Trust that you embody a particular set of approaches, skills and knowledge** that are crucial for understanding – and hence improving – the world.
2. **Don't be afraid to bring colleagues from other disciplines to the field**. Sharing data collection improves joint interpretations and the final text – and it's fun.

3. **Put more effort in translating complex findings and representations into clear recommendations for policy makers and other practitioners**. Generalization remains a key challenge, but language is crucial to change.
4. **Continue doing what you do, from fieldwork and comparison, to finding critical perspectives**. However, search for new areas of research that serve to refine theory and concepts and/or have relevance for society.
5. **Strengthen your influence on the international research agenda.** Identifying the 'right' projects is key to posing the 'right' questions.

About the author

Tanja Winther is Professor at the Centre for Development and the Environment (SUM), University of Oslo. With a background in power engineering (MSc) and social anthropology (PhD), her research centres on the social dimensions of energy, spanning from the social and gendered impacts of introducing electricity for the first time, to sustainable energy consumption in rich countries. She has done fieldwork in Zanzibar (Tanzania), Kenya, Malawi, India and Norway, and teaches at various levels in Norway and abroad. She led the international project EFEWEE – Exploring Factors that Enhance and restrict Women's Empowerment through Electrification, financed by DFID, UK. Winther initiated and currently leads Include – Research centre for socially inclusive energy transitions, funded by the Research Council of Norway (2020–2027).

Notes

1 The team generally agreed that it would be important to use solar power for water pumps and storing medicines, as the area is terribly dry and there is no public health services, but unfortunately, lack of funding and other infrastructure needs (maintaining a cold chain also requires fridge during transport) made this option impossible to realize.
2 In contrast, in gender-blind interventions, the literature shows that electricity tends to be managed by men (Winther et al. 2017).

References

Archetti, E. (1997), *Guinea Pigs: Food, Symbol and Conflict of Knowledge in Ecuador*, Oxford: Berg.

Bhaskar, R. (1989), *The Possibility of Naturalism: A Philosophical Critique of the Contemporary Human Sciences*, London and New York: Routledge.

Booth, D., M. Leach and A. Tierney (1999), 'Experiencing Poverty in Africa: Perspectives From Anthropology', Background Paper No. 1(b) for the World Bank Poverty Status Report 1999, London: Overseas Development Institute. Available online: https://www.odi.org/publications/5025-experiencing-poverty-africa-perspectives-anthropology (accessed 10 October 2017).

Crewe, E. (1997). 'The Silent Traditions of Developing Cooks', in R. D. Grillo and R. L. Stirrat (eds), *Discourses of Development: Anthropological Perspectives*, 59–81, Oxford: Berg.

Douglas, M. (1982), *In the Active Voice*, London: Routledge & Kegan Paul Ltd.

Geertz, C. (1973), *The Interpretation of Cultures*, New York: Basic Books.

Herr, K. and G. L. Anderson (2005), *The Action Research Dissertation: A Guide for Students and Faculty*, London: Sage Publications.

IEA (International Energy Agency) (2015), 'Energy and Climate Change: World Energy Outlook Special Report', Paris: International Energy Agency. Available online: https://www.iea.org/publications/freepublications/publication/WEO2015Special-ReportonEnergyandClimateChange.pdf (accessed 3 August 2018).

Kabeer, N. (2001), 'Reflections on the Measurement of Women's Empowerment', in A. Sisask (ed.), *Discussing Women's Empowerment: Theory and Practice*, 17–57, Stockholm: Swedish International Development Cooperation Agency.

Latour, B. (1988), *Science in Action: How to Follow Scientists and Engineers Through Society*, Cambridge (MA): Harvard University Press.

Leach, E. R. (1984), 'Glimpses of the Unmentionable in the History of British Social Anthropology', *Annual Review of Anthropology*, 13: 1–23.

Melhuus, M. (1989), 'Kjønn, kultur og tilpasset teknologi: En begrepsverden', in T. H. Eriksen (ed.), *Hvor mange hvite elefanter*, 147–56, Oslo: Mostue Bøker AS.

Miller, D. (1998), 'Why Some Things Matter', in D. Miller (ed), *Material Cultures: Why Some Things Matter*, 3–21, Chicago (IL): The University of Chicago Press.

Ortner, S. B. (2006), *Anthropology and Social Theory: Culture, Power, and the Acting Subject*, London: Duke University Press.

Rohracher, H. (2003), 'The Role of Users in the Social Shaping of Environmental Technologies', *Innovation: The European Journal of Social Science Research*, 16 (2): 177–92.

Sen, A. (1999), *Development as Freedom*, Oxford: Oxford University Press.

Sharp, L. (1952), 'Steel Axes for Stone-Age Australians', *Human Organization*, 11 (2): 17–22.

Ulsrud, K. (2015), *Village-level Solar Power in Practice: Transfer of Socio-technical Innovations between India and Kenya*, PhD diss., University of Oslo, Oslo. Available online: http://urn.nb.no/URN:NBN:no-52241 (accessed 15 October 2019).

Winther, T. (2008), *The Impact of Electricity: Development, Desires and Dilemmas*, Oxford: Berghahn Books.

Winther, T. (2015), 'Impact Evaluation of Rural Electrification Programmes: What Parts of the Story May Be Missed?', *Journal of Development Effectiveness*, 7 (2): 160–74.

Winther, T. and K. Gurigard (2017), 'Energy Performance Contracting (EPC): A Suitable Mechanism for Achieving Energy Savings in Housing Cooperatives? Results from a Norwegian Pilot Project', *Energy Efficiency*, 10 (3): 577–96.

Winther, T., M. N. Matinga, K. Ulsrud and K. Standal (2017), 'Women's Empowerment through Electricity Access: Scoping Study and Proposal for a Framework of Analysis', *Journal of Development Effectiveness*, 9 (3): 389–417.

7

AN ANTHROPOLOGIST'S JOURNEY FROM THE RAINFOREST TO SOLAR FIELDS

Sophie Bouly de Lesdain

Even though everywhere in this world we put on clothes, eat, make homes, marry, have children and die, these practices are based on codes, rules and imaginaries that vary from one culture to another. In this respect anthropologists deal with the most intimate aspects of how we live and feel. To borrow the phrase from the French anthropologist Françoise Héritier, 'before existing in a more ordered fashion in our minds, the world exists through our senses' (2012: 87). It explains the often highly affective reactions that occur when one encounters other ways of being and doing. And, since there is more than one way of thinking about the world, dreaming about it and acting on it, anthropologists need to move in between special features and commonalities.

How can we cohabitate with groups that have different practices, visions of the world or social organizations? First, anthropology looks at the way in which a group of people takes its constraints on board, finds its own solutions and invents itself while accepting its difference from other societies. While doing so anthropology allows us to go beyond deterministic discourses, such as those which put forward biological arguments to justify societal facts (e.g. since it is women who are pregnant, it is up to them to take care of children) or tautological culturalist discourses (e.g. 'they' do that because this is the way they are). The discipline can thus help us move away from preconceived ideas and assume alternative viewpoints. Second, despite the fact that the question which lies at the heart of the anthropological project – relating to otherness – is nothing new, the increasing migration and means of communication certainly are. Anthropology is therefore particularly important in times of heated societal debates, but it also has practical applications in industrial and commercial fields, and in relation to public policy. Because the world is constantly changing – and anthropology is a discipline pertaining to the present – anthropology's research subjects constantly evolve. Today, our professional paths call upon us to participate in directing these changes.

In my career, I have moved from academic anthropology to a research organization and, at university, to applied anthropology. The following chapter is based on this experience. First, I demonstrate the value that may be found in applied anthropology for public policy and industry. Second, I briefly present the story that led me to the discipline. Third, I present in concrete terms what my work in an energy company – Electricité de France – consists of. This will allow us to look into the development of solar energy as it is experienced by its users and address the social value and practical implications of anthropology in the world. I will conclude with a few tips for future anthropologists.

Technologies and energy

Let us start with technologies and energy. Change can be found on every street corner today, especially wherever new technologies are concerned. As we are experiencing transition toward the 'internet of things', phones, houses, even whole cities are to become 'smart'. They seem to be invested with a world-changing power that sometimes resembles the form of magical thought. Often, in the corporate world, if the object does not fulfil the predesigned purpose, it is the user who is held responsible for this failure. Typically, 'resistance to change' and 'human error' are then put forward as the explanation for the failure, which could also come from the technical side.

Whenever we use technological devices that transform energy into electricity, such as a hair-dryer, a microwave or an oven, we take care of our bodies. The use of energy is thus underpinned by social and cultural practices (Shove 2003; Shove and Walker 2014), and, as long as these interactions are technologically mediated, they fall within the domain of socio-cultural anthropology. Yet, since decision-makers tend to rely on a universal rationality formulated in terms of technical or economic efficiency, what escapes our attention is the fuller understanding of energy consumption of citizens. Due to the limited involvement of anthropologists, industry and public authorities do not possess the right tools and concepts. Let me give you an example.

When I was leading a field study in Corsica, the inhabitants explained that they had chosen to install a heat pump in order to benefit from a technology that used little electricity and therefore resulted in lower operational costs. It was encouraged by the engineers with whom I collaborated, because it was considered an extremely energy efficient solution. However, one unintended consequence complicated matters: the inhabitants had abandoned traditional cooling methods such as natural airing or closing windows during the hottest periods of the day. Instead, they started using the pump setting at temperatures lower than those to which they were accustomed as 'air conditioning'. Ultimately, the adoption of high-performance technological devices was encouraging more costly uses of electricity. Focussing solely on energy efficiency, engineers had not anticipated that this would lead to a change in indoor temperature norms.

Taking complexity into account

The second key dimension of energy use involves public policies. Let me discuss air conditioning a bit further. As long as the development of air conditioning is closely linked to the concept of a body that must work productively, without sweating and soiling, actors in the construction industry and policy makers responsible for building standards intentionally enforce the use of it (Chappells and Shove 2005; Wilhite 2008). Moreover, in affected regions people install air conditioning to restrict the number of mosquitos entering the home, improve living conditions during pregnancy or adolescence, or because they close windows for fear of a burglary (Bouly de Lesdain 2016). Many anthropologists who studied the proliferation of air conditioning technology have sounded the alarm with regard to its environmental consequences (Hitchings and Jun Lee 2008) and emphasized the need for development of culturally sound technological innovations (Douzou and Bouly de Lesdain 2013). The bottom line of these studies is: all innovations must take into consideration both socio-cultural context and environmental costs.

Anthropology always takes complexity into account. In this respect, it surpasses the behavioural approaches that are so fashionable nowadays. For example, the 'nudge theory', developed by the winners of the Nobel Prize in Economics Thaler and Sunstein (2008), suggests that an initial action in the promotion of energy management will encourage residents to take further actions in order to comply with the trend. Observation has shown that this is not always the case. During research I conducted in Corsica, some inhabitants claimed to set their heating to a maximum of eighteen degrees Celsius. They were doing it to preserve the environment and to conform with a moral[1] maxim of French public policies on energy efficiency (Fodor 2012). However, by having several TVs and computers, an aquarium, a swimming pool, they also multiplied the number of electrical installations and disproportionally increased the overall electricity consumption. An action in favour of the environment (low internal temperatures), is not enough to make people reduce all their uses of electricity, as suggested by the nudge theory. It focusses the attention of individuals on a type of use, on which energy management speeches carry the bulk of their content.

All of these issues about technical innovations and energy consumption tie in with an anthropology of daily life. In this respect anthropology has an undeniable social value. While applied in industrial and commercial contexts, this value is also economic, providing career opportunities for young researchers. But before I expand on my experience with Electricité de France (EDF), we need to visit Mvae in Cameroon.

FROM THE RAINFOREST TO ELECTRICITÉ DE FRANCE

It all began with Marshall Sahlins's book *Stone Age Economics* (1972) when I was nineteen years old. I was living in Paris, studying at the Sorbonne and Sahlins's text was probably one of the first I came across. In the book Sahlins examined the link between economic, cultural and social factors and observed that so-called primitive societies managed to meet their needs, food requirements in particular, without having to produce any surplus, because it is costly in terms of time and energy. In this regard he proposed to use the term 'societies of abundance' in opposition to then commonly used 'subsistence economies'. The conceptual reversal was really very impressive for me. Alongside other influential authors, Sahlins initiated me into the craft of cultural relativism.

Three years later, in 2001, I met Igor de Garine, an ethnologist at the French National Centre for Scientific Research, who also happened to be the next-door neighbour of my boyfriend's parents. Until then I had been studying human sciences and I urgently needed to find an end-of-year internship. Knowing that Igor was running an anthropology of food research programme based in the Southwest of France, I decided to send in my application. However, Igor suggested that I should go to Cameroon. I was surprised by this proposal and saw it as a unique opportunity to discover a world culturally different from mine. At the same time, I also had the opportunity to do an internship in a bank; but for me, going to Africa for six months to work on food practices was definitely more exciting. My first memory of Cameroon is the damp heat in the middle of the night at Douala airport. The red soil of roads. The smell of soaking cassava. The noises coming from the forest. All of that was soon to become so familiar to me.

I ended up living in a remote village on the border with Equatorial Guinea with the Béti-Fang group of the Mvae people. The Mvae live by the coast alongside the Yassa and the 'forest people' (Twa, Aka, Baka and Mbuti), sometimes called Pygmies. The first were farmers, the second were fishermen and the last ones were settled foragers. And these three groups coexisted in the same environment. The economic and technological specialization of these groups could not be reduced to efficiency-based choices. If this was the case, we would find uniform milieu-based practices. This diversity and relativity fascinated me the same way it, supposedly, did Sahlins.

In the early days of my return to France, things that were previously so familiar suddenly started to destabilize me. I remember the yoghurt aisles in a supermarket so vividly: hundreds of types of yoghurt, low-fat, with added calcium, soya, fruit, brewed, plain and so on. How could I choose? I often left the supermarket empty-handed. The consumer society to which I belong suddenly seemed so absurd in contrast to self-sufficient societies. All this is

FIGURE 7.1 Sophie Bouly de Lesdain's first field research in Cameroon, in 1991, in Afan Essokye, a small village on the border with Equatorial Guinea. Personal archive of Sophie Bouly de Lesdain.

history today, but the impression stays with me. Until today, my heart beats faster when I read an interesting article. New questions pop up and I cannot wait to travel to the next fieldwork for answers. In the next section I present my work on solar energy for EDF.

HOW TO DEVELOP SOLAR ENERGY SOLUTIONS AS AN ANTHROPOLOGIST

Having taken a sweeping look at different aspects of the contributions that applied anthropology can make, I am now going to focus on the area that I am currently working on at EDF. With 154,845 employees and owned by the state, the public limited company is the leading producer and supplier of electricity in France and Europe, and is expanding its activities to the Americas, Africa and Asia. Among the employees, there are about twenty researchers: political scientists, semiologists, sociologists and anthropologists. My colleagues and I work on energy transition, fuel poverty, societal trends and their impacts on energy demand and renewable energies. We build some partnerships with academics, but most of the time we are part of internal projects alongside with engineers. One of the key questions I examine is why

(Continued)

local residents install solar panels (PVs) on their roofs even if they are already connected to the national power grid. Drawing on this example I will illustrate the ways in which energy use becomes the subject of industry-oriented and policy-driven research for anthropologists.

The development of renewable energies is the major climatic challenge facing contemporary energy and environmental policies today. In France such energies are sometimes decentralized[2] and respond to the social demand of 'consuming locally'. In this context, one of the challenges for public policies is to encourage residents to become solar energy producers. This raises additional questions: how can we encourage the proliferation of solar power among residents and make them play an active role in sustainable energy transition? What are the profiles of those inhabitants who decide to install solar panels on their roofs? How do these small producers use electricity on an everyday basis? What political interpretation should be given to the local wish to produce electricity? So far we have been addressing these research questions by mobilizing anthropological theories and methods, which primarily means going into the field – something policy makers and engineers often do not do. It means visiting local residents, conducting interviews and carrying out observations of day-to-day life and day-to-day use of energy. After collecting this information, we were struck by the discrepancy between how people are supposed to live and act according to engineers and their actual lived practices. In this respect, anthropological insight allows us to go beyond solar-friendly public opinion polls and shallow cultural knowledge of technologists.

Impacts of feed-in tariff on producer profiles

In France, photovoltaic development at the local level is a minor revolution, because we are moving from a highly centralized nuclear-reliant production (except in the islands) to one which is more evenly spread across society. This development relies on financial incentives for individuals. Small-scale producers sell all the electricity to EDF with feed-in tariffs fixed by the state. When I did my research, the selling price was always significantly higher than the purchase price; between 2006 and 2010 inhabitants sold at between 0.50 and 0.58 euro on a per-kWh basis, whereas they purchased at between 0.12 and 0.14 euro per kWh on the same basis. From 2006 to 2010, purchasing prices were especially high and many people installed PVs on their roofs as if they were investing in the stock market. Since 2010, the decrease in purchasing prices has led to greater diversity in producer profiles and significant increases in self-consumption. We have moved from an essentially financial logic, with people who want to primarily generate money from decentralized production of solar energy, to a domestic logic, with those who install PVs for self-reliance.

Unlike the dominant thinking in the business world, there is no average behaviour based on strictly economic or efficiency-driven logic. Producers are also citizens, mothers and fathers, inhabitants of a region and so on, which helps to build certain anthropological categories to reflect these different identities. The anthropological approach makes it possible to include the notion of commitment, particularly to the environment, as an economic driver. Inhabitants install PVs driven by environmental and citizen awareness, in order to reduce bills, or to boost the inheritance value of their property – the reasons are usually layered. To illustrate the point, among the criteria that affect energy choices is the feeling of agency and independence. In Sweden, Henning (2000) observed that, regardless of the efficiency and low price of communal heating, households refused to have it installed because of the fear of losing control of heating. Returning to France, photovoltaic electricity producers have in common the search for energy autonomy as well. They want to distance themselves from nuclear and fossil energies, the national grid, the fluctuating price of electricity, or even sudden power cuts. In other words, they work towards the dream of freely available solar energy and optimal comfort without harming the environment or one's wallet. As such, PV is not only useful but carries with it the ideal of energy autonomy. However, most small electricity producers overestimate their production capacity. Nevertheless, the search for independence and renewable agency found in various contexts is central to the decision of becoming a power producer.

In short, while trying to develop solar energy generation among residents, public policies and industry cannot be limited to financial leverage alone. Anthropology contributes to the identification of other 'buttons' for the deployment of solar energy, such as environmental values, the search for control and autonomy, or the technologically feasible energy circulation in the system.

Distribution of the produced energy requires a better understanding of use

In the case of solar energy, one of the issues that industry must resolve is the intermittent distribution, that is the fact that the production fluctuates in accordance with the amount of sunlight. Given that periods of sunshine do not correspond with periods of high demand, the difficulty for grid managers lies in correctly adjusting the offer to the consumption. This is accomplished by using technological resources, such as storage, and by locating inhabitants' consumption to specific time periods (Darby and McKenna 2012; Powells et al. 2014). Without the understanding of cultural dimensions, that is how people use their electricity, demand-side management of adapting consumption to suit production is very difficult. Thanks to the in-depth nature of ethnographic methods, EDF can develop predictive tools and incentive programmes for a successful demand management. That said, I will now historicize and contextualize the phenomenon of energy use in France.

(Continued)

Practices and the relationship with energy rooted in a local context

Producers' quest for autonomy stems from the local context as well. Let me take the example of Corsica where the inhabitants are fully aware of their island's limited production capacity. As Molinelli Cancellieri (1995) and Lefevre (2001) suggest, Corsicans are very sensitive to their local environment and this affects the decision to become producers. When I conducted the research in 2013, the interviewees were supportive of local energies, which they considered to be free and environmentally friendly (water, sun, wind) as opposed to imported energies (fuel oil, no nuclear energy on French islands).

The way they envisage solar energy is embedded in the local history of energy infrastructure development. To put it bluntly, in Corsica the electricity grid represents the French state. Since the 1960s, the distribution of Corsican energy has been marked by disputes with the central government, in particular when the Debré government attempted to create an underground nuclear test site south of the town of Calvi. The project was eventually abandoned. Later on, Corsicans protested against the creation of a power line linking Tuscany to Sardinia. Between 1967 and 1969, electricity pylons were among the first targets of bomb attacks (Lefevre 2001; Martinetti 2007). In such a context, small producers give a political interpretation to their decision to install solar panels.

Knowing that Corsica is already connected to Sardinia and Italy, there is a strong conviction that the potential for renewable energy solutions has not been properly examined by the state. Be it as it may, Corsican producers do not wish to cut themselves from the grid – and therefore from the state – but, instead, want to have a freely negotiated relationship with the dominating power. It allows them to use the network as a storage battery or shift certain uses according to the grid's needs. Moreover, it gives the industry the opportunity to develop commercial offerings to meet these needs. Developing PVs at the local level may be one way to give small photovoltaic electricity producers a new role in the grid, because they could thus become network partners. This would, of course, not be a politically neutral solution. In the Corsican context, there is a parallel between these relationships and the island's special political status of a recognized regional authority. The decentralization of energy would thus engender a form of political decentralization.

As I have shown in the case of solar energy, anthropology allows us to study the different rationales behind PV installation or uses of electricity. Small producers have a vision: a vision of electric system and their role in it. Industrialists and decision-makers can learn from this vision, develop well-anchored projects or create commercial offers in line with day-to-day life of local residents. This observation is valid globally, not just in highly industrialized societies but also in the countries where the development of environmentally viable sources of energy is an issue of growth and inequality alleviation. But that is another, albeit important, matter.

FIGURE 7.2 A house with PV panels producing electricity to be sold, Corsica, Borgo's region, 2014. Personal archive of Sophie Bouly de Lesdain.

Energy choices are embedded within technical, social, cultural and political configurations, the study of which essentially falls into the domain of socio-cultural anthropology. This opens up interdisciplinary fields of research, gives us thoughts for collective deliberation and opens the paths towards advancing renewable energy development. At the same time, we need to think of the next generation of social scientists. Why don't we let anthropologists more appropriately influence public and industrial decision-making for the betterment of all?

FIVE TIPS FROM SOPHIE BOULY DE LESDAIN

1. **Be a bridge between the academic world and different spheres of social life.** Make people understand the value of anthropology by translating and interpreting their concerns in such a way that the discipline becomes understandable to them.
2. **Seize opportunities to contribute to a new world.** Present results that economic and political actors can operate with and put into action. This is an opportunity to pass on a message and to drive social change that will make the world a better place.

(Continued)

3. **Don't cross the line.** Taking part in corporate and policy decision-making processes leads to the issues of legitimacy, ethical responsibility and professional pressures. Stay true to yourself.
4. **If you work outside academia, stay active in academic networks.** Applied anthropology needs people to remain active within academic networks to be up-to-date with theories and to maintain healthy distance from the corporate world.
5. **Stay curious.** We are lucky to be involved in an exciting profession. Keep that little flame that inspires you alive.

About the author

Sophie Bouly de Lesdain is an anthropologist and expert researcher at Electricité de France (EDF Lab), where she has been working for about fifteen years on household energy production and consumption. She earned her PhD in social and cultural anthropology in 1996 at the University of Sorbonne, before being a Senior Member at Saint Anthony's College, Oxford. Between 1999 and 2004 she worked as a lecturer at the Sorbonne. After focussing on food production, processing and distribution in agricultural societies she has moved to urban manifestations of economic contexts. She has conducted ethnographic research in Cameroon, Senegal and France.

Notes

1 In French, the notion of 'energy efficiency' is translated as *sobriété énergétique*, which literally means 'energy sobriety'. The term refers to a moralistic discourse connoting the idea of an 'addiction' to energy comparable to alcoholism. The implicit judgement thus renders extensive use of energy as immoral and something that should be 'cured'.
2 Unlike centralized generation, where a large power plant supplies energy to an entire territory, decentralized generation consists of many smaller units connected to the electricity grid to produce local renewable energy.

References

Bouly de Lesdain, S. (2016), 'Le chaud et le froid des politiques énergétiques: des usages de la climatisation à leur prévention', in I. Garabuau-Moussaoui and M. Pierre (eds), *Pratiques sociales et usages de l'énergie*, 215–18, Paris: Lavoisier.

Chappells, H. and E. Shove (2005), 'Debating the Future of Comfort: Environmental Sustainability, Energy Consumption and the Indoor Environment', *Building Research and Information*, 33 (1): 32–40.

Darby, S. J. and E. McKenna (2012), 'Social Implications of Residential Demand Response in Cool Temperate Climates', *Energy Policy*, 49: 759–69.

Douzou, S. and S. Bouly de Lesdain (2013), 'Everyday Life Energy-related Innovations in the Harsh Light of Social Reality: Turning Energy Efficiency Policy Foundations

Upside Down?', *European Council for Energy Efficient Economy*, 3–8 June 2013, Presqu'île de Giens.

Fodor, F. (2012), 'Sustainable Development, Climate Change, Energy Saving: Discursive Developments of an Environmental Ethic', in S. Shmelev and I. Shmeleva (eds), *Sustainability Analysis: An Interdisciplinary Approach*, 179–203, New York: Palgrave Macmillan.

Henning, A. (2000), *Ambiguous Artefacts: Solar Collectors in Swedish Contexts. On Processes of Cultural Modification*, Stockholm: Stockholm Universitet.

Héritier, F. (2012), *Le sel de la vie*, Paris: Odile Jacob.

Hitchings, R. and S. Jun Lee (2008), 'Air Conditioning and the Material Culture of the Routine Human Encasement: The Case of Young People in Contemporary Singapore', *Journal of Material Culture*, 13 (3): 251–65.

Lefevre, M. (2001), 'Écologie et géopolitique en Corse', *Hérodote*, 100 (1): 32–54.

Martinetti, J. (2007), 'Les tourments du tourisme sur l'île de Beauté', *Hérodote*, 127. Available online: http://www.herodote.org/spip.php?article308 (accessed 17 October 2019).

Molinelli Cancellieri, L. (1995), *Boues rouges: La Corse dit non*, Paris: L'Harmattan.

Powells, G., H. Bulkeley, S. Bell and E. Judson (2014), 'Peak Electricity Demand and the Flexibility of Everyday Life', *Geoforum*, 55: 43–52.

Sahlins, M. (1972), *Stone Age Economics*, Chicago (IL): Aldine-Atherton.

Shove, E. (2003), 'Converging Conventions of Comfort, Cleanliness and Convenience', *Journal of Consumer Policy*, 26 (4): 395–418.

Shove, E. and G. Walker (2014), 'What Is Energy For? Social Practice and Energy Demand.' *Theory, Culture and Society*, 31 (5): 41–58.

Thaler, R. and C. Sunstein (2008), *Nudge: Improving Decisions about Health, Wealth and Happiness*, New Haven (CT): Yale University Press.

Wilhite, H. (2008), 'New Thinking on the Agentive Relationship between End-use Technologies and Energy-using Practices', *Energy Efficiency*, 1 (2): 121–30.

8

ANTHROPOLOGISTS MAKE SENSE, PROVIDE INSIGHT AND CO-CREATE CHANGE

Rikke Ulk

Since I became an anthropologist, it has always been my ambition to apply the anthropological approach outside academia and to share its potential to make sense, provide insight and co-create change with as many people as possible. I did not want to join just one company or one organization because I was scared to be bored or to be too much of a rebel within a regulated frame; instead, I wanted to work more creatively than what I had experienced in academia during my years of study. I longed for creating change based on sharing and communicating anthropological insights in an understandable and useful manner. Designing more intense, shorter-term projects, I wanted to be able to invent, test and try new solutions and initiatives with the people involved in the projects. I was not primarily motivated by making money. Actually, I was quite terrified of being commercial, of having to price and package my anthropological insights into deliverables. Still, applying anthropology and making a difference using and re-inventing its methods and approaches in non-academic contexts has become my life-long passion.

My name is Rikke Ulk. I am a Danish anthropologist turned entrepreneur who founded a consultancy company called *Antropologerne* (The Anthropologists) in 2003 as a way of engaging in the world. Today I use my personal drive and anthropological analytical and methodological skills every day to create positive change that matters. In this chapter, I share some of the most important professional principles that have guided my career.

Making sense

Christian Madsbjerg, the co-founder of the Denmark-based consulting firm ReD Associates, presents the following argument to organizations turning towards big data instead of deep insights: 'The more we rely on robots, artificial intelligence and machine learning, the clearer it becomes just how much we need social scientists and humanities experts – not the reverse' (Madsbjerg 2018). Underlining the four essential skills needed in the age of smart technologies – contextualization, curiosity, critical thinking and ethical judgement – he alludes to the core competencies of anthropology. I cannot agree more with Madsbjerg: anthropologists, as social science and humanities experts who foster such skills, are needed now more than ever. In my work, I translate Madsbjerg's four skills into more concrete principles of applied anthropological practice, as I further explain below.

At the 2014 symposium *Why the World Needs Anthropologists* in Padua, Italy, I delivered a keynote speech arguing that there are four basic answers to this question: one, we make sense; two, we care; three, we offer fresh perspectives; and four, we engage people. My practical experience has taught me that the lens of applied anthropology can help to make sense by explaining who the people of concern are, what matters to them, how they act and why they do what they do. Once clients, researchers and communities develop these insights together, they can find ways to use them. In other words, with these four elements in mind, an applied anthropologist can help people to engage and embrace each other in making better solutions for all.

A recent example is our insight and change project focussing on how to ac-tivate more volunteers to become visiting friends on a regular basis for elderly people in need of an important other person in their lives. Creative and engag-ing anthropological approaches to create a new perspective and develop new initiatives and solutions provided the client – Ældre Sagen, a large volunteer organization – with sense, insight and change. Based on our written report and a series of short video portraits, we presented three recommendations on how to attract more volunteers and how to strengthen the organizational setup and flexi-bility by inviting different kinds of volunteers and distributing tasks in new ways. As consultants we did not build these insights alone. By involving those who ask for our help and those affected by the project, such as target groups, end-users of a product or those taking part in a civil society movement, we always sense-make with the people who are part of our studies and projects.

At my company the project development unfolds in the following steps: we *go out* to do field visits; we *hand out* to engage our informants in discovering the unknowns using tours and exercises; we *try out* by building prototypes and ex-periments with new solutions; and finally, we always have an ambition to *stand out*, when we facilitate and build useful results that can serve as an engaging point of departure for a change or an improvement of the service, the product or the movement we study. While Christian Madsbjerg formulates the four points using academic lingo, our four principles – *go out, hand out, try out, stand out* – deliberately use a different and more actionable vocabulary. You may see the connections between the two linguistic strategies: *go out* connects to the impor-tance of acknowledging the context, *hand out* stands for exploration and curiosity, *try out* is an equivalent to critical thinking, and *stand out* indicates the need to make a positive difference in the world. In today's world, where quantitative, 'big data' approaches dominate in the decision-making of governments, organizations and companies, we should be very careful about the powers that influence the creation of evidence. Instead of invoking numbers and ready-made academic authorities, the challenge for applied anthropology is to work out more actionable spaces for collective sense-making, insight generation and solution delivery.

Tensions between working inside and outside academia

Anthropologists are trained to do ethnographic fieldwork and make sense out of observations, conversations, reflections and, generally speaking, all kinds of interactions with and among the people they study. In short, there is a three-step process by which anthropologists work:

1. Data generation and co-creation: we take part in our participants' endeavours and document these experiences.
2. Sense-making and analysis: we write up notes, report on the field experience, analyse the patterns and cluster the data. In short, we make sense of the empirical data, interpreting and translating them into narratives and insights.
3. Sharing and communication: we communicate the insights with our partners to enable them to better comprehend the social and cultural aspects of the participants' motivations, decisions and practices.

While these are the key tools of anthropological research, there are differences in how academic and non-academic anthropologists understand and use them. In step one, data generation and co-creation, I see the following productive tensions: fieldwork duration and the level of collaboration with participants. In academia, at least traditionally, data generation and co-creation are done during long-term fieldwork (Wilk 2011) and the authorship of analytical insights is often attributed to a single researcher. Even if being in-and-out of the field and doing multi-sited research is gradually becoming the new norm (see Falzon 2009; Marcus 1995), 'the longer, the better' principle persists. In consultancy and applied settings, we generally develop shorter-term engagements. They can also be framed as field visits. In our practice, a field visit consists of one- to five-hour long visits while meeting people in their everyday contexts. We would typically do eight to twelve field visits and design anthropological focus group events.

Furthermore, outside academia, informants are usually treated more explicitly as project participants and co-authors. The term *co-creation,* first coined to describe the emerging relationship between customers and enterprises where value is co-created when a customer is able to personalize his or her experience using a firm's product or service proposition (Prahalad and Ramaswamy 2000), is central today. However, as it is carried into the applied field, it seems to be used in less instrumental and less industrial manner. Morphing into the newly worshiped approach to social change, it is put in practice to challenge long-established power structures. For instance, every municipality I worked with talks about how to address and achieve co-creation with citizens and organizations to reshape all sorts of issues ranging from energy, welfare, health, housing and education to integration, unemployment and loneliness.

In step two, sense-making and analysis, the productive tension is the importance and application of theory. In academia, analysis usually takes more time because it involves peer discussions and considerable use of theory. For many academic anthropologists, refined theorizing is their primary goal. In applied settings, that is usually not the case. The main goal we strive for is to produce, share and make useful the insights based on solid anthropological approaches. Indeed, applied anthropologists do read cutting-edge studies, even if they tend not to discuss theory to the same extent as academic anthropologists. Theory-in-action is often used as an informed implicit perspective on the given subject matter – think of taboos, values and rites of passage – and intersects with the principle of co-creation. Along the way, anthropologists working as consultants usually rely on the collaboration of project participants more than academic colleagues conducting more theoretically-informed studies. These practices, however, should not be seen as 'better' or 'worse', but as the edges of a single theory-practice continuum where theory informs practice and vice versa. Moreover, the pressure to accelerate the pace of knowledge production is facing both anthropologists in academia as well as those outside of it; we are all increasingly exposed to the 'gig economy' (Kwok 2017), which might require us to adjust some of our research approaches.

In step three, sharing and communication, I see the tension in the relevance of different media. In academia, thanks to the increased popularity of media and visual anthropology as well as the growing interest of anthropologists in artistic practices (Schneider 2015) the terrain has been shifting dramatically. Yet, even though multimedia and multimodal approaches are expanding, written communication is still dominant. Applied anthropologists do use text and produce reports but given the preferences of their diverse audiences, they often employ 'more-than-textual' ways of sharing findings and communicating insights – such as video, audio, pictures and quotes – to engage recipients on an emotional level. The use of tangibles, visualization and different media formats ensures that non-anthropologists embrace and integrate the insights and knowledge that we generate. Pictures with quotes, videos with statements and recordings in real-life contexts give access to a new level of identification, empathy and understanding.

Practising outside academia, we generate and analyse data, and shape and communicate our results slightly differently than researchers within academia do. We work with clients asking for knowledge, direction and help, which obligates us as consultants to make our insights transferable and useful to those who sought them and are affected by them. This is an ethical stance and an important contribution of applied anthropologists who navigate between lands of co-creation and directed social change.

Who are clients?

There is no such thing as a typical client of a consultancy company like ours. Clients are diverse in age, gender and their personal and professional profiles. That said, usually the project owner, the project manager and/or the management behind a study has some academic experience, like us anthropologists. Typically, clients tend to be open-minded, curious people who want to understand who, what, how and why from an outside, human-centred perspective, just like we do. Five years into my career a wise person told me that to attract clients and to provide real value to them, I should look deep inside myself and explore the mirroring between the client and the consultant. This exploration still drives and nurtures me. Meeting new collaborators in an organization, I ask myself, *Is she brave, different, visionary? Is he sensitive, well-connected, struggling? Is he or she perhaps a parent like myself? How does the client resemble me or us and how does he or she differ from us personally and professionally? What attitudes, motivations, preferences, dreams and strategies are at stake in this group and among these individuals?*

Ultimately, clients are real people with intentions, rationalities, objectives and values, usually willing to learn and to change while, at the same time, they are professionals with formal organizational mandates. This is why it is important to always start by reflecting on who the client is and what will make a difference to him, her or them when working on a project. Beware that what a client explicitly wants usually shifts throughout the project, which is why as consultants we should engage in a continuous analysis of the client. For instance, a general question may morph into specific ambitions or a focus on the end result and the end product may reorient towards finding value in the shared learning and relation-building. To give an example, in a project formally focussing on work safety and security policy among firemen in a big Danish fire department, the staff ultimately worked together on the most important strategic theme: having more dialogue. Moving the team from internal differences and fear of change towards experiencing a common gain and developing enthusiasm, we experienced the healing powers of breaking hierarchies and of being brought together. It was an achievement in itself.

This example touches on another aspect of this tenuous social terrain. Clients are people who work hard to understand whom they tend to call their 'users' and who are eager to use the deep insights generated in an anthropological study to support their decisions and direct change. However, it sometimes happens that the partners we engage with are at first sceptical about or express low expectations for the project we embark on. If this is the case, the following questions can help us to understand them: What drives them? What frustrates them? Why are they sceptical? Are they reluctant, resisting to engage or just reserved in their attitudes? Getting closer to them, you will usually discover that sceptics either do not understand or simply do not agree with the premise of using an anthropological study to shed new light on a given subject. They may fear that it will not be worth the money and time spent, that anthropological research will be just another development project draining resources without significantly changing anything, either in the mind-set of the leadership or in their understanding of key customers. Developing relationships and building trust over time has proven to be the most useful remedy for such situations. When the employees are truly invited in and get to know the anthropological team, we have seen that being heard, getting involved and imagining a common future alleviates distrust and leads to better collaboration. I have experienced this sudden transformation from resistance to engagement very often.

The most rewarding part of conducting an applied anthropological project is thus being able to guide people from one point to another through continuous communication: by listening and observing, involving them in the study and the questions asked, and creating input for new services, products, strategies and alternative futures.

Users – or patients, members, customers, fellow citizens, neighbours?

How to think of the people we meet and engage with while doing an anthropological study for and with a client? The trick is to handle diversity in the right manner. As applied anthropologists, we meet people who interact with various places, services and products. We meet health service and care-taking providers, leaders and employees, volunteer workers, community builders, students, children, seniors, various interest groups and organizations. Basically, citizens of all kinds. We meet political representatives, start-up innovators, researchers and various kinds of experts. The list is almost endless.

As for Antropologerne, for example, we map five different types of users using new prototype maps and geodata in Greenland. We meet hearing aid users and health care professionals in Japan, Germany and the United States. We listen to refugees in Denmark telling stories at public events and follow citizens of a municipality invited to discuss openness and involvement with the City Council. In one project for the Danish Crime Prevention Council, me and my colleagues engaged with a group of young people that was developing a sexual consent campaign among the 15–17-year-olds. In other studies, we focussed on understanding operators of sensor technology-based lightning systems in different working places and we generated insights into the experiences of people living with bone marrow cancer and their significant others.

It would be an act of utter reductionism to think of these people as mere 'users' – as operators that need to be taken care of – like marketing agencies do. They are much more than users. They are real, complex human beings engaged in both simple and complicated endeavours of their everyday lives. By inviting us into their private spheres, they accept to share their thoughts, knowledge and expertise. In our fieldwork, analysis and communication, we make sense of it and give meaning to experiences of others. In this way, we assist in an ongoing process of discovering how both clients and their constituents interact and do what they do in various contexts. No ordinary market research can match the wealth and credibility of such insights.

WHAT SET ME IN MOTION

For many years, I was uncertain about what to devote myself to during the five years of university studies. I was thinking of philosophy, journalism and media studies, but I could not decide. Why did I finally choose anthropology? What motivated me to become an anthropologist? I think it actually happened by accident.

For a non-Dane, it may seem strange not knowing which field of study you are headed for. But since Denmark has a relatively high level of taxation and university education is basically tuition-free, the selection of your higher education programme is based either on your interests or on your high school grades. I was graduating from an unconventional high school where the choices and combinations of study subjects and topics were in our own hands. The students came from all sorts of backgrounds and were of all ages, with very different reasons for pursuing their studies. I was looking for a field of study that could meet my interests and challenge my personal profile, my independent character, social skills and intellectual capacity. However, graduating with very good results and thus being able to choose from all university programmes available did not help me much in deciding on my future degree.

Despite my young age, I had at that point already spent more than a decade as a leader in political student work. I had done an exchange study programme in Brazil, living with a host family in a culturally very distinct Brazilian society. I had been a driving force in all kinds of peace work efforts as well as a singer and percussionist in Soukous, a big tropical dance band playing African music, with fourteen fellow members. Back then, my goal and preferred choice of studies was a brand-new line of educational degree at an experimental university, the Roskilde University Centre (RUC), situated some distance away from Copenhagen where I was living. I knew I wanted to do something relevant for society, for the world, but I did not know what it was – and the relatively new idea of modern culture and media seemed like something that could point me in the right direction.

But one of my concerns about the studies at RUC was the format. The curriculum was built around collective learning, which would mean more collective work, more group dynamics and sociality. Perhaps it will come across as antithetical to what an anthropologist-to-be should prefer, but I was also becoming more individualistic: I felt an emerging profound need, almost a longing inside of me, to focus on my individual learning and development rather than on social groups and group work.

Anthropology as a path to myself

While at a friend's bachelorette party celebrating her transition from an unmarried to a married woman, I met Johanne. She was just finishing her studies in anthropology and told me how much she loved it. From her I learned that as an anthropology student, I could study modern phenomena including mediated relations between people. I suddenly realized how I could make a future while honouring my main area of interest, that is communicating and making sensible changes in society. As we chitchatted about my personal history, my dreams and ideal future, a bubbly feeling took over. On a beautiful day in the early summer of 1992, in the final hour before the application deadline, I decided on a new direction.

In the last month before high school graduation, I learned that the grade requirements for admission to anthropology studies were almost the highest in Denmark at the time. This motivated me even more to choose anthropology. Moreover, I found it very promising to think and learn about cultures in a more structured way. My experience from Brazil and my passion-driven engagement were revived and re-invigorated me. I could do it. It was difficult and special, but I could do it.

After a period of nervous waiting, my admission was granted. Coming from a background where both my parents were schoolteachers and my grandparents belonged to a working class, I was now signing up for a university degree in anthropology at the University of Copenhagen. That was so empowering to me! The department used classical methods of teaching based on individual studies and learning, which felt more like the 'real thing' than the new group-based style at RUC. Anthropology shed light on my social engagements in the world and I suddenly saw my experiences from Rio and Brazil in a new way. It even seemed to resonate with the power of spreading joy as a musician in the dance band.

Back on that warm summer night of my friend's bachelorette party, the first intriguing anthropological idea I learned from Johanne was participant observation. It meant to me that the discipline also provided me with the possibility to simultaneously be an insider and an outsider, to be special and not-so-special, to participate and not to participate in other peoples' worlds. It was weird, but it triggered me and to some extent liberated me. Could I be 'more myself'? I knew I wanted to become an anthropologist – through my own interpretation of what the studies could lead me to professionally.

JOINING THE EFFORTS OF THE ENERGY ISLAND

Samsø is an island in the middle of Denmark where the Vikings used to live and meet. In fact, Samsø stands for 'samlings-ø', an island of gathering and getting together, the point of departure to new adventures and the point

(Continued)

of return. Until 1997, Samsø was entirely dependent on oil and coal, both imported from the mainland. In 1997, however, Samsø won a government competition to become a model renewable energy community because the local community came together in an unprecedented way.

Today, Samsø is an energy island. This means that its residents have successfully become self-sufficient. At Samsø, the collective investment in renewables meant that the resources such as biomass, solar and wind power secure all energy needs of the population and surplus can be slated for export. This transition has been led by the island's Energy Academy, which aims at managing change without using management tools or formal decision-making, instead continuously developing engagement with public, private and educational aspects in mind. At Samsø, they have tried and succeeded to lead and to set an ambitious plan that thoroughly and patiently involved fellow citizens in collective buying, owning and administrating of the large windmills.

After over twenty years of efforts, the people of the small island started to seek an outside perspective on the movement and the accomplishments of the community with regard to building their own sustainable solutions. The leaders of the transition, members of the Energy Academy, felt a need to explore and understand the socio-dynamic aspects of what makes up the local pioneer community in order to inform and shape future developments. Because we have worked on sustainability topics such as electric cars and citizen involvement in local planning in Antropologerne before, I was invited to this Danish island to join the Wisdom Council of the Energy Academy. The anthropological perspective we could offer to the collective meaning-making in the community was in demand. In the Wisdom Council, we helped the Energy Academy to investigate their way of gathering people in a circle, using eye contact, the talking stick and equality as unifying tools (even visiting delegations of European kings and queens were invited to take part!). As anthropologists, we also fine-tuned their model of using past, present and future as the core elements in the process of change.

Antropologerne's contribution to Samsø

Our engagement with Samsø's local pioneer community began with my colleague Maria Koch Jensen and me going to the island to conduct a short study on leadership and followership. We investigated whether the typical islander sees himself or herself as a part of 'the Energy Island' and of the local pioneer community. The second dimension explored the perception of personal leadership. The study focussed on when and how a person was first introduced to the Energy Island project, whether and how they knew the Energy Island's founding figure, Søren Hermansen, and where the relative importance of state or municipality, market and civil society was located. We

FIGURE 8.1 Maria Koch Jensen and Rikke Ulk, two anthropologist consultants, during field work at Samsø, the Energy Island of Denmark, in a project exploring leadership and participation, 2014. Courtesy Antropologerne.

collected qualitative data based on interviews, mapping exercises and participant observation, talking to and doing exercises with 27 islanders in their homes. Based on our study, we delivered an article on personal leadership in pioneer communities (Ulk and Koch Jensen 2007) and a leadership compass, of which more below.

The study has shown that the person who exercises personal leadership must know the place and the community well in order to motivate others towards a common goal. Samsø became the safe-haven for pioneering because its members worked closely together. With pioneering leaders showing the way, stronger social capital enabled higher social cohesion and enforced interpersonal trust. Our contribution to this process of self-understanding was the concept of 'here'; both as the sense of place and as the commitment to the cause. To maintain the extraordinary level of cohesion in the future, the insights led to the creation of a leadership compass consisting of five main elements: North, East, South, West and 'here' at the centre (Figure 8.2.).

The leadership compass is to be read from the middle. The centre represents the place and the cause – a starting point for participating in a common project. The different directions extending outwards raise critical questions about the community's identity (who are we?), its abilities and potentials in the face of change (what can we do?), the community's desires (what do we want?), and the community's capacity to achieve the goals in practice (what do we do?).

(Continued)

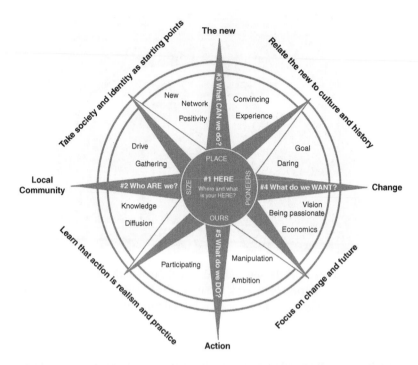

FIGURE 8.2 Leadership Compass created for Samsø community.

Today, the 3,700 inhabitants of Samsø not only produce their own energy but export it and have the ambition to become completely fossil-free by 2030. They are developing solar energy and biofuel projects, their own broadband solution and are looking into investing in a large biofuel centre. In addition, other visionary small and large projects are being taken on, such as ecological farming, dairy production, slaughterhouse and a School for Sustainability. Seeing the community develop visions of building an opera house and an educational institution for lifelong learning, the nature of improvements does not seem to stop with energy innovations.

Love local, reach global

Admittedly, I was not the first one in my family to become a part of the sense-making in the transformation of Samsø. My husband Tor Nørretranders previously co-wrote a book with the founder of The Energy Academy Søren Hermansen titled *Commodities = Commons + Communities* (Hermansen and Nørretranders 2013). Privately, we have both wanted to walk our talk for some time. Finally, in the summer of 2018, my husband, our youngest daughter and I moved to Samsø. We are not outsiders anymore, but newcomers who are settling down in the place that is not unfamiliar to us anymore thanks to our previous research and the relations it engenders.

In the autumn of 2018, Antropologerne moved to Samsø, too. With no full-time employees and no headquarters in the old city centre of Copenhagen, where we used to be – and loved to be – we created a new version of consultancy. Antropologerne reshaped itself into a project-network–based company with a commitment to loving locally and reaching globally from our 'here', the place and the cause of the fossil-free island Samsø. We continue working to provide insight and create change together with our clients and the people we study while operating from various inspiring places. We keep on exploring and finding more reasons for why the world needs anthropologists, bringing anthropologists together at the island of the Viking gatherings.

FIVE TIPS FROM RIKKE ULK

1. **Go out.** Go in and out of your field and subject. Try to do this as often as possible. Explore your surroundings and interactions of social groups – share, dwell, follow, travel, talk, chitchat, observe and participate in their everyday life.
2. **Hand out.** Hand out your agenda, your questions and your thoughts. Use new formats of doing so – pictures, words, exercises, hypotheses and generative tools that open up to a common exploration between you and your participants.
3. **Try out.** Try out some of the possible solutions that will inevitably emerge out of your analysis. If there is a need for more ownership, try to mock it up, build it and create it. Dare to just test and explore with tangibles – it will help you improve your analysis and recommendations.
4. **Stand out.** Dare to be different. Dare to stand out, share, care and give. As anthropologists we should stand out more, side-by-side with our clients and their constituents.
5. **Reach out.** Accept your own limit and the limits of anthropology as a discipline. Reach out to other people and professions. Embrace and invite others' skills into your endeavour. As an entrepreneur or a freelance researcher, you will need help from people with skills to communicate, visualize, sell, do accounting, manage or develop.

About the author

Rikke Ulk is the Founder and Director of Antropologerne (since 2003), the first and female-led anthropological consultancy in Denmark and Europe. After spending time in Brazil and the United States, where she conducted fieldwork and performed as a singer and percussionist, she obtained master's degree in anthropology from the University of Copenhagen in 2002. Driven by the need to make contributions towards societal change, she has worked actively as an anthropologist consultant for more than seventeen years. Rikke has been a member of several professional networks and associations, among them the REACH Network, f-i-x.dk network, the Danish Management Society, Design Denmark, the Wisdom Council of Samsø Energy Academy (2015–16) and the Jury of the Danish Design Award.

References

Falzon, M. (ed) (2009), *Multi-sited Ethnography: Theory, Practice and Locality in Contemporary Research*, Farnham and Burlington: Ashgate Publishing.

Hermansen, S. and T. Nørretranders (2013), *Commonities = Commons + Communities*, Samsø: Samsø Energiakademi.

Kwok, R. (2017), 'Flexible Working: Science in the Gig Economy', *Nature*, 550 (7676): 419–21.

Madsbjerg, C. (2018), 'Thanks, Robots! Now These Four Non-Tech Job Skills Are in Demand', *Fast Company*. Available online: https://www.fastcompany.com/40533471/thanks-robots-now-these-four-non-tech-job-skills-are-in-demand (accessed 26 February 2018).

Marcus, G. E. (1995), 'Ethnography in/of the World System: The Emergence of Multi-Sited Ethnography', *Annual Review of Anthropology*, 24: 95–117.

Prahalad, C. K. and V. Ramaswamy (2000), 'Co-opting Customer Competence', *Harvard Business Review*, January–February. Available online: https://hbr.org/2000/01/co-opting-customer-competence (accessed 24 October 2019).

Schneider, A. (2015), 'Towards a New Hermeneutics of Art and Anthropology', *EthnoScripts*, 17 (1): 23–30.

Ulk, R. and M. Koch Jensen (2007), 'Energi Akademiet: The Outsider's Perspective'. Available online: http://www.pioneerguide.com/ (accessed 24 October 2018).

Wilk, R. (2011), 'Reflections on Orderly and Disorderly Ethnography', *Ethnologia Europaea*, 41 (1): 15–25.

9

OPEN UP THE TREASURE OF ANTHROPOLOGY TO THE WORLD

Jitske Kramer

A lot has been written about organizational culture. It has been discussed, debated, defined and redefined. Interestingly enough, the anthropological view has been missing for the most part in the management literature. Leaders, managers, change managers, team leaders, human resources experts, project leaders – all are working on creating a 'culture of excellence' without the in-depth understanding of how people shape culture and how culture shapes people. This is where the knowledge and methods of cultural anthropology kick in. This is a valuable and essential angle, especially in nowadays organizations with great global challenges and ever-increasing diversity. For the past twenty years, I have been applying anthropology in culture change processes within organizations, and wrote, together with Danielle Braun, the book *The Corporate Tribe* where we talk about corporate anthropology. Our view: no challenge is entirely new. In human existence, nearly every problem we face in modern business has already been seen and solved. We just have to figure out how to apply that age-old wisdom to our current circumstances (Braun and Kramer 2018).

The corporate tribe

In anthropology, a 'tribe' refers to a group of people who share the same language, customs and beliefs. It is made up of different families and relatives and may include individuals outside the immediate family members as well. I am aware that for some the word 'tribe' may carry negative connotations, due to colonial history and misuses of the terminology. However, I do like to use it in a more neutral and matter-of-fact way. People organize themselves into tribes all over the world. Tribes in which people live, work, believe, love, fight and change together. This happens in a similar way in organizations and I find it very useful to talk with business leaders in terms of tribes, totems, clans and rituals instead of the more technical and rational management terms like departments, mission statements and project planning. After all, in organizations, people are still people – social and emotional animals who organize themselves in groups, using stories, symbols, habits and ranking systems. People are tribal beings, also in office spaces, as Martin Page described decades ago in his thought-provoking book *The Company Savage* (Page 1972).

Corporate anthropologists look at companies as living communities formed by the ideas and behaviours of people. At the same time, the prevailing ideas and norms in organizations influence the people. This is what we call culture. Tribes and cultures shape themselves in interaction, dialogue and decision-making. And this is the actual core business of most organizations: to talk, interact and get to agreements in order to deliver the best services and create the greatest product. However, in many organizations moments of actual connections and meeting of minds and hearts are rare. People are too busy with their key performance indicators (KPIs), targets, spreadsheet and back-to-back meetings to find the time for a heart to heart. Content driven meetings—not emotion driven meetings—are the norm.

Corporate anthropology

Corporate anthropology comes out of the application of cultural anthropology to management and consultancy. This relatively new professional field goes by various names: organizational anthropology, business anthropology and corporate anthropology (Denny and Sunderland 2014; Neyland 2008; Simon 2016). I prefer to call myself a corporate anthropologist for no other reason than that I like the sound of it.

Cultural anthropology is the discipline that asks itself what it means to be a human among humans. It is a discipline with a rich history. Back in the nineteenth century, we spoke of 'armchair anthropologists', that is anthropologists who would write books about faraway peoples, without ever having met them, from the comfort of their armchairs. Then, at the beginning of the twentieth century, the 'real' anthropologists arrived. They went out into the world, lived for months in villages and communities, among the local people, to get to know the local habits and customs from the inside out. They were looking to understand the meaning that people give to the world around them and how this is expressed in symbols, behaviour and rituals. Corporate anthropology examines organizations, companies, boardrooms and board members with the same wondering gaze that anthropologists use for examining 'tribal' societies.

Corporate anthropology illuminates the dynamics of an organization that are at work beneath the surface. It reveals the difference between the formal organizational structure and informal sources of power. It allows us to identify and analyse patterns of behaviour, rituals, relationships and defining narratives at work within the organization. With such knowledge of group processes, we can offer up fresh solutions for building or maintaining a 'strong' organizational culture or stabilizing an organization's culture when it is in crisis or transition. Indeed, this approach is indispensable for achieving sustainable cultural change. For example, aligning different corporate cultures in a merger process can be tough and is the cause of many failed mergers. By understanding the anthropological insights regarding the need for leaders to hold space during the liminal stage of a change process, the human need for rituals in times of chaos and stress, and that a merger is in many ways similar to the stages to come to a marriage, managers will lead this process more effectively.

Anthropologists do not look so much at the individuals in an organization but rather at 'the spaces between people'. We look at the relationships between people, the kinship systems, the expectations, the unwritten rules and the judgements that seem to hang in the air. Anthropologists listen to the small details to get the bigger picture. As their starting point, they take the dynamics between different worlds – teams, departments, sub-cultures, the realities 'on paper' and the experienced realities. There is always tension between these worlds through which the anthropologist moves as an interpreter of (sub)cultures and social systems. There are clashing worlds not only between client and provider, management and the work floor, information technology division and the rest of the organization but also between men and women as well as different age groups, ethnicities and religious worldviews.

Making the strange familiar

Anthropologists make the strange seem familiar and the familiar seem strange. They do this so that space may be created for new ways of seeing and new ways of dealing with issues. I like to start from the premise that the challenges we face in our organizations are both new and, at the same time, centuries old; they are both unique and universal within human experience. Just look at cultures around the world. Nomadic leaders have been managing network organizations where no one has a fixed workstation for hundreds of years. Countless communities across the globe have figured out how to broker successful mergers; we call them marriages. The truth is, as humans we know how to solve these perennial problems; we have just forgotten how to apply them in our office spaces and meeting rooms. With anthropological knowledge and methods, we can revive this age-old human wisdom within our organizations. By focusing on people and how they shape cultures, we can build 'strong tribes', safe for diversity and ready for change.

It is the anthropologist's fate to always be in-between things: cultures, countries, languages and even realities. The aim is to get to know and understand every (sub)culture from the inside out and to understand it as someone would understand their own work and life without any outsider judgements. Any interpretations, comparisons and analyses may be attached later by looking at a culture from the perspective of the outsider to determine whether the usual way of working is really desirable and to decide if change is needed. To summarize this, if you let an anthropologist look at organizations it is as if you switch from black and white to colour TV. Challenge the obvious. Every day.

The desire to change organizational cultures

Where there is organizational culture, there is cultural change. Just Google the term 'organizational change'. The number of hits – over 6.5 million at the time of writing – indicates tremendous interest in this area. Why? Because in the process of rolling out transitions and instituting change in an organization, all kinds of things can – and do – go wrong, leading to frustration and wasted capital resources, among other negative consequences. Depending on which research you read, about 50–70 per cent of cultural change processes fail. From this, you might deduce that organizational culture, or culture in general, has an inherent tendency to be unshakeable and immutable. Although more recent articles question this failure rate of 50–70 per cent (see e.g. Tasler 2017), it is still fair to say that these culture change processes typically take much longer than estimated and often do not lead to the desired outcomes. I believe this is because leaders and managers of organizations are making a mistake when it comes to understanding culture and implementing cultural change.

If a strategy fails to work time after time, we need to look at the basic assumptions and underlying principles that are guiding us. This is why the world needs anthropologists. Anthropologists can make the connection between the *planned* organization and the *experienced* organization. The planned organization shows itself on paper, in KPIs, figures, strategies, mission statements and vision. The experienced organization appears in stories, emotions, patterns of behaviour and relationships. Anthropology can help people understand how cultures are constantly changing and how important the spaces between people are; the spaces that are filled with 'invisible lines' between people, which make a group more than just the sum of individuals. Anthropologists focus on the assumptions, beliefs, rules and norms that people share, that make the group act as a collective and ensure that each group member knows the intention of the collective and how he or she should behave within it. These are valuable views and anthropological insights to create workplaces in which people love to work and provide an additional value for the world.

Anthropology shows us that to create change we need to understand that the change we are looking for is probably already happening somewhere in the tribe. People are not stupid. If things don't work anymore, some of us will already be trying out something new. Leaders not only need to think where to go to with the organization but also need to see what is already there. Sustainable culture change does not happen by cascading down the 'new corporate values', by training people 'the new competencies', or by 'getting the information out there' through posters and slides. Real culture change is a change in our sense of the world around us, in our story, which will express itself in a change in our collective behaviour. And this type of change does not travel through slides and information. It travels through stories, through copying behaviours, through emotions. Anthropologists know that you don't need to involve the whole management to get things moving. You just need to focus on the most well-connected people and they will spread the change through their behaviours and stories, which is also wonderfully described by Leandro Herrero in his book *Viral Change* (Herrero 2008). Since culture comes in patterns, if you change one pattern, more will follow. When going through change, it will not follow a clear linear process. There will be chaos, but this chaos can be structured with the anthropological knowledge of liminal stages and rites-of-passage (van Gennep 2010 [1909]). When managers understand how rituals help people go through change, change management programs get a different flow and structure. When you add age-old anthropological knowledge on how people shape cultures and how those cultures shape people, and when you use anthropological methods to understand the cultural dynamics, cultural change programmes become a lot easier to handle.

Creating inclusive cultures

There is a saying we jokingly make among our anthropology colleagues that if you put two anthropologists in a room, they will start talking about ethics within two minutes. Many of my fellow anthropologists ask me about ethics. Do you work with all types of organizations on all types of (cultural) change? To me, this is in part the same type of question as 'do you study all types of cultural phenomena, ethnic groups and tribes?', to which the academics' answer is usually 'yes'. In addition to applying anthropological wisdom and methods to create certain movements of change within organizations and therefore within society, there is the element of questioning yourself if your contribution is making the world more beautiful or not. I guess this is a question all of us have to answer. My answer is that I will always choose to work with culture change processes in which an element of more inclusion of different (sub)groups is desired and more inclusive decision-making is in sight and thus, no top-down roll-out of the new corporate values but a true conversation about the purpose of the organization unfolds. Including the views of the professionals, for example the teachers, technicians, nurses and the clients. Not going around the difficult conflicting desires but holding genuine conversations about this.

This is to me another reason why the world needs anthropologists: because the way anthropologists look at the world makes people appreciate our cultural variety. This is a much-needed attitude to tackle wicked problems and solve global issues like war, climate change, refugee crises and so on. In addition, at a smaller scale, to stop bullying, overcome silo-thinking and create workspaces in which all people are welcomed and able to contribute to the best of their abilities.

To help create inclusive cultures, I have defined eight inclusion principles (Figure 9.1.), which I use as guidelines to start and deepen conversations about our differences and our commonalities. These inclusion principles are based on

1. DO NOT CLONE

- Understand how your preferences influence your decisions.
- Stretch your preferences.
- Deliberately work with people who are different.
- Judge an idea, not a person.

2. SEE THE POWER OF POWER

- Be conscious about who decides what is normal.
- Discuss rules and behaviour that exclude people.
- Use your privileges and your position for the greater good.

3. CHALLENGE THE TRUTH

- Dare to question your own opinion and the group norm.
- Have honest conversations about differences and similarities.
- Actively seek out where you are wrong.
- Accept that there are multiple truths.

4. ENJOY THE UNKOWN

- Break fixed patterns and try out new things.
- Create confidence by being open to learning.
- Acknowledge and recognize uncertainty and anxiety.

5. NOT EITHER/OR, BUT BOTH/AND

- Don't see another viewpoint as an obstacle.
- Think and/and, keeping the collective goal in mind.
- Start from your own preferences and add the value of others.

FIGURE 9.1 Jitske Kramer's eight inclusion principles to start and deepen conversations about human differences and commonalities.

6. HUNT FOR ALTERNATIVE VIEWS

- Don't push divergent views under water.
- Say respectfully what needs to be said, without fear of rejection or for your position.
- Engage the people who are affected personally by your decisions.
- Truly listen to their opinion.

7. VARY THE RHYTHM

- Tune into each other, the goals and the situation.
- Adjust the work process, not the people.

8. DO IT TOGETHER

- Create connections.
- Openly support good initiatives.
- Create the space for informal, human contact.

FIGURE 9.1 *(Continued)*.

psychological and anthropological insights (Kramer 2013, 2019) and are an example of how to translate academic research into words and easy to understand images and stories so that people in organizations can directly apply these insights to their daily practice.

Emic and etic

To conclude, I would like to stress the importance of the concepts of emic and etic to a broader context than just anthropology. *Emic* refers to the perspective from inside out, to how an insider to a particular culture or subculture experiences something herself or himself. *Etic* stands for the perspective from outside in, for how an outsider sees a specific reality. In an etic description, you offer an explanation, an analysis. In the corporate world, this may even extend to a moral judgement because the CEO who hired you to conduct an ethnography of the organization usually wants to fix a problem and wants you to tell him or her if the current corporate culture is effective or not, based on what you have observed.

FIGURE 9.2 Jitske Kramer delivering a master class to Russian human resources managers about how corporate anthropology could help them in their business development programmes. Personal archive of Jitske Kramer.

To me, this is where applied anthropology in business is different from academic anthropological research. A corporate anthropologist cannot stop at researching and describing cultural patterns and phenomena, as many academic researchers can, but will always be asked for advice on how to improve things. And sometimes not only asked for advice but also to actively design the narrative of change or even to implement the activities to reach the desired change. My business clients demand advice on how to make their company and their corporate culture more effective and how to get rid of the so-called dysfunctional cultural behaviours. That's why they hire consultants or corporate anthropologists: to help them with their problems. A corporate anthropologist can use all kinds of theories, models and explanations from different disciplines and frameworks to do this. The anthropological researcher collects the subjective emic stories during fieldwork and then analyses them using etic theoretical frameworks in order to reach a more objective description of general human characteristics and dynamics, often in order to get to an advice to move towards the desired culture. In this process of describing the culture, I am always very careful to be clear on the difference between emic and etic descriptions, and the way I phrase things. The language we use to talk about others has an impact not only on perceptions of their culture and frameworks for understanding it but also on our own observations.

In my experience, working with leaders and professionals, explaining this way of looking at the world to organizations proves to be extremely useful. Being aware that you can look from an insider's and an outsider's view at a department, at a team, the whole organization, frees up the notion that you can have different perspectives on the same reality. It allows people to speak more openly, to explore different views instead of fighting about them. And it opens their eyes to the fact that the only way you can truly learn about yourself and your own cultural assumptions, is through meeting people who are different. And that's another reason why the world needs anthropologists.

HOW TO BE A HUMAN AMONG HUMANS

Since I can remember, I have been intrigued by various questions. Why do people do the things the way they do? Why not do them differently? Why do people fight over their worldviews instead of enjoying the variety? Who gets to define the norm – and why and how? There is also a more philosophical one: what does it mean to be a human among humans?

As a teenager, my curiosity for people took me into acting. I joined a semi-professional theatre group and was getting ready to go to the academy of dramatic art. Then I stumbled over anthropology. It was love at first sight. My parents were not surprised. Apparently, when I was a kid, my reply to the question of what I wanted to be when I grew up was that I would travel to faraway places to learn everything from the people there and that only a photographer could join me.

I have a deep and never-ending curiosity about the fact that the world has such a variety of people and cultures and yet we human beings have not found a nice way to deal with all these differences yet. We are all unique individuals who somehow like to work and be with likeminded people. We love creativity and the search for new ways, but most of us don't like sudden great changes or conflicts with people who view things differently. In fact, most of us are very bad at dealing with real conflicts and with people who hold basic assumptions that strongly oppose ours. This is something we see in families, teams, whole organizations, global business and politics. I hope that I, somehow, can contribute to fixing some of our human fragmentation, at micro, meso- and – who knows – at one point maybe even macro-level.

Currently, I am very intrigued by the issues arising around 'truth', 'fake news' and 'alternative facts'. I am also interested in the human reflex to search for strong autocratic leaders in times of chaos and doubt. Since nothing has meaning in and of itself, and people create and construct their systems of meaning together, sharing facts and stories is a vital element of building

(Continued)

FIGURE 9.3 Conducting research to learn from nomadic leadership in the Sinai desert, Egypt, 2015. Personal archive of Jitske Kramer.

communities and tribes. In our recent book *Building Tribes*, we describe how people build tribes through interaction and decision-making (Kramer and Braun 2018). My search for the coming years will be directed towards how we can improve these processes in the age of internet, and how we can face all the wicked problems that are waiting for us to be solved at a global level: climate change issues, refugee crises, ongoing ethnic and religious conflicts, and so on.

So, why did I become an anthropologist? I guess I have felt like an anthropologist all my life.

DO SHOW, DO TELL: MY CAREER AS A CORPORATE ANTHROPOLOGIST

I studied cultural anthropology at Utrecht University in the Netherlands. I was trained as an ethnographer, did research in Botswana and specialized in the theatre of development in Uganda. After my time in Uganda, I started my career as a trainer and consultant with a large Dutch consultancy firm, working in the field of communication and leadership development. In this company, I was the only anthropologist. All my colleagues were psychologists or business economists. In a way this wasn't easy. I noticed that I looked at our clients, their corporate cultures and leadership issues in a different way than my colleagues. But since I was new to the field of consultancy, I thought that I might be looking at it the wrong way; so, I trained myself in psychology and the MBA-management language my corporate clients spoke. I kind of forgot about anthropology and blended in with my new business tribe. It was only a few years later that I recovered my anthropological background.

As a trainer and consultant, I started to work more and more in international settings, focusing on intercultural competences, post-merger and culture change programmes. Then it hit me that no one was using anthropological theories and methods to understand the dynamics of culture and culture change. This not only made me curious but also slightly irritated at myself and at my fellow anthropologists. How did we let it happen that in this huge field of work around organizational cultures, leadership, internationalization and innovation processes, the anthropological views were close to absent?

I decided to embark on this quest by myself. I started calling myself an anthropologist again, used the title Corporate Anthropologist on my business card, and founded my own organization called HumanDimensions in 2006. The organization initially focused on global leadership and international teamwork. Then I got the assignment to help improve the production process in several Indian factories. A complex issue in which my assignment became 'find the story on how information travels through our organization'. And I decided to approach this as an ethnographer. In this project, I was asked to visit three similar factories in different regions of India, with a week's time per factory. Obviously, this is a very short time frame for a thorough ethnographic research, but a very long timeframe for my client, who was expecting quick interventions. I looked for advice from my fellow anthropologists through LinkedIn and Facebook, but the main response was, 'It is not possible to do that in three weeks, I wouldn't do it, can't be done, don't go'. Again, my irritation grew, but it was also a great source of creativity. How to apply the anthropological view and methods in the context and timeframe of my business client with the maximum scientific thoroughness and a clear business frame of good-enough information to build on for further improvement? Therefore, I just started working in India and learned to be a corporate anthropologist while doing it.

Now, I not only work in organizations applying anthropological skills to understand and maybe change my clients' corporate cultures together with my team of colleagues but also travel all over the world, by internet, Skype and plane, to learn from traditional healers, leaders, surprising innovators, peers and random passers-by. I experience special rituals, everyday actions and age-old dialogues, to learn about the treasury of human wisdom. It is these cultural 'best practices' that I then translate into practices for teams,

(Continued)

departments, projects and chain cooperation in our training courses, vlogs, books, keynote speeches and master classes. These are different ways of using my anthropological training to find and understand micro-stories and vignettes that I can take into other contexts to help build stronger 'tribes', safe for diversity and ready for change.

FIVE TIPS FROM JITSKE KRAMER

1. **Be proud and show it.** For all trained anthropologists out there: be proud of your academic training. Put 'anthropologist' on your business cards. Get out of the closet if you're in it; do show, do tell.
2. **Combine anthropology with another skillset.** Anthropological views and methods can be very powerful outside the academic world, especially when combined with another skillset like project management, journalism, teaching skills, facilitation techniques, leadership. Or the other way around: make sure that other professionals can learn how to think and act like an anthropologist, for example by offering 'anthropology for managers' courses just like psychologists started designing 'psychology for managers' trainings years ago.
3. **Be creative.** Allow yourself to mix and blend different approaches, theories and research methods in order to find the best possible way to apply anthropological wisdom in a certain context.
4. **Be holistic, but don't get lost.** In academic contexts, it is vital to cross all the t's, connect all the dots, include all actor perspectives and triangulate to the maximum. And it should be vital. In the context of organizations, however, your research findings, your report, your cultural description, your ethnography, are not the end results of a research project. Reports should be accurate and true and triangulated as much as possible, but good is good enough to proceed with any cultural dialogue. You work with what you have. Your informants will talk back, your observations are the input for the larger and continued corporate story. Even one day of participant observation and informal interviews can be of great value to a client.
5. **Be judgemental and level up.** What? Really? But isn't anthropology all about postponing judgement and cultural relativism? Oh yes, no question there. But working as a corporate anthropologist, you need to be able to give clear emic ethnographic descriptions *and* be willing and

able to share your personal views, your advice, your judgement and your vision on how to improve broken teams or organizations. So, get comfortable talking with leaders, boards of directors and politicians. Make sure you truly understand all, high and low rank actors' perspectives and become the business and sparring partner of higher management if needed.

About the author

Jitske Kramer is a corporate anthropologist, a speaker, an entrepreneur, a facilitator and the founder of HumanDimensions. She travels around the world searching for ways to build strong tribes and to reinforce the relationships between people. And then she brings that knowledge back to the world of organizing, cooperation and leadership through challenging keynotes and master classes to improve the strength of individuals and groups (and to make the world more inclusive and beautiful). Author of *Managing Cultural Dynamics* (Dutch title: *Normaal is Anders!*), *Deep Democracy – de wijsheid van de minderheid* (Dutch only), *Wow! What a difference*, *Jam Cultures* and co-author of *The Corporate Tribe* (management book of the year 2016) and *Building Tribes*.

References

Braun, D. and J. Kramer (2018), *The Corporate Tribe: Organizational Lessons from Anthropology*, London and New York: Routledge Taylor & Francis Group.

Denny, R. and P. Sunderland (eds) (2014), *Handbook of Anthropology in Business*, Walnut Creek (CA): Left Coast Press.

Herrero, L. (2008), *Viral Change*, London: Meeting Minds.

Gennep, A. van (2010 [1909]), *The Rites of Passage*, London: Taylor & Francis.

Kramer, J. (2013), *Wow! What a Difference: Diversity Works*, Utrecht: HumanDimensions Publications.

Kramer, J. (2019), *Jam Cultures, Inclusie: over meedoen, meepraten, meebeslissen*, Deventer: Management Impact.

Kramer, J. and D. Braun (2018), *Building Tribes: een reisgids voor organisaties*, Deventer: Vakmedianet.

Neyland, D. (2008), *Organizational Ethnography*, London: Sage Publications.

Page, M. (1972), *The Company Savage: Life in the Corporate Jungle*, London: Cassell & Company LTD.

Simon, A. (2016), *On the Brink*, Austin (TX): Greenleaf Book Press.

Tasler, N. (19 July 2017), 'Stop Using the Excuse "Organizational Change Is Hard"', *Harvard Business Review*. Available online: https://hbr.org/2017/07/stop-using-the-excuse-organizational-change-is-hard (accessed 20 October 2019).

10

THE PRACTITIONER'S ROLE OF FACILITATING CHANGE

Anna Kirah

When I was in my twenties, I remember telling my father, an academic, that I wanted to be an anthropologist. He thought it was a waste of time and that I would not be able to find a job. But my father was wrong. When I get asked today what you can do with anthropology, my answer is simple: 'You can do anything you want!' Anthropology can enhance anything and everything. The list of possibilities is endless; we find anthropologists in politics, in health, financial, public and private sectors, in governmental and in non-governmental organizations. In all these positions, anthropologists have been adding value to the talking, doing and making of products, policies, services and organizations. Engaged in such work, I myself was dubbed, at the end of the previous century, a design anthropologist. Yet, today, most anthropologists still need to write their own job descriptions because the understanding of how anthropology and anthropologists can contribute in these sectors is still weak. This has, unfortunately, much to do with how anthropology is taught and academia having little experience outside the boundaries of theory. Theory is critical, but so is practice; our ability to connect theory with practice is the clue to how we, as practitioners, can involve ourselves in the changes taking place around us, instead of only describing them.

It is my belief that, as practitioners, anthropologists are in a position to, and responsible for, guiding and facilitating reflected change for the good of individuals, communities, nations, societies, non-human beings and our planet. Not only does our job require the understanding of perspectives other than our own and being humble about how our differences can give room to new and unknown solutions, but we must also facilitate the verbalization of tacit knowledge and understand the multiple identities and roles of an individual in different settings. In this way, anthropology can – and should evolve – from merely describing culture and change, to facilitating change that sustains humanity and ensures the involvement of the people who will be affected by change. Because anthropologists keep zooming in and out of the issues and contexts we are studying, we are well equipped to reflect on the consequences of actions taken – or to be taken – and can mitigate the unintended consequences. In addition, our formal training is imbued with ethics and ethical considerations much needed in the public debates of today. This makes anthropologists crucial in informing and facilitating change for the better.

Anthropologist high up in the sky

Becoming an anthropology practitioner and seeing the world through the eyes of anthropology, my career began high up in the sky studying the behaviour of passengers, pilots and flight attendants on Boeing airplanes. My job was to research the experience of long-haul air travel in order to inform and improve aircraft design. While I had initially been asked to conduct a quantitative survey, I was able to convince Boeing of the value of observation and dialogue with passengers, pilots and flight attendants. I had realized that while numbers gathered through surveys could point Boeing in the direction of *what* might be important to these individuals, the qualitative data provided the explanations and understanding of *why* things were important and *how* the company could improve on existing conditions.

My subsequent career has taken me into thousands of homes, places of work, shops and places where people move about, such as parks, airports, cafes, houses of worship and modes of transportation. At the onset, each project has a specific question or set of questions to be answered. To address them, I would inevitably meet an informant at their home – or another place relevant for the study – and follow them around for a day looking for clues. No matter what the original research question, I would end up with rich data about human behaviour, often reaching crucial insights beyond what had been assumed to be important based on the initial question. For instance, in a study about the use of MSN Messenger amongst the elderly, I not only understood how they made use of the software but also learned about the qualities necessary for long-lasting love. Researching the usage of email, I ended up discovering patterns in how, why, when and where people communicate using different modes of communication, rather than only finding out about their emailing practices. Working on a project aiming to reduce the risk of infection in patients using a particular medical device, we found out that there was nothing really wrong with the device or its application, which is what the medical company had assumed. Nurses could predict which patients would have infections based on which surgeon performed the surgery. It was the particular way a surgeon performed the surgery that caused the increase in infections, not the device. In a study of an airport, it was discovered that no one had ever talked to the security guard about what he had seen and experienced around a difficult transfer point for passengers. He had stood there day in and day out and had a multitude of observations and ideas that – once we talked to him – ended up resolving the challenges that had been there for years.

The work, over time, led me to study life stages and life events all over the world. The ability to provide both deep insights into the issues under study and a thorough understanding of the broader context became increasingly useful no matter the sector I was employed by. So did understanding the people from their perspective – rather than that assumed in the research question – and the ability to synthesize and connect the dots, that is, finding answers in a chaotic, messy data set. Each step of the way, I have always taken participatory observation on the road – or in the sky – with me. From my experiences of working closely with people, I have subsequently dedicated myself to one cause: to change the belief that an organization or a government can design *for* the people without involving the people, to the principle that an organization or a government can design *with* the people they serve in order to develop meaningful, relevant and sustainable solutions that create value. Where did this cause come from? It came from my childhood and the way I grew up, it was inspired by my anthropology studies, it was imbued by my teachers, my fellow students and my informants, and was infused by my colleagues within and outside of anthropology circles.

Anthropological thinking instead of design thinking

Unlike many disciplines, the skills of an anthropologist are developed and discovered over time. As anthropologists, we have a constant need to invoke curiosity and an inclination to question what we see, even when we think we understand what we see. During our studies, this came about from reading classic and contemporary ethnographies and from our fieldwork adventures where we tested our own boundaries of understanding through participatory observation. It also comes from our discussions with colleagues, informants and teachers when we jump into the chaos of trying to find meaning in our data. One result is that a practitioner of anthropology is not able to accept assumptions or absolutes. An anthropologist is never comfortable assuming anything but requires a deep dive into whatever is being questioned until she has the necessary data and an understanding that either substantiates or dismisses the assumption. Our fieldwork approach helps us to fail forward into discovery, hop into chaos and untangle it, and uncover a set of truths. While we are writing down and explaining our own and others' truths, we develop and obtain the anthropological mindset, quite different from the practice of design thinking. Design thinking, as prescriptions for the innovation of products and services within the business context, is a diluted and commercialized version of our mindset.

As practitioners of anthropology, we often express our observations by seeing things from others' perspectives. This quality is about making the known unknown and the unknown known – and it is the fundamental basis of our work. We are translators of that which is known and that which is unknown. What appears to be known, when described with a new lens, can suddenly bring about new explanations and deeper meaning for the people we serve. What is initially explained in one way can also be explained in another one – and this is how the will to change comes about. The anthropological mindset is bound by the way we ask questions, by the way we immerse ourselves in understanding and meaning. We bring forth new perspectives by viewing the obvious with new filters. We have an ability to describe culture in a manner that is understood by both our informants and those we share our views with because we continuously validate our findings and adjust our understandings along the way. We have an ability to help others to see the exact same things they have always been seeing with new eyes and new understanding – and this is how we facilitate change.

This is why the world needs anthropologists: we need to look at things people do on this planet at a macro and micro level, and describe them with different filters in order to find new possibilities to sustain humanity, all living things and our environment. And our work always starts by asking 'why'.

The dynamics of culture

One tenant of anthropology is that there is no one truth other than 'culture is dynamic'. Anthropologists thrive in contexts of cultural change and transition because we are comfortable with change and are always searching to untangle that which appears impossible to untangle. As anthropologists, we learned that culture is not something created in a leadership meeting or a task force in order to better the organization's working environment. Culture is not tangible, it is not a thing; it is more like a fluid space, continuously (re)created and negotiated by people through social interactions (see e.g. Brightman 1995).

As practitioners of anthropology, we are able to identify the mechanisms in groups of people that create culture as a part of the dynamics of everyday life. Culture can be in the dynamics of two people or within an entire corporation. In entering the space as practitioners of anthropology, we first observe and then we start interacting and doing. In our questioning, we are actually turning things upside down and shaking them up a bit, only to calmly bring forth some observations. This is our way of revealing the culture we are in the midst of. We also uncover what is being taken for granted amongst the people involved. I have been called many things in this practitioner role, one of my favourite aliases being a 'fortune teller'. I laugh and I explain that I am not a fortune teller, I am just extremely curious and I follow the threads until I find the answers. The journey is magical, but the results, when revealed, are actually quite pragmatic and understandable to the people involved.

The act of revealing may cause friction, even when our work unveils the tension that already existed and only makes it more explicit. Why does this happen? Again, as practitioners of anthropology, we are never looking at just one perspective but at a multiplicity of perspectives, thereby revealing that how culture is perceived is dependent on the roles, levels of power and knowledge of the people we interact with. Our role is to manoeuvre and manage this newly formed understanding of existing practices and arenas where the latter come into play.

In doing so, we affect the organizations we work in or with and this is critical to the understanding of our own practices.

With our competencies and multiple perspectives, anthropologists enter into a dynamic box that is viewed by others as static. In this box, we are both a force and a challenge. Our influence creates a space where tension appears. Our 'magic' happens in the tension point between the anthropological perspective and the organization or people we are engaging with. This magic, however, can only occur if both the anthropologist and the people who are involved can handle the tension. To mitigate the dangers, we need to spend quite a long time establishing and maintaining trust. In fact, it becomes our role, as practitioners, to only unveil the tension point if we are to do it together with the people we work with, for this is when magic appears. Thus, knowing when and how to reveal the tension becomes a delicate process where our understanding of classical ethnographic works can help.

Learning from the classics

History repeats itself over and over again – and so does culture – even when the stories and cultures are from a different era. I am a member of a small group of Norwegian anthropologists – all of whom are practitioners – who gather together to read and discuss classic works of anthropology from the previous century and try to connect the dots to the present. What we have learned and continue to learn in our meetings is boundless. We have learned that we are not only able to connect the past with the present, but that we can also create anthropological visions of the future. We realized that the articles and ethnographies we read as students have acquired new meanings for us after years of experience in the workforce. We now see how they helped to shape what we observe, how we think and how we utilize anthropological skills to solve challenges in our places of work and in our policy-making.

To exemplify the connection between the classic anthropological literature and what we do in our places of work, The Guru and the Conjurer by Fredrik Barth (1990) is a fantastic point of departure. In reading this classic text, we found ourselves comparing the two different ways of transferring knowledge described in Barth's article to how we transfer knowledge or facilitate the transferring of knowledge in our places of work. We discussed our experiences and the impact of leaders who act as the Guru, standing before an audience, transparent about their knowledge. We also shared our experiences and the impact of the Conjurers, leaders who discuss strategy and the future with a 'chosen' audience behind closed doors, where knowledge is mysterious and only for those who have passed 'an initiation rite'.

One of the biggest challenges for anthropologists working in organizations is to discern when to be the guru and when to be the conjurer. It is in our nature to want to be the guru, but that becomes a dangerous game when the politics of innovation and organizational politics are at play. It is at this point that the subtle dance of the facilitator comes on stage and our experience guides us in dancing two roles at the same time: depending on the context, we transform ourselves between the two roles of the guru and the conjurer. The smoother we are in this transition, the better the dance between the facilitator and the group involved in facilitation.

What do practitioners bring to the table?

Almost every day of my working life, I am faced with the consequences of having a set of eyes and ears that see and hear things from different perspectives. I am also faced with the consequences of knowing that no one story is absolutely correct, that stories are always interpretations and that they are thus only partially true. This is the liability of becoming an anthropologist, of being trained to observe and listen, and to connect the dots without judgement. The description of culture is something that is dynamic and our descriptions tell *a* story, not *the* story.

Our tools are many, but perhaps the most important tool we offer to a rapidly changing world is our ability to see things from different perspectives and to connect the dots. It is our ethical responsibility to create scenarios based on these dot connections and to facilitate change in transdisciplinary settings. As practitioners, we are bound to work in transdisciplinary environments and when collaborating across disciplines, small miracles can and do happen: we transcend our own methods, models and processes, and find ourselves in new realms.

Practitioners often work on the edge. We are neither fully integrated into an organization nor placed completely outside of it. Rather, we stand on the edge looking inwards and outwards at the same time while focussing on making sense of things. In my first job at Boeing, I remember observing passengers, pilots and flight attendants. I also remember observing the behaviour of Boeing employees. The corporate culture had strict processes and their own set of rituals and methodologies to get 'the job done' which did not always align with the needs of their customers (the pilots, flight attendants and passengers). This culture was very foreign to me. I remember thinking that to be successful, I must find a way to connect these two worlds and to facilitate an understanding inside the company of what they do not know they do not know they need to know in order to create an experience that would be meaningful and relevant to the people they serve when designing aircraft. And thus started my journey of working on the edge. The most powerful changes made to products and services in my career came not from my expertise but from my ability to facilitate understanding and knowledge between different worlds in new ways.

Thus, the reason we need anthropologists is that when we listen to the multitude of ideas, thoughts and theories that come our way, we ask questions and we reveal the dynamic nature of theory in practice. In any field, in any area, an anthropologist will question and will in this process be a catalyser, an unexpected interventionist, helping people to see the same old things with new eyes and new understandings. This is how we can facilitate change by the people and for the people.

Although the world of humanity has always been a dynamic and changing one, we are witnessing the exponential speed by which change is happening that has had, and will continue to have, significant consequences (see Eriksen 2001). Below, I try to capture the nature of today's changes within four areas – globalization, environment, healthcare and balance between technology and humanity – all of which would benefit from greater engagement of anthropologists.

Globalization

Globalization has been here for a long time and is here to stay. Recently, Thomas Hylland Eriksen reminded me of the fears of globalization in the United States in the 1930s and how easy it was to see the parallel to our fear of things foreign today. A prominent anthropologist, Ralph Linton (1937), wrote the article One Hundred Per Cent American during that time to demonstrate the irony of fear of all things foreign by demonstrating how much of an individual's life is based on products and behaviours acquired from all around the world (another example of what I wrote about earlier when referring to the importance of anthropological classics today).

A TV series called *Beforeigners* (2019) puts yet another spin to what we are experiencing by introducing people of the past in the present and changing the dynamics and definition of 'us' and 'them'. Whereas now 'us' and 'them' often refers to communities at a national level, in the show 'beforeigners' – people from the past – pop in to the present and 'us' becomes everyone who is from the 'now' time and 'them' refers to everyone who is living now but comes from the past. To mitigate, the term 'trans-temporal people' comes into action in order to find a place for the 'beforeigners'. And to make it even more interesting, what do we do with the people from the 'now' time who want to identify themselves as those from the 'past'? This series is a must for any anthropologist or anthropology student.

In a sense, we are already trans-temporal and trans-local. We can travel the entire world at the touch of a finger and that same world invades us in a nanosecond. The human brain was never meant to have to negotiate so much information, so many different people – and yet we are continuously inundated with information and stories about people and places. Grassroots movements occur when people perceive the world moving too quickly and when they feel a sense of fear or lack of understanding; we respond by going retro, by eating local, by going national. When we do not know how to negotiate what is happening around us, we react. With the exponential growth of technology, cultures are brought even closer together and are therefore more likely to collide. The result is severe polarization manifesting itself in a world of 'us' and 'them', and flourishing nationalisms.

It is important for anthropologists to come in and help to facilitate the understanding of different cultures. Our attempts, however, are often thwarted by our inability to move beyond cultural relativism which prompts us to grasp cultures in their own terms. Anthropology must understand cultures through cultural relativism, but we must also move beyond it and help policy makers, institutions and people find ways to negotiate the vast differences we find ourselves confronted with. Are there universals? Are there spaces where the practice of universals should happen and other spaces where cultural relativism can pervade? Can we find ways to communicate across our boundaries, ways that are fruitful and not harmful?

Sustainability

We have an environmental and climate crisis related to our usage of resources at our doorstep, we are witnessing climate change affecting our planet. As anthropologists, we can participate in understanding the consequences of change but also in informing and facilitating the transformation necessary to address environmental and climate issues. The only thing that will save the planet is a change in human behaviours; technology alone is unlikely to do the job.

Sustainability is not just about our environmental needs, however, it is about saving humanity. I refer the reader to the seventeen United Nations Sustainable Development Goals for inspiration on all aspects of sustainability (United Nations 2015). All the goals are relevant to all disciplines. Under each goal is a starting point where anthropology has a place at the table to facilitate change that is meaningful, relevant, useful, desirable and sustainable to our common future. To illustrate, Goal 1 is to eliminate poverty. We, as academics and practitioners, need to be asking ourselves how we can participate with our skillset as anthropologists to eliminate poverty. And so on and so forth, with other goals related to health, education, equality, access to clean water and affordable energy, economic growth, decent work, sustainable communities and new business models.

Healthcare

We face demographic challenges with an increasing aging population and new demands on healthcare for all ages. How do we sustain our rapidly growing population on this planet? How do we care for our elderly in societies that no longer observe elders as the wise ones? How do we mitigate the increased level of stress, depression and anxieties correlated to rapid change and advancement of technologies? How do we deal with chronic illnesses or geriatric illnesses such as dementia? How do we deal with death and dying? At what point should we stop saving lives and allow for death? Is it acceptable that people can start to live to 120 years of age? How will society, governments and the private sector ensure healthcare for all? How do we define healthcare? What are the consequences of welfare technologies? How do we look at short term technology solutions and long-term effects? A safety alarm sounds like a good idea to keep an old person home alone as long as possible, but who wants to live home alone, abandoned and lonely for another ten years with an alarm around their neck? There is a place at the table for anthropologists interested in these types of questions.

The exponential growth of technology

Things are moving fast and human beings do not have the capability to mitigate or understand the effects of exponential growth in technologies. Thomas Hylland Eriksen actually forewarned about these changes already in 2001 when he wrote about technology and how the need for immediate reciprocity can become tyrannical (see Eriksen 2001). These challenges affect our places of work, our communities, our nations, our globe and humanity.

Are we coding blindly our way into the future, creating technologies without thinking of their consequences? What does eugenics mean in a context where we can find out our genetic coding or sequencing and change it? How far do we go with these possibilities? Are technology advancements only benefiting the wealthy? Are they increasing divides? Who defines technology for the good or for the evil? What do we do with future megacities, smart cities built on the premise that technologies are good? Who is looking at the societal consequences of these megacities? How will we feed the masses in these cities? Will cities be able to grow their own foods? How can they grow their own foods? Technology is not void of culture. Anthropologists belong in the intersection between people, technology and culture.

FIGURE 10.1 Anna Kirah explaining at the *Why the World Needs Anthropologists* event how manipulation of data gave us Donald Trump, Lisbon, Portugal, 2018. Courtesy Dan Podjed.

The role of practicing anthropologists now and in the future is one of engagement. As practicing anthropologists, it is our duty to facilitate change, understanding all the possible ways in which we are affected by it. Technologists alone should not create technical solutions. Here, there is a need for transdisciplinarity; anthropologists, historians, psychologists and designers should work with technologists to foresee potential risks to society and to co-create and test out technological solutions that are relevant and meaningful in the context of society and culture – and not just because they are technologically feasible.

Connecting the past and the present, shaping the future

I do not believe that anthropologists are better suited than any other profession to solve the challenges we face today. I do, however, believe that we have an equally important role as other professions in furthering the development of sustainable products, services, organizations, governments and policies for our planet. Our role is to connect the past and the present and to help to shape the future based on our understanding of culture and human behaviour.

We need to take anthropology forward into practice and raise our voices while being willing to involve ourselves in facilitating the directions we propose. Our ability to connect the dots and fail forward is crucial to learning about and adjusting to the change that is upon us. As anthropologists, we do not purport to have the answers, but we listen, we observe, we keep going until we have answers that are recognizable from the many different perspectives that may push against each other – and only then can we facilitate and participate in change.

We are bombarded by easy solutions that might have short term positive effects but which might fail in the long term. These easy solutions rarely give us the whole picture. The media and social media are disturbing examples of providing us with simple answers and simple thinking to complex challenges where there is a need for holistic understanding of what is actually happening around us.

As anthropology practitioners, we have both a moral and ethical responsibility to contribute with our tools and our skills and to develop these tools and skills further. We have a moral and ethical responsibility to connect with educational institutions, governments, political leaders and private and public sectors, in order to facilitate the creation of meaningful, relevant, useful, desirable and sustainable solutions to the challenges we face in the world today and in the future.

ANTHROPOLOGY AS A DESTINY

I have been told that I am clever at scanning a situation, scanning a room, and within seconds be able to generate a story, a wholeness in what I saw. I note what fits and what does not fit and become curious about discrepancies.

(*Continued*)

I have no qualms at walking up to a complete stranger and asking them to tell me about … whatever I am curious about. This scanning capability combined with insatiable curiosity is the premise of what I am passionate about in my work: the search for patterns and non-patterns, making sense of what I observe and then applying it to the development of products, services and organizational change. Same basic procedures, different outcomes for different clients and always centred around the very people I serve, their behaviours, aspirations and motivations.

I learned this skill of scanning when I was a little girl. I was growing up in various parts of Asia and my parents put me in local schools. Each time I moved to a new country and new school, I had to start all over again with making friends, learning the language, understanding cultural codes. Scanning – through observation and learning – was my survival skill.

Later on, at a critical time of my life, when I was fifteen years old, I had an art teacher, Barry Moser, who gave me the book *The Shape of Content* (Shahn 1957). In the book, there was a chapter called The Education of an Artist. I took it as a bucket list, as things I needed to do before I made up my mind about what I wanted to do with my life. It told me to keep my hands in the earth, it told me to travel and see the world, to read books in other languages, to sit in cafes, listen to other people's conversations and to draw. That list woke me up and created an insatiable curiosity in all that was around me: people, objects, services, religions, policies – and the list goes on.

FIGURE 10.2   Anna Kirah's first attempt at fieldwork in Taiwan, 1964. Personal archive of Anna Kirah.

How do these two things explain why I became an anthropologist? The truth is that I did not intend on becoming one. I had to choose a minor subject when studying education and someone told me anthropology was both easy and fun. On the first day of my introductory course in anthropology, my professor and later advisor, Axel Sommerfelt, explained that anthropology was about understanding the 'natives' from their point of view and not our own. I questioned Professor Sommerfelt as I thought this was something everyone did naturally. There was an odd pause in the room broken by Professor Sommerfelt's voice saying, 'Well, actually, no'. The light bulb went on and I realized that anthropology was already my life, my soul, and thus became my destiny.

Becoming a practitioner also happened by chance. I had the opportunity to work at Boeing during my doctoral studies. I was actually studying clinical psychology and Boeing needed help with a quantitative customer survey. Suddenly, I connected the needs of Boeing with my passion: observing and learning from people. Before I knew it, I was flying around the world observing and talking to passengers, pilots and flight attendants, and was given the title of Design Anthropologist. Since then, I have had so many adventures and have learned so many things that I feel really quite blessed. My word of advice to readers of this book is: be open to possibilities and have no regrets, just accept that some paths need rerouting.

THE THREE CORNERSTONES: HONOUR, ETHICS AND INTEGRITY

My jobs since I became an anthropologist have been diverse, but the clue is that I have always been an anthropologist: a consultant at a labour department working on immigration and refugee policy, a teacher of written and unwritten rules in the Norwegian workplace, a clinical psychologist for children and families in distress, a design anthropologist for Boeing and Microsoft, a designer of a radical innovation school for leaders in the public and private sector, a rector of said school, a vice president of a design company, a problem solver in the private and public sector, a board member in various companies and public funding programmes, a jury member of a design prize, a consultant working with services, strategic initiatives and research and development of collaborative tools for businesses and organizations. All along this journey, I have passionately promoted design anthropology as a

(Continued)

discipline, co-creation as a methodology and people-centred approach to design, innovation and organizational change as a mindset.

When I journeyed down this path, worldwide, there were only a handful of anthropologists who had attempted to take a public stance as practitioners. There was only the method of trial and error and the strong sense of honour, ethics and integrity which I got from my professors, fellow students and the curriculum associated with my studies. In the beginning, I received a lot of critique from those same students and professors for helping the 'devil', that is capitalism, governments, the system. I spent many days questioning myself from an ethical standpoint. But I am proud to be an anthropologist and I realized that what I gained from the University of Oslo during my studies – besides a deep understanding of anthropology – was that very sense of honour, ethics and integrity, and I have not allowed this to be abused or taken from me. I have taken a stand and I have fought many battles where I was willing to walk out of a job if I could not remain ethical, honourable and have my integrity intact.

However, one question remains: is it my own or is it a collective sense of ethics, honour and integrity? I have a stronger conviction than ever that using anthropological skills to better the world is acceptable only as long as the very people who we aim to 'help' are not only involved but actually direct the process from their perspective and not our own as anthropologists. As an anthropology practitioner, I act as a facilitator of change, not the actual change agent. That said, I believe it is time to create ethical guidelines for practitioners as the needs for our services are increasing, along with the complexities of the challenges that need to be addressed.

FIVE TIPS FROM ANNA KIRAH

1. **Throw away your ego** and grab on to copious quantities of humility.
2. **Watch out for your expert blinders** and hone in on collaboration skills.
3. **Be open to possibilities**. Ask questions, be curious and be willing to learn
4. **Keep your hands in the dirt or in organic matter**. It will ground you.
5. **Co-create**. Continuous involvement of the people you serve will give you the optimal chances for success.

About the author

Anna Kirah is an internationally renowned design anthropologist and psychologist known for pioneering the people-centric approach to innovation and change management. She started her career at both Boeing and Microsoft. In 2004 she was voted contributor of the year at Microsoft. Her passions are co-creation and working with transdisciplinary teams with the motto 'If you understand people's motivations and involve them in your process, you can create meaningful, desirable and sustainable solutions for and with the people you serve'. Anna returned from the United States to Norway in 2010 where she has her own consultancy, teaches at the Oslo Metropolitan University and is a board member of Design without Borders.

References

Barth, F. (1990), 'The Guru and the Conjurer: Transactions in Knowledge and the Shaping of Culture in Southeast Asia and Melanesia', *Man*, 25 (4): 640–53.
Beforeigners (2019), [TV series] Dir. Eilif Skodvin, Norway: HBO Europe.
Brightman, R. (1995), 'Forget Culture: Replacement, Transcendence, Relexification', *Cultural Anthropology*, 10 (4): 509–46.
Eriksen, T. H. (2001), *Tyranny of the Moment*, London: Pluto.
Linton, R. (1937), 'One Hundred Per Cent American', *The American Mercury*, 40: 427–9.
Shahn, B. (1957), *The Shape of Content*, Cambridge (MA): Harvard University Press.
United Nations (2015), *Transforming Our World: The 2030 Agenda for Sustainable Development*, New York: UN Publishing. Available online: https://sustainabledevelopment.un.org/post2015/transformingourworld (accessed 16 October 2019).

11

DO WE REALLY NEED MORE ANTHROPOLOGISTS?

Riall W. Nolan

We don't really need more anthropologists. But if we're going to save the planet, we need more anthropological thinking. Let me explain.

Our world is increasingly run by numbers, but the reality to which the numbers refer often gets overlooked. Do we know, for example, where the numbers come from? Many years ago, a British government official said this:

> The government [is] extremely fond of amassing great quantities of statistics. These are raised to the nth degree, the cube roots are extracted, and the results are arranged into elaborate and impressive displays. What must be kept ever in mind, however, is that in every case, the figures are first put down by a village watchman, and he puts down anything he damn well pleases. (attributed to Sir Josiah Stamp, 1840–1941, Her Majesty's collector of inland revenue)

Numbers are a favourite way for economists to measure wealth and poverty, but anthropologists know that it is much more subjective and contextually based than that. Even when we have a number, do we know what it really means? If you're asked in a restaurant how spicy you want your food on a scale of one to ten, you can certainly provide a number. But does that number mean the same thing to the cook in the kitchen? When it comes to wealth and poverty, people around the world seem somehow reluctant to accurately report money income to foreign questioners. In Indonesia, for example, development planners learned to assess prosperity not in terms of money, but with reference to the materials used to build one's house, what the floor was made of and what people used for transportation (Honadle 1982; Soetoro 1979). At around this same time, I was helping design household surveys in Sri Lanka, where we used similar measures, including particular pieces of furniture, as quite accurate ways of determining relative levels of prosperity.

Numbers, always and everywhere, depend on context for their meaning. And anthropology is very good at uncovering context. Anthropologists know that observed phenomena are not isolates, but are connected in complex and often invisible webs. We know that whatever we think we are looking at may look entirely different to the person next to us.

And we know a variety of ways to uncover this, to reveal the cultural meanings under the surface. We suspend judgement, we look for wider connections and we build understanding from the ground up. We do all this by talking and interacting with the 'different others' who we want to understand. Above all, we seek to see the world through someone else's eyes.

These are some of the hallmarks of anthropological thinking. It's second nature to most of us, but not, apparently, to most other people in the world. It is, however, a learnable mind-set, and once acquired, it tends to stay with people, for one simple reason: because it's useful. Anthropological thinking doesn't replace other ways of thinking; it complements and enhances them.

Who could deny that this ability is sorely needed today, as we face a growing number of global grand challenges, each of which arises in part at least from human cultural difference?

Anthropological thinking helps people do what Wendell Berry (1981) called 'solving for pattern'; in other words, situating the solution to a problem within its overall context in such a way that change does not ignore or disregard the larger connections of which it is a part.

Many of our current problems arise because we don't think very anthropologically. The reality of numbers may be 'out there', but what the numbers actually mean is 'in here' – that is, inside the heads of human beings.

Anthropology is, indeed, sometimes a science of verification, but most often, it's a science of discovery. It finds, reveals, unearths and discovers stuff we didn't really know was there, and in doing so, it extends and enhances our understanding of the world. If it turns out that what we uncover was stuff that some people already knew all about, well, that was the point, wasn't it – to bring the diversity of human thought and experience into view?

Anthropological thinking often comes across as elaborated common sense, the kind of insight that, once one sees it, we tend to say, oh yes, of course. Prior to that, of course, we generally *didn't* see it.

This is the century in which we need to figure out how to make human diversity work for the collective resolution of our global problems. And simply put, anthropology is going to be one of the best ways to do it. How to do it is the issue.

What sorts of steps should we be taking, now and in the future, to get anthropology into the mainstream, and encourage more people on the planet to start thinking anthropologically?

Here are three suggestions.

Broadening our message

Across Europe and North America, difference is no longer remote; it has moved in next door. Most of us, today or tomorrow, will work with or for someone of a very different background. We buy and sell to different others across the globe. We collaborate with them, and we compete with them. We are largely unprepared to do this, but anthropology can help.

One of the easiest things to do to help our fellow citizens start thinking more like anthropologists is to get anthropology into our primary and secondary schools. We know that humans are hard-wired to be curious about the folks living over in the next valley, so why not capture some of that as early as possible and explain to young people – while there is still time – how and why they should take an interest in the lives of others.

It's a bit like sex education. You can either approach it intelligently and get out in front of things, or you can let kids get educated by whoever they meet on the street. Right now, we do very little in our schools to help students understand the world's diversity, with the result that our children grow up, oftentimes, with no real ability to make sense of an increasingly diverse and contested world.

At the same time, they are bombarded by media messages which are essentially designed to provoke fear and distrust of people not like ourselves. They are also taught a bunch of other stuff which isn't really helpful, and which promotes and reinforces a kind of naïve realism – the belief that the way your culture views the world is the way the world really is. They're probably taught, for example, that there is something like the Law of Supply and Demand, or that there's a phenomenon called the Tragedy of the Commons. But any anthropologist can point out that these aren't laws or inevitabilities, but cultural value orientations, and that there are plenty of societies around the world where neither of these patterns exist.

Once you understand that other people out in the world manage to live lives which are happy, spiritual, productive and fulfilling, and that they do all this on a very different basis from you, you eventually realize that you, too, could live your life on a different basis if you so choose.

Becoming a profession

To spread our message and gain influence, we also need to start acting more like a profession. It doesn't mean giving up 'the discipline', but it does require a shift in both focus and attitude.

A profession solves problems. Professions work in clearly demarcated domains, they bring specialized knowledge and techniques to their work, and they do all this for people – clients – who value what they do and are willing to pay for it. Early in my career, I worked with a group of American irrigation engineers who were designing an irrigated tomato project in northern Senegal. They had gone to a great deal of trouble to map out and survey a complex system of water pipes, and when they had finished this, they also drew up a schedule for turning the water on and off, which required people to go into the field and manually operate the valves. They then showed the schedule to the villagers, who looked uneasy and began to mutter among themselves. The chief engineer turned to me. 'You're the local expert', he said. 'Tell 'em this is how they have to do the water'. I looked at the schedule and shook my head. 'They'll never do this', I said. 'You have them going out to the fields at twilight'. 'That's the ideal time', one of the engineers said. 'Maybe', I replied, 'but it's also when the evil spirits come out. Move the time either earlier or later, but not at twilight'. The engineers weren't convinced, so I took them in the jeep up on a small knoll overlooking the village, and as we sat there drinking beer and smoking cigars, I drew their attention to what was happening in the village below. As night gathered in, people disappeared into their houses, only to re-emerge again once it had become fully dark. 'Well, I'll be damned', said the chief engineer. 'Looks like you earned your money today'. And he changed the watering schedule.

We're not yet a profession, and we may never be one in the same way that, say, physicians are. But we are able to solve problems by solving for pattern, and we need to do more to train our anthropology graduates to do this, in a professional manner.

Fortunately, this process is well underway in many places, with the emergence of training programmes for applied and practicing anthropologists. These programmes, in addition to providing a first-rate grounding in anthropology per se,

FIGURE 11.1   Riall W. Nolan discussing health education with a group of Senegalese village elders, as part of Peace Corps project in 1967. Personal archive of Riall W. Nolan.

also train students in how to actually use what they know, and how to operate effectively in the non-academic workplace. These programmes, many of which are excellent, are an ever-evolving work in progress, and represent in many ways the cutting edge of the discipline.

But most of our departments, unfortunately, still prepare their students less well than they might for the opportunities existing outside the academy. There is still, as one writer put it, a 'jarring disconnect' between graduate education in anthropology and the needs of the market (Muehlebach 2013: 305).

Many of the skills needed for practice – for example, networking, collaboration, design, problem-solving and communication – are either not taught at all in many of our programmes or are not taught in ways which are relevant for practice.

Paying attention to practice

Finally, we need to take non-academic anthropological practice seriously.

Practice is still regarded warily by the more conservative members of our discipline – viewed as ethically suspect, lightweight and theoretically empty. The fact that it is sold on the marketplace is, for some, the most serious transgression.

But most of what is new in anthropology is coming from practice, including new approaches to the collection and interpretation of data, and the development of frameworks and procedures for planning, forecasting and design. Practice is giving us in-depth looks inside the operation of many of the large and powerful organizations which shape our lives. Practitioners are also accumulating valuable experience about the internal processes and dynamics of organizations large and small, and about how the implementation of plans and policies can be done successfully.

Many of our hard-science colleagues take a somewhat rational-directive approach to getting things done, assuming that good data will speak for itself, and carry the day. Anthropologists know – or learn – that, as one of my mentors put it, 'It's easier to ride a horse in the direction it's already going'. Getting a sense of what matters to an organization and how it likes to receive new information, is often a crucial part of getting anything done. When I worked with Indonesians, for example, I learned to respect their method of consensus-building (*musyawarah-mufakat*) as a key element in negotiations. Attempting to reach decisions in a more North American way almost always resulted in disappointment. Later, in my work for the US Army, I realized that I had to tailor everything I was attempting to communicate in terms of its direct effect on mission accomplishment. Anything else was likely to be ignored or, much of the time, not even heard at all.

As we have seen, the work that practitioners do, and the way they do this work, is quite different from traditional academic endeavours. Collaboration and interdisciplinarity, and the need to co-think and co-create with others – these and other characteristics of practice have brought practitioners into contact with new ideas and perspectives. But much – nay, most – of this does not find its way back into the discipline. As a result, what practitioners learn from the field – the stuff which, in previous generations, helped the discipline advance – has been largely absent from the academic curriculum.

At work, practitioners face the challenge of making the anthropology in what they do more visible. Their published accounts of practice in various domains are providing us with valuable glimpses into how this actually occurs. To the extent that practitioner contributions are seen as instances of what anthropology can accomplish in the workplace, the image of the discipline is strengthened, and with it, future opportunities for practitioners.

The fieldwork that early anthropologists did helped fuel and propel early discussions of theory, method and ethics, and was fundamental to the shaping of a young discipline. One might ask today whether the discipline is now able and willing to use the information coming back to them from practice in order to develop and extend theory, improve methods and refine our sense of ethics, of ourselves and of our place in the world. The opportunity to do this lies before us.

Years ago, Erve Chambers (2009: 376) pointed out that 'the notion that anthropology is ours [i.e. the academy's] alone to define and to bless and then turn out into the world cannot prevail'.

It is from the world of practice that disciplinary energy, innovation and – most of all – influence are emerging. At the moment, little of this is finding its way back into the academy in the form of recognition, training or acceptance, but this is almost certainly a temporary phenomenon. The sooner we fix this situation, the better.

Thinking like an anthropologist

The years to come are going to challenge all of us. The global system which we have created – or allowed to emerge – is one driven by finance and markets, which is to say by numbers. It frames our choices as bottom-line issues, and obscures anything local, which is to say cultural, unless it relates directly to profit or loss. It assumes that there will be winners and losers, and the system, once in place, tends to run more or less on its own, being headquartered nowhere in particular except in cyberspace.

Anthropological thinking is the very antithesis of this approach to human affairs. Anthropology has moved, in the last 100 years, from being an obscure and quirky discipline whose purpose appeared to be mainly that of bringing back exotic and unusual information from the far corners of the earth, to an emerging profession, able and – at least to a degree – willing to put its knowledge and tools to use in the wider society.

In that sense, the world definitely needs anthropological thinking, and more of it. Not just by anthropologists but by citizens, voters and decision-makers at all levels, across society.

Getting an anthropological way of thinking out into the world will, as I've suggested, require us to take some steps, by introducing it into our primary and secondary schools, by transforming our academic training and by paying more attention to practitioners.

Some may object that none of this sounds much like 'real anthropology'. As the last several decades have shown, however, it's no longer our grandparents' anthropology, and today, practitioners and academics alike are less worried about purity. They are more concerned with finding ways to use what they know in helping resolve human problems, while at the same time showing other non-anthropologists how to do the same.

In the end, anthropological thinking is thinking that enhances our ability to understand the world around us in more grounded and authentic ways. One definition of intelligence is the ability to make finer and finer discriminations that actually matter. If this is true, then anthropology makes us smarter.

Smart people make better citizens. They're better at their jobs, and they do more exciting and creative work. They have more fun, and they're more interesting as friends and colleagues.

They're just the kinds of people, in other words, that you'd want helping us save the planet.

ONE WAY OF BECOMING AN ANTHROPOLOGIST

Early spring in 1965 in the Chenango Valley in upstate New York, and my undergraduate advisor and I are sitting in his office. He'd just asked me what my plans were for after graduation.

I said what many young men of my generation might have said. 'Well, sir, if I can't think of anything else to do, I guess I'll just join the Army. Get my military obligation out of the way'.

His pipe came out of his mouth. 'You don't read the papers much, do you?' he said.

'What do you mean?'

'In case you hadn't noticed', he said drily, 'there's a war starting up in Southeast Asia. If you want to be part of a war, then joining the Army would be just the thing'. A pause. 'Otherwise, think of something else'.

Later in life, this moment would appear for me as a kind of epiphany, where worldviews connect – or in this case, collide – and new meanings arise, at least for one of the participants.

We talked, and half an hour later, the idea of joining the newly formed Peace Corps had taken shape. I signed up, and my fortunes took a strange and wonderful turn.

Waking up – halfway around the world

I lived in a thatched hut in a remote part of Senegal, with people who were compassionate, skilled and industrious but whose lives were often hard and uncertain. From time to time, I'd see outsiders coming in on the twice-weekly

DC-3 airliner from the capital, development experts with some kind of project they wanted to talk over. Most of their ideas wouldn't work, of course, because they just didn't fit with the local culture. And by that time, I had understood that if you wanted things to work, the local culture wasn't the problem, it was the solution.

The outside experts, for the most part, knew nothing about the local culture. Nor did they seem to care very much. They didn't see opportunities, in other words; they saw obstacles.

But then one day a new group of Westerners came to town. Four of them, in fact, driving a battered jeep and dressed in faded work clothes, very much like my own. They turned out to be a group of French anthropologists, from the Musée de l'Homme in Paris, and they were doing fieldwork.

They had a camp on the outskirts of town down by the river. I had just learned to speak passable French (albeit with an accent straight out of the Fouta-Djallon region) and so I started hanging around. And fairly soon, I was invited to go with them on a *sortie* up into the hills, collecting data.

We wound up deep in the bush, in a small Malinké village. One old man came up, touched my arm gently, looked into my blue eyes, and asked in halting French if I was a Mauritanian. 'Why does he think I'm from Mauretania?' I asked the interpreter. He shook his head. 'You didn't understand, *monsieur*', he said. 'He wasn't asking if you're from Mauretania. He's asking if you're dead'.

I spent all afternoon watching the anthropologists working with their interpreters to collect stories from the older men and women. They worked slowly and patiently, and in between sessions, they explained to me the significance of some of the stories, dealing with origin myths, spirits and legendary heroes. This is great, I thought; these guys know how to find out all sorts of useful stuff.

On the way back to town I asked the obvious question. 'What are you going to do with your field data?'

'Why, send it back to the Museum, of course'.

'But then what happens?'

They seemed puzzled. 'What happens? Nothing happens. The data go in the archive, that's all'.

Ah. I thought about all of this in the days to come. On the one hand, I thought, we have Westerners with hard-core practical knowledge of things like crops and machinery but who don't know how to fit what they know into the local context. On the other hand, we have my newly found anthropologist friends who know how to learn about the local culture but have no practical purpose in mind for what they learn.

Finding my calling

That's when I decided to become an anthropologist. All my life I had enjoyed tinkering with things – taking them apart to see how they worked

(Continued)

and putting them back together, sometimes in new ways. Now, I wanted to fit development projects into culture, so that they stood some chance of succeeding. I knew that I would need an advanced degree to do this, and so, from my thatched hut on the edge of nowhere, I set about investigating university programmes.

I began with US universities. I learned that I would need a doctorate and that this might take six years or more. I learned that because I had only minored in anthropology, I would need additional courses to bring me up to an acceptable level. I learned that these programmes had very few, if any, courses relating to development, and that most folks on the teaching faculty had experience with either Native Americans or Mesoamerican communities. And I learned that I would need to 'qualify' in all four fields to get my degree.

I wrote to the admissions committees. I don't want to be an archaeologist, I said. Or a linguist. And I don't plan on working with either Native Americans or folks in Central America. I speak French, and I want to do development work. Too bad, they replied; this is the programme. This is what you do.

Only if I come there, I wrote back, and crossed them off my list.

Finally, it dawned on me. If I want to work in Africa and Asia, and I want training to prepare me to do that, why not turn to the seat of empire? And so, I applied to half a dozen UK universities, and in the fullness of time was given a Fulbright scholarship to study at the University of Sussex, just then building its reputation in the field of development studies.

FIGURE 11.2   Riall W. Nolan on the waterfront in Hanuabada Village outside of Port Moresby, during his time as a Lecturer in Community Development at the University of Papua New Guinea, 1973–1977. Personal archive of Riall W. Nolan.

Originally, I had wanted only a master's degree, so that I could get back into the field quickly. My tutor wisely persuaded me otherwise, and so I chose the doctorate, which in the UK can be done in as little as three years. And the rest is, as they say, history.

Once in a while a student asks how I managed to plan my career so successfully. I generally don't tell them the truth: that life can be terrifyingly random, and that happenstance plays a huge role in shaping who we are and what we become. My springtime conversation with my undergraduate advisor probably saved my life and sent me on my way to Africa. The kindness of the Senegalese enabled me to develop my understanding of very different ways of life, and an interest in development. My encounter with the anthropologists showed me how insight into these different ways of life could be gained. And my tutor at Sussex pointed me in the right direction in terms of professional qualifications.

But I don't generally say these things to my students. Instead, I talk about the interplay of agency and contingency in people's lives, and how it's important not only to have an overall goal in mind but to be able to recognize and capture those moments when life sends you opportunities. Louis Pasteur said it best: 'Le hasard ne favorise que les esprits préparés'. *Chance favours the prepared mind.*

THE MOST ANTHROPOLOGICAL PROJECT I EVER DID

Like many practitioners, I never had the word 'anthropology' in any of my job titles. And a lot of what I did, likewise, didn't have 'anthropology' written all over it. But the anthropology was there, nonetheless.

The international affairs network

This was the best project I ever did, and it took place in the former Soviet Union in the early 1990s. I was working at the time at the University of Pittsburgh, directing the International Management Development Institute inside the Graduate School of Public and International Affairs.

Prior to this, I'd been involved in quite a few development projects in Asia and Africa, and although sometimes anthropology made a significant difference, there were always major constraints to, as I termed it, 'doing things right'. There were budget constraints, there were personnel issues, there were design flaws that couldn't be undone, there were dysfunctional agency and/or host country regulations and procedures. Given all of that, it's a wonder that any development projects work at all. And in fact, many of them don't, as we know.

(Continued)

FIGURE 11.3 Riall W. Nolan (on the right) in St Petersburg, Russia, on a cold and snowy day in 1992, during series of international affairs workshops for academics and officials from Russian and Eastern European universities. Personal archive of Riall W. Nolan.

Not so with the International Affairs Network. We began it in 1990, before the breakup of the Soviet Union, and by the end of the 1990s, it was still in operation. It was an outstanding example of a capacity-building project that really worked. It worked for several reasons: it had developed in response to real, as opposed to imagined, needs; it was planned and carried out collaboratively as a true partnership across different cultures; and it was fundamentally anthropological in concept and operation. We took the time to engage with our partners and to understand what questions and concerns mattered most to them, before the programme planning began.

It began in a rather odd way. In the year prior to the collapse of the Soviet Union, we were approached very discreetly by several high-ranking Baltic officials to see if we could respond to requests from their foreign ministries. The Baltic countries were still Soviet republics, but the handwriting was on the wall, and some within these governments were already planning for what might come next.

We were asked to provide training to foreign ministry officials in Estonia, Latvia and Lithuania, in three specific areas: how to set up foreign diplomatic offices abroad; how to formulate national foreign policy; and how to negotiate troop withdrawal with the Russians. In this, we enjoyed a degree of active but invisible collaboration with some key Russian officials, who understood, I think, that having stable states on their border was better than the alternative.

We conducted these programmes at the time that the 'Singing Revolution' was reaching its climax in the Baltics. The Singing Revolution involved mass singing demonstrations in all three Baltic states, and was in part responsible for restoring independence to them. The movement was largely – although not entirely – peaceful; indeed, we were in Lithuania during the Russian siege of the television tower, and our ministry driver had to manoeuvre around Russian tanks in the streets when we went to the training site each day.

I've said elsewhere (Nolan 2002) that development projects often resemble cross-cultural plays in which the actors don't entirely know their lines at first. This was certainly true for us as we began to work with people who, although outwardly similar to us in many ways, turned out to think very differently at times. As the lead person on this undertaking, I was in a position to frame what we were doing in fundamental ways, and because we were in most respects entirely free to design and implement the project as we saw fit, this seemed to be an excellent opportunity to 'do things right'.

Our teams initially spent a great deal of time learning, interacting with participants, interviewing them, developing an understanding of their perspectives, and incorporating that into the design of our training. Unlike a lot of what passes for 'executive training' in US universities, where 'experts' present the current orthodoxy to passive trainees, or what happens in many development projects, where plans made in Washington or Paris are unloaded on local communities, ours was an extended reflective conversation with our counterparts, and our goals, methods and procedures reflected this.

One rather amusing example will illustrate how we changed the programme as we interacted with our colleagues. While organizing sessions in negotiation with our Estonian partners, we asked them to list the top five characteristics of a good negotiator. Number three, it turned out, was the ability to drink large amounts of alcohol and remain functional. When we asked why, the Estonians explained the Russian concept of the soul (*dusha*) to us and its relation to alcohol. They also explained the ritual of the toast, the drink and the *zakuski*. If you want to talk seriously, they said, you should expect to drink. Although our foundation grant technically didn't allow expenditures on alcohol, we found ways to make sure that some was available at all of our meetings, in the spirit of *dusha-dushe* (conviviality).

By the time we'd finished the training programmes, the Soviet Union had more or less dissolved. Statues were being taken down all over the Baltics, Cyrillic road signs were being replaced, and new banknotes were appearing. We had learned a great deal about a great many things, and out of our discussions with our new-found Baltic colleagues, an interesting idea for a possible next step together had emerged.

(Continued)

Teaching international relations in the post-Soviet era

With the collapse of Soviet control over university curricula, a void had appeared in the area of international relations. Individual countries now had the task of defining for themselves what international relations actually was, and how it should be taught to reflect national rather than Union issues and priorities. Materials – textbooks, curricula and case studies – needed to be developed, and this required access to new and previously off-limits sources of information.

All of this emerged slowly, over late-night discussions with our colleagues. Once the idea had taken shape, our team began a series of site visits to countries in the region, interviewing government officials and university faculty, to better understand both the issues and the mechanisms for addressing the issues. This took many months, as we – and they – felt our way towards mutual trust and understanding.

In the end, we worked together to design a five-year capacity-building project to improve the teaching of international relations in eight partner universities across the region, from Estonia in the north to Ukraine in the south. The project included training, collaborative research activities, visits to partner countries, fellowships and the provision of technical assistance to help our partners get connected to the then-emerging internet.

Four years into the project, I met with an old friend, now the USAID mission director in one of our partner countries. 'I've been hearing excellent things about your international affairs partnership', he said. He added wistfully, 'We could never do anything as good as that through this agency'.

Anthropology as a key factor in design success

Years ago, Conrad Kottak (1991) showed us that development projects which take account of social factors are more successful than those which do not. Sometime later, in her study of US foreign aid to Eastern Europe, Janine Wedel (1998) showed us what happens when these social factors are ignored.

What happened with American aid in Eastern Europe was what the philosopher Reinholt Niebhur warned us about many years ago:

> The same strength which has extended our [American] power beyond a continent has also ... brought us into a vast web of history in which other wills, running in oblique or contrasting directions to our own, inevitably hinder or contradict what we most fervently desire. We cannot simply have our way, not even when we believe our way to have the "happiness of mankind" as its promise.

> *(cited in Kaplan 1997: 60)*

The Americans misunderstood many things about the Eastern European context in which they had begun to work, but in particular, they underestimated the strength and significance of existing relations among people in the region. I had a similar problem in the late 1980s when I tried to explain to my colleagues at the World Bank that the 'misuse' of Bank funding by the Senegalese was not a breakdown of the system, it *was* the system; a system based on the core value of *bokk*, or sharing, whose operation took precedence over whatever might be contained in the World Bank agreements.

Our project in Eastern Europe was not overtly anthropological, but it was led by an anthropologist, and it incorporated some essential design features which are part and parcel of the anthropological approach. These include considerable time spent interacting with project partners before plans are made, a deep-seated understanding and appreciation of local-level perspectives and priorities, the gradual building of trust and reciprocity among partners, and – perhaps most importantly – a willingness to modify frameworks as both sides learn.

Was it dramatic? No. Was it effective? Everyone said so. Was it anthropological? Most definitely.

FIVE TIPS FROM RIALL W. NOLAN

1. **Learn to work collaboratively with other specialists to co-create with them.** Think about how what you know might be added to their frameworks, and how what they know might be added to yours.
2. **Organizations are complex cultures; become an expert at learning about how they work.** You will get your most important work done, most of the time, through organizations.
3. **Learn how to be influential and persuasive within your organization**, as a means towards developing leadership skills for change and improvement.
4. **Get involved with ground-level implementation**, so that you understand exactly how ideas get turned into tangible realities.
5. **At the same time, develop skills in policy-making**, rather than simply continuing to be a policy critic.

About the author

Riall W. Nolan is Professor of anthropology at Purdue University. He received his doctorate in Social Anthropology from Sussex University, and lived in North and West Africa, Asia and the Southwest Pacific for nearly twenty years, working in higher education and international development. He teaches courses on international development, work and learning in cross-cultural environments, and the application of anthropology to global issues. He writes and consults frequently on issues of international development, international education, cross-cultural adaptation and applied anthropology.

References

Berry, W. (1981), 'Solving for Pattern', in *The Gift of Good Land: Further Essays Cultural and Agricultural*, 134–45, New York: North Point Press.

Chambers, E. (2009), 'In Both Our Possibilities: Anthropology on the Margins', *Human Organization*, 68 (4): 374–9.

Honadle, G. (1982), 'Rapid Reconnaissance for Development Administration: Mapping and Moulding Organizational Landscapes', *World Development*, 10 (8): 633–49.

Kaplan, R. D. (1997), 'Was Democracy Just a Moment?', *The Atlantic Monthly*, December: 60.

Kottak, C. (1991), 'When People Don't Come First: Some Sociological Lessons from Completed Projects', in Michael M. Cernea (ed.), *Putting People First*, 431–64, Washington (DC): World Bank and Oxford University Press.

Muehlebach, A. (2013), 'On Precariousness and the Ethical Imagination: The Year 2012 in Sociocultural Anthropology', *American Anthropologist*, 115 (2): 297–311.

Nolan, R. (2002), *Development Anthropology: Encounters in the Real World*, Boulder (CO): Westview Press.

Soetoro, A. (1979), 'Prosperity Indicators for Java', Washington (DC): Development Alternatives Incorporated.

Wedel, J. (1998), *Collision and Collusion: The Strange Case of Western Aid to Eastern Europe 1989–1998*, New York: St. Martin's Press.

CONCLUSION

Back to the future of applied anthropology

Pavel Borecký and Carla Guerrón Montero

In more than one way, *Why the World Needs Anthropologists* is about foreseeing the future of applied anthropology worldwide. Yet, to have a vision for the future of anthropology, we need to look at its past. The introductory chapter in this volume revisits the discipline's contested history, and it evocatively jokes about the popular imagery of 'pith-helmet-wearing colonial adventurers' and 'bearded, long-haired men' only to remind us of the possible negative impacts such imaginative baggage may unleash on the upcoming generation of anthropologists. In fact, anthropologists are not only 'lone wolves' who explore the world in search of data about the 'Other'. Forming a specific socio-cultural group in its own right, its very sense of collective identity and purpose can be expressed in the exercise of storytelling (see, for instance, the anthropology of anthropologists in Green et al. 2015). In order to offer a publicly convincing answer to the question 'why does the world need anthropologists?', we need to go beyond binary dichotomies regarding what constitutes 'good' or 'bad' anthropology, or how anthropology can be practiced "inside" and "outside" academia.

The chapters in this volume follow a common outline wherein each author was asked to share their experiences structured along four main themes. First, we invited the contributors to provide answers to our presumably vain question, the question that brought us all together in the first place: why *does* the world need anthropologists? We then asked them to share with us a story that epitomizes the reasons that motivated them to become anthropologists, and to give examples from their careers on how they have applied their anthropological skills and knowledge in practice. Finally, each of them proposed five tips for developing skills and knowledge that fledgling anthropologists should consider.

In the introduction, our colleagues Dan Podjed and Meta Gorup teased out the self-contained qualities of individual contributions. In the concluding section,

FIGURE 12.1   Pavel Borecký (middle) with Laura Korčulanin (left), the event co-convenor and financial manager of Applied Anthropology Network, who hosted a speed-talk format called Future Cities, and Muntasir Sattar (right), an independent researcher and a volunteer at *Why the World Needs Anthropologists*, Oslo, Norway, 2019. Courtesy Mariana Bassani.

our task is to explore the commonalities and differences in the recommendations provided by our contributors. In an effort to see 'through' and 'in-between' and to locate points of connection and divergence, we identified five axes that matter greatly to this group of accomplished anthropologists. In doing so, we invite the reader to leave the 'ivory tower' behind and reflect on the ways in which the contributors propose to apply anthropological insights to change the world for the better. These axes include navigate the ethics of change; own it; expand the skill set; collaborate, co-create and study up; and recommend.

Navigate the ethics of change

Be it straightforward normative statements or latent undercurrents of their thoughts, the personal ethics of these researchers are uncovered through their life stories. For Thomas Hylland Eriksen, despite the assertion that anthropology is not primarily a problem-solving science, writing ethnographies about what constitutes a (good) life elsewhere is ultimately about making alternatives visible and conceivable for others, including cold, rich, well-organized and almost empty Norway. His is the ethics of listening to the outcasts and of cross-cultural comparison. Launching 'eBay for help' (Breidenbach, this volume), Joana Breidenbach's story exemplifies directing the disruptive potential of the digital revolution towards the enabling qualities of civic activism. She offers an anthropological translation of the ethics of democratic action and solidarity exchange into a virtual space to allow as many people as possible to work collaboratively against capitalist social relations. Whilst Breidenbach stands in defence of anthropology being a 'movement studying movement' (this volume), Sarah Pink's academic nomadism of working across institutions, fields and disciplines, literally embodies the point. Forging anthropology that is keen on learning, hers is the ethics of possibilities. Pink employs concepts of trust and hope as the means of navigating the unknown and 'voicing possible ways forward into an uncertain future' (Pink, this volume); in doing so, she makes the explicit bid for an ethics of responsibility. Finally, a fresh breeze comes in with Rikke Ulk and Anna Kirah, who invite us into a world where one goes for a walk, trusts loose thinking and is willing to 'fail forward into discovery' (Kirah, this volume) by not forcing things to happen. This reasoning strongly echoes the commentary on the 'darkness of the long contemporary moment' made by Arjun Appadurai, one of the major theorists of globalization. When Appadurai reflects on the significance of activism, he defines the ethics of possibility as being grounded in 'those ways of thinking, feeling, and acting that increase the horizons of hope' (2013: 299). The interlinked ethics of listening, responsibility, possibilities and of the unexpected found in this volume help us navigate desirable changes and reshape our world's futures.

Authors in this volume highlight the look towards the future lingering at the edges of the present and the way in which anthropologists are firmly entrenched in its making. However, let us not be fooled by a picture of cohesion and correspondence. Whereas a handful few would disagree with the statement that 'doing social research' mandates moral and political commitment to 'socially responsible science' (Partridge 1987), how such commitment is practised varies. To paraphrase Kirsten Hastrup and Peter Elsass, who said 'a commitment [to] improving the world is no substitute for understanding it' (1990: 307), a full circle is drawn when one simply inverts the equation: 'a commitment to understanding the world is no substitute for improving it'. Reaching this crossroad, we arrive at the heart of a scholarly battlefield in which the key ethical tension is the one between acceptable ways of 'knowing' and 'acting on knowledge'. Here the 'academic' and 'applied' labels are placed as polar opposites, as if 'understanding' is always at odds with 'changing'. For example, when Kirah shares the story of being accused by academicians of 'helping the "devil"' (this volume), be it the system, capitalism or governments (for discussion on 'dark anthropology', see Ortner 2016), the hammer of ethics is being raised against the relationships 'well-mannered' researchers shall never even consider. Yet, turning the weapon of her intellectual adversaries into her own source of power, to Kirah it is precisely the constant movement between 'applied' and 'theoretical' that is the tool that allows her to constantly refine a sense of ethical engagement. Working actively against an idea of ethics that is elevated as a form of 'battle cry against practice' (Hill 2000: 4), she ultimately reintegrates both traditions into 'a continuum of practice' (Rylko-Bauer, Singer and van Willigen 2006).

Recognizing the need to negotiate the pressures of policy and decision-making, contributors make the argument for not shying away from complicated power dynamics. Breidenbach, Steffen Jöhncke and Riall W. Nolan address this challenge by suggesting some answers: working around 'healthy hierarchies' (Breidenbach, this volume), anthropologically recasting other people's problems (Jöhncke, this volume) or using leadership skills to get the 'most important work done' through organizations (Nolan, this volume). However, as much as the intention to 'do the right thing' in a turbulently accelerating world prevails, the stakes of such engagements are undeniable. Despite walking a long way in refining the codes of ethics, of theorizing and employing multi-vocality, participatory methods, and cultural decolonization, the 'colonial hangover' (Podjed, Gorup and Bezjak Mlakar 2016: 54) still looms large as one of the key hindrances of social anthropology. What can the history of complicity with obtaining economic and political dominance by 'knowing the Other' do for us and our partners today? First, let us pause for a moment and not see the past as a limitation. Instead, let us see the past as the fuel for reformed wisdom and recast identity. Since any ethnographic research is always already embedded in plurality and transience, let us be more upfront to broadcast the values of the anthropological project more transparently and facilitate the change that protects cultural multiplicity, diminishes suffering and challenges the abuse of power.

Own it

Be it trust, pride or sense of ownership, the most commonly shared trait the contributors to this book set to boost is the sense of identity of anthropologists themselves. While thinking about links between research, education and entrepreneurship, we realize that all of our contributors place great attention on self-esteem. Jöhncke, Tanja Winther and Pink hail the uniqueness and usefulness of anthropological training, which they see as their main source of professional identity. To use Jöhncke's words, the real self-confidence comes from doing 'with anthropology what *you* think is important' (this volume). Only through the alignment of one's values, societal aspirations and creative attitudes towards the 'toolbox' (Eriksen, this volume), the ever-evolving practice of anthropology can stay both grounded and in constant motion. The second important trait is the need for enhanced visibility made by Lenora Bohren, Ulk and Jitske Kramer, whose entrepreneurial careers taught them to constantly search for new opportunities. As they argue, it is necessary to say, 'Hello, I am an anthropologist' more often, be daring and outspoken in professional contacts and show one's expertise without reluctance. If executed with dexterity and persistence (and a grain of luck), what might start emerging is the public voice and, even, the popular role of the public intellectual Breidenbach advocates for. Yet, for Breidenbach all of these passionate excursions need to boil down to the *self* again, to a careful recursive examination of where I am and what I am doing, an activity very much akin to meditation practices.

If anthropology is such a magnificent complexity-cruncher, why is there a need for a self-esteem boost at all? First, as several life stories in this volume attest, those who aim to produce impact-oriented ethnographies or work as policy consultants, may be contested and symbolically labelled as 'polluters'. In extreme situations, as the authors of this conclusion have personally witnessed, the argument can basically go as follows: if one resorts into 'applied' business, one virtually opposes any theory-driven aspirations of anthropology and, therefore, forfeits the right to call oneself an 'anthropologist' altogether. Second, as of today, educational systems often blindly reproduce the misconception that non-academic career pathways are 'alternatives'. In other words, doing anthropology as a professional occupation is rarely celebrated and students are too often left wondering how useful all that 'critical thinking' is going to be in the job market. Third, leaving the university, it suddenly becomes rather complicated for many students to do the beloved ethnographic fieldwork they were asked to master. Structuring anthropology programmes too narrowly and connecting excellence with hard-to-reach academic positions brings about a sense of failure and shame that often lingers for years to come in the minds of those anthropology graduates who 'did not make it'. Consequently, one of the biggest challenges for the Applied Anthropology Network of the European Association of Social Anthropologists (EASA) is to simply locate anthropology practitioners, who, against all odds, actually 'made it'. Let us face it. Combining all these factors together, a rather worrying picture emerges. Who owns anthropology? Or, better said, who has the opportunity to be involved in its making and how does it affect those who are not? Ultimately, to borrow the words of Nolan, who benefits from the persistent clinging to academic versus non-academic distinctions that render the non-academic as 'ethically suspect, lightweight and theoretically empty' (this volume), basically not so good?

In the conventional story of social science, the hero-researcher was a single gender-neutral scientist who dedicated years to theory-building in close engagement with research informants. Usually, the hero's power and framework of action were interlinked with academic institutions, which provided a safe space for so-called objective studies. This trick of modernity led to the expansion of a particular dominion, which, directly or indirectly, subjugated other knowledge systems (Foucault 1976). However, as influential feminist scholars such as Donna Haraway and Lila Abu Lughod have argued, under the guise of neutrality and objectivity a very specific position of a white male heterosexual human was hidden. Even *culture*, the very flagship term of anthropology, has come under heavy fire as being too-Western, coherent, timeless and bounding (see, for instance, Abu Lughod 1991). The counter-argument posits that all kinds of knowledge that people produce are neither transparent, nor absolute. They are always already situated in the planes of ontology, epistemology, ethics and politics (Haraway 1988). There is always bias and position. There is always incompleteness.

As Podjed and Gorup point out in the introduction to this book, the ways in which our community of practice is received and discussed co-create the public image of the discipline and the range of options to which our anthropology graduates are exposed. However, the imprecise public understanding of contemporary anthropology cannot be blamed on faceless crowds. On the contrary,

FIGURE 12.2 Carla Guerrón Montero at the seventh international symposium *Why the World Needs Anthropologists* in Oslo, Norway, 2019. Courtesy Rafael Estrada Mejia.

it touches the very serious question of ownership. It touches the questions of identity, belonging and the mechanisms of othering, which are internal to anthropology itself and must be first transcended.

Expand the skill set

As most contributors to the book highlight, the problems we face as humans are not completely new. History provides us with blueprints to understand how people have shaped cultures and how cultures have shaped people. However, it is important to recognize that – in many ways – we are living in unsettled and unsettling times. Ambivalence, ambiguity and unpredictability are – paradoxically – certitudes in today's context. Thus, anthropologists need to be more flexible and creative than ever. Contributors to this volume propose that the challenges faced by anthropologists today include developing cultural contextualization and deep immersions on relevant issues in a short period of time. The days when the lonesome anthropologist needed to prove his (and it was, indeed, mostly 'his') ethnographic abilities in isolation, in faraway places and for lengthy periods of time are long gone. Now an anthropologist needs to understand problems through a cultural lens quickly and efficiently. How is that achieved? For Breidenbach, it is essential to keep anthropology lean and flexible, attentive to the internal and external structures of life as constructed and thus, as contested and contestable. Pink proposes that interdisciplinary work is the answer. Her work with emergent technologies focusses on possibilities rather than solutions; her brand of anthropology is informed by theory and rooted in ethnography while remaining resolutely centred on interventions. And this collaborative work can only be achieved through methodologies that go well beyond traditional anthropological training. Some of them include experimental visual, sensory, digital and design ethnographic methodologies. How else to venture into technologies of the future? How else can anticipatory models be proposed? Certainly, our contributors side with John Comaroff (2013) who stated, there is no such thing as a post-ethnographic anthropology just like there is not such a thing as a post-theoretical anthropology.

This conversation brings to the forefront the urgency of transforming anthropological training so that it becomes up to par not only with the current employment opportunities offered to anthropologists but also with the endless possibilities available for envisioning and constructing the future. As Nolan asserts, although being incessantly trained to be 'critical' is very important in academia, most anthropology programmes ignore the logical following step: developing skills for constructive application. Anthropology programmes are in dire need to develop curricula that prepare students for intensively collaborative interdisciplinary applied work. For instance, Kramer stresses that the deep engagement with 'the spaces between people' (this volume) that anthropology provides can be applied to the corporate world, as corporate cultures are living communities just like the so-called exotic locations where anthropologists used to work almost exclusively. New generations of anthropologists should be prepared to work with the same ease in a small village half the world away as in a board meeting room full of businesspeople. Being in-between cultures, countries, languages and realities is what we know how to do best, and our training and methodologies should be elastic enough to provide this flexibility. As David Lempert (2018: 48) states, we need to ensure that we teach and model 'active applications of skills and morality in practice'.

Moving towards the realm of collaboration, Jöhncke reflects on the ways in which his team has approached anthropology. For him, the view of anthropology as a discipline with a fixed set of tools that are applied or 'put to use' is not productive (this volume). Indeed, the constant need to customise, reinvent and assemble anew is the core thriving skill in the market-driven environment where applied anthropologists often operate. Considering how rapidly some nature-culture environments may shift, the refusal to commit to one perspective or one set of cherished skills may very well be the sign of a pre-emptive strategy. For instance, it has been reported that coastal communities that experience the drastic impacts of climate change (as embedded in ongoing economic and cultural transformations) need to learn how to trust volatility, flexibility and improvisation (Krause 2018). The same goes for highly specialized environments such as academia. The European Union's research funding scheme Horizon 2020 was built precisely around the concept of transdisciplinarity, as the prophetic creativity vector to challenge the complexities of current social problems. The conversation on the variations of post-disciplinarity and un-disciplinarity engender both excited and anxious responses. Regardless of whether such developments are the sign of increased vulnerability or resilience, our proposal for anthropology at large is to benefit from the assertion that 'making is thinking' (Sennett 2008).

Collaborate, co-create and study up

Anthropology is a profession based on 'principles of science and discipline that work towards real technical solutions for long-term human survival and sustainability rather than just serve as dogmas that actually promote acceptance, passivity and inaction' (Lempert 2018: 48). A common thread among several of the contributors to this volume is the emphasis that they place on collaboration and co-creation. Contributors stress the need for anthropologists to partner with the industry, the government and the public sphere. As Pink asserts, the world needs a new kind of interventional anthropology, one where anthropologists work as diligently on their cherished specializations as on generalized knowledge that allows them to work in interdisciplinary teams. For instance, Bohren provides an impressive series of examples of applied projects on topics as varied as carbon emissions, refugee relocation, and especially, car culture, where she contributed—among many talents—the holistic approach that characterizes our discipline or, as Breidenbach states, the anthropological multiperspectivity.

Collaborative work that co-creates is not an easy task. Winther's example of a transdisciplinary project to establish a village-scale electricity system in Kenya illustrates the potential structural, intellectual and practical blocks that can surface. This example also illustrates that while collaborative projects might be normative in terms of their objectives, they need not become normative in terms of their methodological approaches. If long-term fieldwork is not an option, the use of mixed methods is a potential solution.

Laura Nader recommended in her ground-breaking essay, 'Up the Anthropologist' (1972), that anthropologists should be as concerned about asking the question 'Why are some people poor?' as the question 'Why are other people so affluent?' In line with this invitation, some contributors to this volume take the challenge of studying up. Many of them work with clients who are more powerful and wealthier than the anthropologist working with them. Others collaborate closely with colleagues in different disciplines and, in order to work productively with them, they find fruitful ways to 'study sideways'.

The current generation of applied anthropologists is informed by the lapses of colonialism and does not eschew complicated power dynamics. However, Ulk rightly points out in her elaboration of the co-creation concept that, if the method becomes 'worshiped' (this volume) by powerful social actors such as cities and municipalities, the commitment to collaborative service needs to be carefully revisited. For instance, nowadays the participatory principles in urban planning are being mainstreamed across Europe and the promised land for applied urban anthropologists is opening up. Yet, the space between top-down political aesthetics and true bottom-up informed actions can be extremely slippery. How often are trained anthropologists-facilitators hired to run all-inclusive planning gatherings only to mask the true development intentions of the political establishment?

Recommend

Ulk stresses that, 'The biggest challenge for our discipline is to provide recommendations' (this volume). How do practising anthropologists grapple with the role of advisors and consultants? Why is 'offering a recommendation' such a challenge and what do the authors recommend doing about it? The question is tied to research ethics and the importance of a contended hallmark of anthropological theory – the concept of cultural relativism. Whereas for Eriksen the sensitive examination of cultural differences is central to what anthropologists shall be communicating to the world, to Kirah and Kramer the issue is more complicated. 'Our attempts ... are often thwarted by our own inability to move beyond cultural relativism', claims Kirah (this volume), a design anthropologist who built up her career as an in-house researcher at Boeing and Microsoft. To cut this Gordian knot, corporate anthropologist Kramer goes as far as stating 'Be judgmental!' Despite the differences in what acting on knowledge means, we recognize that the process of evaluation is present in either case. Debating solution-oriented research, Bohren considers anthropology as an applied discipline that does provide solutions. Pink, however, proposes that anthropology should actually go beyond providing solutions and, instead, offer possibilities and envision better futures. In the case of Winther, we face a paradox: on the one hand, anthropologists are to inform policy-making; on the other, her anthropology is explorative and not in search for solutions to pre-determined questions. Jöhncke ends the debate reminding anthropologists that the world does not need anthropologists *per se*, unless they 'are willing to contribute to the collaborative effort of saving the planet, creating a more just world, or whatever fair cause [they] choose' (Jöhncke, this volume). In short, the contributors to this volume move in between two contested positions – proposing a resound *yes* or *no* to providing recommendations.

'The ultimate, hidden truth of the world is that it is something that we make, and could just as easily make differently', wrote Occupy Wall Street anthropologist David Graeber (2009: 514). Assuming the role of one of the spokespersons for the movement, Graeber transformed cross-cutting social theories into easily digestible claims that helped to diagnose the socio-political situation in the United States and clarify the demands for anti-capitalist activism. Certainly, this impactful example of civic engagement may stand today side by side with an alarming text on the future of applied anthropology written more than ten years prior by James Peacock: 'If the discipline is to gain recognition and a valuable identity, it must accomplish things; it must be active beyond its analytical strategy' (1997: 12). To whom and when anthropologists decide to recommend and how such recommendations are to be formulated remains a matter of personal preferences and, as we have shown, varies widely. Nevertheless, in an era of societal upheavals, it is extremely insightful to grasp the perspective of those who move as well as those who are moved.

Is anthropology the next big thing?

In 2018 Podjed and Gorup stepped down as Convenors and became Executive Advisors of the EASA Applied Anthropology Network. Created out of enthusiasm and willingness to communicate to wider audiences, now the internationally recognized event *Why the World Needs Anthropologists* fell into the laps of four new convenors. The successive generation of 'cheerleaders' for application and engagement consisted of the founder of Antropología 2.0 Verónica Reyero, artivist Laura Korčulanin, expert on political violence Pardis Shafafi and Pavel Borecký, the founding member of the Czech applied anthropology organization Anthropictures. Being new blood in knowledge production, both inside and outside academia, some of the questions the collective started discussing were the following: How to navigate power, ethics and professionalism to build credibility within the community and help anthropology at large? What kinds of anthropologies and what kind of anthropologists does the twenty-first century need?

To answer these questions on local scales, the network offered – in addition to the main annual symposium – a new toolbox, called *Why the World Needs Anthropologists: Satellite Event*, which follows successful formats, such as TEDx, PechaKucha and Creative Mornings. The main point of these events is to advocate, negotiate and disseminate the value of anthropological thinking beyond

FIGURE 12.3   The moment filled with enthusiasm for the common cause, and the day when the network representatives proclaimed, 'It's not just a network anymore, it's a movement!' EASA Applied Anthropology Network meeting, Oslo, Norway, 2019. Courtesy Mariana Bassani.

one annual 'gig'. In short, these smaller and local events enable *Why the World Needs Anthropologists* ideas to go viral in different countries, regions and cities. Having no time to waste, under the guidance of urban anthropologist Hélène Veiga Gomes, the first two spin-offs of the annual symposium were created in Lisbon in 2018 and Bucharest in 2019 – and there are several other 'satellites' on the horizon, which will help making anthropology 'the next big thing' on various levels.

Hello, are there any anthropologists out there?

If *Why the World Needs Anthropologists* international symposium and its 'satellites' set the task to convince people that anthropology has significantly changed, reaching this point one shall reflectively ask, 'Has this book achieved what it promises to deliver?' Indeed, change, transformation and transition have always been popular conceptual lenses through which the discipline aims to grasp the experience of being human across time and space. After all, concepts to 'think with' can be extremely practical. However, as the authors exemplify, the question of 'why' can no longer withstand the ethical challenges of the present moment. In other words, anthropologists need to continue to become change-makers themselves. One of the crucial reasons for this is the unparalleled change that humankind is experiencing.

One way to evaluate the impact of this book is through a thought experiment. Imagine yourself in a distant future as you are picking up this volume from a bookshelf. Are anthropologists still out there? Did we succeed in challenging the 'pith-helmet-wearing' and 'sandals-with-socks' (Strang 2009: 1) stereotypes that incessantly loomed over the discipline for decades? Are anthropologists respected members of the knowledge community and sought-after public intellectuals and practitioners, or has their labour become outsourced by big-data crunchers and AI humanoids? Has our work in the troublesome years of the early twenty-first century been of any transformative value?

We leave you with your own answers to these questions. However, our hope is that this volume becomes a catalyst that contributes to making anthropology the discipline that collaborates, co-creates, envisions, forms and transforms world futures. Why? Because we are pretty much convinced that the future world will still need anthropology– perhaps even more than it needs it now.

About the authors

Pavel Borecký is a social anthropologist and an audiovisual ethnographer. As a holder of an MSc in Sustainable Development and an MA in Social Anthropology, he completed various primary and applied research projects in the fields of ethnobotany (Peru), civic society building (Estonia) and urban development (Czech Republic). Receiving a Swiss Government scholarship, he currently works on his PhD at Walter Benjamin Kolleg and teaches at the Institute of

Islamic and Middle Eastern Studies, University of Bern. In his communal practice, Borecký curates the film programme EthnoKino and serves as the convenor of the Applied Anthropology Network of the European Association of Social Anthropologists. His latest films *Solaris* and *In the Devil's Garden* have been presented at numerous festivals and conferences in Europe and abroad.

Carla Guerrón Montero is Professor of Anthropology, Africana Studies, Women and Gender Studies, and Latin American Studies at the University of Delaware. She is a cultural and applied anthropologist trained in Latin America and the United States. She has conducted extensive research on the anthropology of tourism and the anthropology of food in Latin America (Brazil, Ecuador, Grenada and Panama) and collaborative interdisciplinary applied research on food sovereignty and cultural heritage in Ecuador, Grenada and Peru. She has served the American Anthropological Association (AAA) and the Society for Applied Anthropology (SfAA) in several capacities, including member of the Executive Board of both associations. Since 2015, she has served as a member of the Advisory Committee of the *Why the World Needs Anthropologists* international symposium, and since 2016, as the United States liaison to the EASA Applied Anthropology Network.

References

Abu Lughod, L. (1991), 'Writing against Culture', in R. G. Fox (ed), *Recapturing Anthropology: Working in the Present*, 137–54, Santa Fe (NM): School of American Research Press.

Comaroff, J. (2013), 'The End of Anthropology, Again: On the Future of an In/Discipline', in P. A. Erickson and L. Murphy (eds), *A History of Anthropological Theory*, 4th edn, 524–38, Toronto: University of Toronto Press.

Foucault, M. (1976), *Society Must Be Defended: Lectures at the Collège de France, 1975–1976*, New York: Picador.

Graeber, D. (2009), *Direct Action: An Ethnography*, Oakland (CA): AK Press.

Green, S., P. Laviolette, E. Papataxiarchis, A. Kuper, C. Gregory, D. Miller et al. (2015), 'Forum Rethinking Euro-Anthropology', *Social Anthropology*, 23 (3): 330–64.

Haraway, D. (1988), 'Situated Knowledges: The Science Question in Feminism and the Privilege of Partial Perspective', *Feminist Studies*, 14 (3): 575–99.

Hastrup, K. and P. Elsass (1990), 'Anthropological Advocacy: A Contradiction in Terms?', *Current Anthropology*, 31 (3): 301–11.

Krause, F. (2018), 'Hydrosocial Volatility in the Mackenzie Delta'. Available online: https://www.agenda.uzh.ch/record.php?id=39477&group=46 (accessed 18 December 2018).

Lempert, D. (2018), 'The President's Mother the Anthropologist and the Anthropologist's Son: Anthropological Issues and US President Obama', *Anthropology in Action*, 25 (1): 41–8.

Nader, L. (1972), 'Up the Anthropologists: Perspectives Gained from Studying Up', in Dell Himes (ed.), *Reinventing Anthropology*, 284–311, New York: Pantheon Books.

Ortner, S. B. (2016), 'Dark Anthropology and Its Others: Theory Since the Eighties', *Hau: Journal of Ethnographic Theory*, 6 (1): 47–73.

Partridge, W. L. (1987), 'Toward a Theory of Practice', in E. M. Eddy and W. L. Partridge (eds), *Applied Anthropology in America*, 211–36, New York: Columbia University.

Peacock, J. (1997), 'The Future of Anthropology', *American Anthropologist*, 99 (1): 9–17.

Podjed, D., M. Gorup and A. Bezjak Mlakar (2016), 'Applied Anthropology in Europe: Historical Obstacles, Current Situation, Future Challenges', *Anthropology in Action*, 23 (2): 53–63.

Rylko-Bauer, B., M. Singer and J. van Willigen (2006), 'Reclaiming Applied Anthropology: Its Past, Present, and Future', *American Anthropologist*, 108 (1): 178–90.

Sennett, R. (2008), *The Craftsman*, New Haven: Yale University Press.

Steffen, W., J. Rockström, K. Richardson, T. M. Lenton, C. Folke, D. Liverman, C. P. Summerhayes, A. D. Barnosky, S. E. Cornell, M. Crucifix, J. F. Donges, I. Fetzer, S. J. Lade, M. Scheffer, R. Winkelmann and H. J. Schellnhuber (2018), 'Trajectories of Earth Systems in Anthropocene', *PNAS*, 115 (33): 8252–9.

Strang, V. (2009), *What Anthropologists Do*, Oxford and New York: Berg.

INDEX